The Celtic Rising

1965: The year Jock Stein changed everything

by

David Potter

CelticStarBooks.com

The Celtic Rising
1965: The year Jock Stein changed everything

by David Potter

Published by The Celtic Star
in cooperation with Matt Corr Media.

First Published in the UK in 2022 by The Celtic Star.

ISBN 978-1-8380207-5-0

A catalogue for this book is available from the British Library and the Irish Library in Dublin.

Cover & page design and typesetting by Stephen Cameron.

Edited by Matt Corr.

Foreword by John Fallon.

Publisher - David Faulds: email editor@thecelticstar.co.uk

Bookstore Website – https://celticstarbooks.com

Visit https://thecelticstar.com for the best Celtic news and views every day.

Printed in England by CPI

Dedication

This book is dedicated to all Celtic players and supporters who were alive at the time and remember the events of 1965, possibly the most momentous and certainly the most dramatic year in our history.

Acknowledgements

A whole host of people have helped me in the making of this book, some of them without even realising that they were doing so! They have done so by making a remark in conversation about this great year, which has then triggered a memory in me. I thank them all.

Sources have included the files of The Celtic View, The Evening Times, The Sunday Post, The Scottish Daily Record and The Scottish Daily Express. I have also consulted The Scottish Football Books edited by Hugh Taylor and various other books including Billy McNeill's For Celtic and Scotland, the first Celtic book that I ever read.

Those who have consciously helped me in this book (over a period of years) include Matt Corr, David Faulds, Stephen Cameron, Liam Kelly, Tom Campbell, John Fallon, Yvonne Blackburn and (posthumously) John Hughes, Charlie Gallagher, Bertie Auld and my late father Angus Potter, who shared every kick of the ball with me in 1965.

Mention must also be given to the intrepid members of the Joseph Rafferty Celtic Supporters' Club of Kirkcaldy, who share my agonies and ecstasies today.

There are many others whom I have forgotten to mention. To them I apologise and offer my thanks.

David Potter
Author

Contents

Introduction

As a Stadium Tour Guide at Celtic Park, I frequently reference Billy McNeill's comments around the Centenary Season, when he spoke of the "fairytale" that surrounds the club founded in Glasgow's east end in the late 19th century for the most wonderful of reasons. And of course, he is quite correct.

From the earliest days of Celtic Football Club, it has been defying the odds, and often logic, to deliver incredible moments which we as supporters will never tire of recounting or reliving.

At Celtic Star Books, we take real pride in being at the forefront of making sure that incredible history is shared across the Celtic diaspora. Our stories and our songs, honouring our heroes who wore those famous green and white hoops across so many generations.

From the record-breaking Alec McNair, Celtic's defensive Icicle for more than two decades, through the dazzling skills of Willie Fernie, as he turned on the style throughout the Fabulous Fifties to Harry Hood, weaving his own brand of sorcery as Jock Stein's side evolved from Lisbon Lions into a second magnificent team which played at the very top level of European football a decade later. And in the more recent past, of course we had the wonderful, magical Invincibles, undefeated as they brought home the first of what would eventually be a quadruple of domestic Trebles.

And not forgetting the Celtic heroes who pre-dated those iconic hoops, Willie Maley's Bould Bhoys, who kicked the whole thing off in such dramatic style in our very first season, proud and fearless as they took on the establishment clubs of the day to reach the Scottish Cup final at the first attempt. It is a truly incredible history, which simply must be shared, devoured then passed on for the next generations of Celtic supporters to enjoy.

Perhaps for the first time but definitely not for the last, Billy McNeill himself is a key figure in this latest Celtic fairytale of which he spoke many years later. Since Willie Fernie's man-of-the-match display at Hampden in the Sun back in October 1957, the Parkhead cupboard had been bare in terms of major honours. Seasons came and went but still those at the helm of our club could not find a way to write the next chapter of Celtic success. By the end of 1964, those with green blood flowing through their veins could see no end to the dominance of the club in the south-west of the city, and indeed could only look on as teams from Edinburgh, Dundee and Dunfermline were providing the main challenge.

Like all fairytales, The Celtic Rising needed some magical ingredients to spark it off, and they would duly follow as the Hogmanay Bells sounded the end of one era and the beginning of something so special no-one could possibly have foreseen.

Author David Potter was one of those long-suffering Celtic diehards who dreamed of the glories to come, and then witnessed the change which delivered those dreams…and then some. Like so many of our triumphs of the past, it was as unexpected as it was thrilling, a wonderful old club rising from the depths of so many heart-breaking defeats and false dawns to once again become the dominant force in Scotland and position itself for an even greater adventure to follow. David will take you with him every step of the way of that journey through 1965, each emotion, each setback, then each of the fabulous, joyous moments which are now Celtic folklore. There is no one better placed to do so.

Matt Corr
Editor

Foreword

It was my great honour and privilege to be part of 1965.

Sadly, so many of my teammates and friends from back then are no longer with us, but I can recall the various moods of 1965, beginning from the despair of January to the excitement of everyone when we heard that Jock Stein was coming back; the euphoria of April and the sustained happiness of that glorious summer; then the ups and downs of later in the year, which finished with Celtic once again a power in the land.

On a personal note, I clearly recall that glorious day of April 24 (and my wife giving birth soon after!), especially my save from Alex Edwards in the second half, which was probably the most important in my career. I also recall my "rivalry" with my good friend Ronnie Simpson for the goalkeeper's jersey, and how we always sat together on the team bus and talked about goalkeeping. Wonderful times.

We always knew that Jock Stein would bring changes, and we hoped that success would accrue.

We did not know just quite how much success Jock would bring!

And it all started in 1965!

Read and enjoy!

John Fallon
Celtic FC

1965 IN CONTEXT

The year of 1965 was a reasonably quiet one in Great Britain certainly, if not in the rest of the world. The death of Sir Winston Churchill in January seemed to say that it was now time to consign to the history books these horrendous conflicts of earlier in the century. Twenty years had passed since 1945, and the world was now different. There was still what was called the "Cold War" between East and West, but fortunately, it was not in 1965 showing any signs of heating up any time soon.

Britain's Prime Minister was the benign Harold Wilson, who was holding on to a very slim Labour majority in the House of Commons. He was in charge of a very talented Government and he himself was a very astute politician. Wilson was not necessarily appreciated at the time by everyone, but later historians have come to see his value. He made one decision that really should earn our respect, and that was the decision not to join the USA in its crazy war in Vietnam. Australia was not so clever – to its cost – and in 2003 one of Wilson's successors, Tony Blair, in a similar position, made the fatal mistake of aligning himself with the USA in a war in Iraq, which both he and the country would have been better out of.

More of the Vietnam War later, but the Conservative Party changed its leader in July from the aristocratic Sir Alec Douglas-Home to a rather strange character called Edward Heath, who beat Reginald Maudling and Enoch Powell in a leadership contest. He was a bachelor with interests in music and sailing, and did not come across as an easy man to like in the way that Harold Wilson did. It was clear that Wilson would have to go the country soon for a mandate (he did this in March 1966) but for the moment, it was clear that he was keeping his head down, introducing a few reforms and proving quietly that Labour was fit to govern. Inflation was definitely a factor, but was still under control.

There was one particularly nasty problem which would be kept under the surface for the moment, but which would blow up in a year or two's time and it concerned race, particularly in the Midlands of England. Since the Second World War, immigration had been a big issue with Commonwealth citizens arriving from the West Indies and elsewhere. Most people welcomed them, but there were those who didn't and there was no lack of unscrupulous politicians around to spread myths like *"they are here to take our Jobs," "they are here to scrounge off the Welfare State," "they breed like rabbits"* and other such offensive rubbish which deceived and beguiled the gullible.

Historic events occurred in Ireland in January. Ireland had been at peace for several years now, since the IRA had abandoned its campaign against the border. We were beginning to hope that the mighty deeds of Sean South and Kevin Barry would be given their deserved place of honour in the songs of Celtic Park but would be kept there. And those of us who wondered why there had to be two Irelands at all were given encouragement by the sight of the two leaders meeting each other first of all in a snowy Belfast in January and later on in Dublin in February.

Captain Terence O'Neill of the Ulster Unionists, although well aware that he presided over a corrupt and indeed rotten regime, was a thoroughly decent man, it seemed. And so too was Sean Lemass, the Taoiseach of the Dublin Government. They met, handshakes were exchanged, and there was even a hope expressed that a united Ireland, which had been pursued in vain by violent means in the past, might now come about by peace and common sense, with everyone having the right to go to whatever Church they wished. It did not seem to be beyond the wit of sensible people to guarantee the religious rights of everyone in a united Ireland, to work out a woolly compromise to allow anyone to recognise the anachronistic Queen if they wanted to, and then the new Ireland could get on with the important things like standards of living, education, health services etc.

A peaceful solution seemed possible, but unfortunately the Ulster Unionists had a lunatic fringe. It tended to centre on a loud-voiced Minister called the Reverend Ian Paisley, who seemed to be afraid that Captain O'Neill was selling Northern Ireland down the river to people called *"Papists," "Popeheads"* and *"Fenians."* Although generally laughed at in mainland Britain for such nonsense, he obviously was a charismatic gentleman in Ulster and attracted a lot of people (including some who should have known a lot better) to his cause, and his constant ranting over the next few years eventually achieved what he wanted all along in a major renewal of "the troubles" in 1969. In later years, Dr Paisley as he then was, became tolerant, sensible and even likeable. In 1965 he was far from that.

The United States had two major problems in 1965 for President Lyndon B Johnson to deal with, and both of them would plague him for all of his Presidency. One was the endemic one in the Deep South, where the irresistible force of the Civil Rights movement came up against the immovable object of the Ku Klux Klan and other white supremacists. The problem was bad enough, but it was a historic one going back to before the Civil War of 100 years ago. Far worse was the problem that Johnson brought upon himself in Vietnam. To be fair, it was possibly John F Kennedy who had started the whole business but Johnson did little to extricate himself as the problem escalated.

The Vietnam War was a horrible one. It was also very odd in that there was never any outright declaration of war. There was never any "invasion of Poland" or "Twin Towers" moment to start the war. It just seemed that the USA allowed itself to drift into it without any realisation of just what exactly they were doing in their support of the capitalist but corrupt South Vietnam against the prickly and communist North. A whole decade later, the North would win, and what a gross and unnecessary amount of suffering would happen in the meantime!

Rhodesia caused some problems in 1965. Their Prime Minister, Ian Smith, was wanting independence. Normally in the 1960s, this would have been granted, because Britain was beginning to realise that colonial involvements, particularly in Africa, were a great deal more bother than they were all worth. But the Rhodesians refused to make any promises about "unimpeded progress towards majority rule." This meant that what Smith and the Rhodesian Front party wanted was the continuation of white rule so that Rhodesia would effectively become another South Africa. Laudably, Britain said *"No,"* but Rhodesia issued a Unilateral Declaration of Independence in November anyway, and things were at an impasse. It would be many decades before this one was sorted out and the outcome in Zimbabwe (as it became) was not at all what the white Rhodesians would have wanted and indeed they could have had, if they had softened their line.

Europe - France's General de Gaulle in particular, had said *"No"* a couple of years earlier to Britain joining the Common Market, as it was then called. Since then, arguments raged on, boringly and inconclusively, about whether it would be a good thing or not, with most intelligent people believing that it would make sense for Britain to join the Union at some time in the future.

Paul VI was the Pope in Rome, having taken over from Pope John XXIII in 1963. He was a kindly man, made a few concessions towards the Eastern Orthodox Church, but the barriers between the Catholic Church and western Churches still remained as stark as ever, although everything was generally peaceful and even tolerant. Intelligent Roman Catholic women were now, however, in the wake of the recent appearance of the contraceptive pill, beginning to ask questions about the Church's rigid stance on birth control. In Scotland, the Church of Scotland had well over 1,000,000 members and was actually in 1965 at the peak of its power.

Queen Elizabeth II had now been on the British throne for 13 years. She now had four children – not that she saw very much of them – and they had not yet disgraced her as they would sadly do in future years. Her husband, Prince Philip or the Duke of Edinburgh, was looked upon as an amiable sort of buffoon who endeared himself to many people by saying things like the *Daily Express* was a *"bloody awful newspaper."* Curiously, in spite of the grotesque wealth of the Royal Family, there were no great republican sentiments expressed, and those of us who suggested, ever so gently, that possibly one of the palaces might be used for some useful purpose like a hospital or a school were greeted with either pity or anger! The Royal Family, much loved by Rangers supporters, had one thing in common with them – in that they did not open their doors to Roman Catholics – and amazingly, no-one saw any problem with that!

And of course, there were The Beatles! 1965 was arguably their best year, with songs like *"Ticket To Ride."* They had now moved on from their early simple music and had not yet reached the strange stuff that they would produce later on. They were now accepted by most people, although it was very difficult for anyone, particular a young person, to say that they did not like them. Social pressures were such that one would be excluded as a pariah if they dared to say that he or she did not like the Beatles. But there were also Marianne Faithful, Manfred Mann, The Shadows, The Rolling Stones and Bob Dylan, whose *"The Times They Are A'Changin"* seemed to sum up the new world that was developing.

Most households in Scotland now had a television. Colour TV had not yet arrived and there were only two channels, BBC and STV (or Grampian or Border, depending where you lived), but news programmes, sports programmes, soap operas and Scottish programmes involving Kenneth McKellar and Andy Stewart were devoured with enthusiasm and relish. Some working-class households were now beginning to aspire to own the two other symbols of prosperity which were hitherto considered to be the prerogative of the middle-classes – namely the motor car and the telephone. People were living longer, the National Health Service had eradicated a lot of the preventable horrors of the 1930s – there had been a notable success with TB, for example – and in every respect things were a lot better than they had been even ten years ago.

The prevalence of television gave an added boost to sports, football in particular – if any such boost was required. Attendances at football grounds were beginning to fall, but this was emphatically not because of any decline in interest in the game. It was certainly a comment on the appalling facilities at most grounds and the realisation that there were now other things that one could do on a Saturday afternoon. But there was still the desire to listen to a radio commentary of a game, to watch the Saturday night highlights and to read the Saturday evening and Sunday morning newspapers.

In England, Manchester United, now totally recovered from the Munich Disaster of 1958 and with ex-Celt Pat Crerand on board, won the First Division. Everyone was delighted for the courageous Matt Busby, and it was another Scottish Manager who won the FA Cup. This was Bill Shankly (whose brother Bob was the Manager of Dundee and then Hibs in 1965) who, having won the League in 1964 for Liverpool, now lifted the trophy, almost unbelievably for the first time, by beating Leeds United in a game where both captains were Scottish – the huge Ron Yeats and the diminutive Bobby Collins. And just to compete the set, as it were, the Manager of the winners of the League Cup was also Scottish – Tommy Docherty of Chelsea, but it would be fair to say that the League Cup in England did not as yet enjoy anything like the esteem that the other two trophies did, or indeed that of its Scottish equivalent. The final, for example, was played over two legs, and it was not until the trophy was awarded a Wembley final in 1967 that it began to be as prestigious as it is now. In Scotland, Stirling Albion won the Second Division and were promoted along with Hamilton Accies to replace Airdrie and Third Lanark. Sadly, the famous old Cathkin outfit now only had a couple of years to live and would never see the First Division again.

And of course, everyone was excited about the World Cup to be held in England next July. Plans were being drawn up, venues organised, TV coverage arranged. It promised to be the most exciting World Cup yet. England, of course, qualified automatically as did Brazil, the current holders. Both Irelands and Wales failed to make it, and the loss of Scotland in December of this year was a blow to the finances, but nevertheless everyone looked forward to the tournament with relish.

Boxing provided quite a talking point in 1965 with the man called Cassius Clay (who had now changed his name to Muhammad Ali) taking on Sonny Liston twice and winning both bouts, in February 1964 and May 1965. There were the usual allegations of "fixing," but Clay/Ali at least was good box office material, in that he talked a lot, and kept the television companies happy.

Scotland had a very poor season in the Five Nations (as it then was) Rugby Union Championship, losing to everyone except England, with whom they shared an appallingly dull 3-3 draw on the same day that Celtic drew with Dundee at Dens Park by the same score! The difference of course was that the football 3-3 was great entertainment, albeit full of errors. The rugby 3-3 was similarly full of errors, but lacked any kind of entertainment whatsoever!

Test Cricket saw England beat New Zealand in the first half of the season without any sort of problem, but they found the South Africans in the second half of the season to be a different kettle of fish altogether. More and more people began to protest about apartheid at cricket matches where South Africa were playing. In Scotland, West Lothian won the County Championship, and Ferguslie and Edinburgh University respectively won the Western and Eastern Leagues. In the other summer sports, it was all about Australia, with Roy Emerson and Margaret Smith winning at Wimbledon and Peter Thomson clinching the British Open Golf Championship at Royal Birkdale.

In general terms, although one has to say that there were plenty of changes, most of them for the better as the healthy "baby boomers" were now growing up and claiming places in universities, the word "revolution," if it could be applied at all, would have to be qualified by words like "slow" and "gradual." It took some time to persuade working-class youngsters, particularly girls, that they were entitled to go to university. Once again, it was a quiet, slow and almost unnoticed development.

At Celtic Park, however, the changes were dramatic, obvious and quite breathtaking!

PROLOGUE

SEVEN LEAN YEARS

The deliriously happy Celtic End of Hampden on Saturday, 19 October 1957 could hardly have believed just exactly what was coming. Those who said that that game would be talked about as long as football would be played had a point. It had been an absolutely glorious performance from a team at the height of their form with everyone playing the kind of football of which they were capable. If anyone was to be singled out, it would be Willie Fernie, but that is not to imply that there were any weak links, and the team of *Beattie, Donnelly and Fallon; Fernie, Evans and Peacock; Tully, Collins, McPhail, Wilson and Mochan* rightly have their place among the best of Celtic teams.

The journey home was spent in cheerful predictions of the glorious future that was beckoning. Rangers seemed to be broken and damaged irreparably. Hearts were good that season, but how nice it would be if Celtic could mount a League challenge! It almost went without saying that there would be an attempt on the Scottish Cup, Celtic's favourite trophy and already won 17 times. The future looked rosy, but now was the time to relish and revel in that great 7-1 triumph, and to crack all the jokes about the time being *"Seven past Niven"* and how poor old George Niven (not, in truth, the worst goalkeeper, in the world) had to consult his doctor about back pains caused by too much bending to pick the ball out of the back of the net.

But by New Year, little more than two months later, Celtic were already out of the League race with four defeats in a row over Christmas and New Year, and then a defeat by Clyde in the Scottish Cup on the opening day of March meant that the 7-1 game was going to be the only triumph that season. Injuries played their part in this sudden and dramatic decline, but it was also true that some players were now past their best, notably Sean Fallon and Charlie Tully, for example. These two Irishmen had contributed immensely to the team, and Fallon of course had a great part yet to play in the management of the club, but their playing days more or less ended with the 7-1 cup final.

It was a disappointing end to the season – a certain amount of humour being caused by the alliterative pair of full-backs called Meechan and Mochan – but there was still the glow of 7-1 to keep the supporters happy. And of course, there was the always potent factor that Rangers hadn't done well either, as Hearts, the lesser of the two evils, won the Scottish League and Clyde won the Scottish Cup. Scotland then had neither its first nor its last disappointing World Cup in the summer of 1958.

It was one of life's supreme ironies that Celtic who had destroyed Rangers in October 1957 were also the team that resurrected them in April 1959. It was the last day of the season. Hearts who had won the 1957/58 Scottish League Championship and the 1958/59 Scottish League Cup in fine fashion, had not quite dominated the League this year and were seemingly losing out to a Rangers team which had improved only very slightly and even when winning games were often leaving the field to the catcalls and boos of their own supporters!

The last day of the 1958/59 League season saw Rangers play Aberdeen at Ibrox, and their only challengers Hearts play Celtic at Parkhead. If both teams won, drew or lost Rangers would win the title in a somewhat unconvincing way. As it turned out, Rangers lost to Aberdeen and their supporters were trudging away home disgusted and unhappy until they heard the news that Celtic, (yes Celtic!) had done them a favour by beating Hearts.

It was possibly Celtic's best result of the season, but paradoxically also their worst. It had been a dreadful season, and yet there had been good results too. Such things are likely to happen with a youth policy and this was the first year that Celtic had declared that they were operating such a policy.

The idea was a good one, and if the policy had been better organised, it might have produced results a great deal sooner than it did, but there was no real thinking behind it with the Chairman giving the impression that he was quite happy to write off this particular season. Mr Kelly had clearly been impressed by Manchester United's "Busby Babes" and his youngsters were called the "Kelly Kids," men like John Colrain, Jim Conway, Alec Byrne, Pat Crerand, Billy McNeill, John Hughes and Charlie Gallagher, some of whom made it, and some of whom didn't.

Part of this plan, however, involved the selling off of experienced players like Bobby Collins and Willie Fernie. Both of these decisions were colossal mistakes, as events would prove, but there was also the fact that Celtic had belatedly decided that they needed floodlights at Celtic Park. They turned out to be the best in the business, but of course they had to be paid for, and however much it was officially denied, the sale of Collins and Fernie did help to pay for these necessary improvements. The folly of it all in footballing terms was made apparent when Fernie was brought back from Middlesbrough two years later, whilst Collins was still playing for Scotland as late as 1965, the same year in which he led Leeds United to an English FA Cup final appearance!

Celtic, although they played the "kingmaker" role at the end of the season 1958/59, were never themselves considered as challengers after so many awful performances. At the start of the season, they had qualified from their League Cup section but lost to Partick Thistle in the semi-final. As is often the case, it was the Scottish Cup after the New Year which provided the main hope of a major honour for Celtic. And things looked good when Celtic put Rangers out at Celtic Park on the last day of February with the goals scored by John Divers and Matt McVittie, two of the "promising" Kelly Kids. It was a well-deserved victory and did little to dispel the current Glasgow belief that Rangers were going nowhere.

But then came the semi-final on April 4 at Hampden, when a ragged Celtic team collapsed 0-4 to an experienced St Mirren side who would go on to win the Cup. Phrases like *"little boys lost"* were used and comparisons made with the pantomime "Babes In The Wood," as the traumatised youngsters had simply no answer to the St Mirren onslaught. Some experienced players like Evans and Peacock did what they could to stem the tide, but this was a chastening experience for the much vaunted "youth policy."

And yet the defeat of Rangers at the end of February and the defeat of Hearts which gifted the title to Rangers showed what could happen on a good day. Another good day came when Celtic won the Glasgow Charity Cup by beating Clyde 5-0, but what hurt was that they couldn't win on the days that really mattered.

Still, it was one bad season. We had had bad seasons before, we reckoned, and maybe it was necessary to have a bad season in order to blood the youngsters. Next season would be better as the youngsters would have grown up a little in the tough unyielding, unforgiving environment that Scottish football certainly was. But would they?

The answer was a resounding *"No."* The start to this season had been much heralded, as always, but the immature Celts managed to lose their first four games, the worst start that anyone could remember. Effectively when the weather was still warm, the cricket season was still going strong and before a single leaf had dropped from a tree, Celtic were out of the Scottish League Cup and the Glasgow Cup. They never really recovered from all this, lost twice to Rangers in the League and generally drove their support crazy with form that the charitable called *"inconsistent"* and the more honest simply called *"awful."*

And yet a few players were beginning to emerge. Young McNeill was beginning to challenge Bobby Evans for his place (and that was possibly one of the reasons why Evans departed in summer 1960 after 16 years with the club) and up front, Divers, the son of an earlier John Divers and the grand-nephew of Patsy Gallacher, and a speedy character called Chalmers were beginning to hint at and promise something. It was just, as yet, a promise, though.

The Scottish Cup came round again and hope kept springing eternal. Last year's conquerors, St Mirren, were defeated but we needed three games to do it! Then a very narrow squeak at Elgin in a game where The *Evening Times* described the young Celtic side as *"frightened,"* a reasonably good performance against Partick Thistle, and then Rangers in the semi-final at Hampden.

It was last chance saloon for both Glasgow teams, for the League Championship was heading slowly but definitely towards Tynecastle, the place where the League Cup had also gone, and the first game was a respectable draw made memorable by a wonderful Steve Chalmers header of which Jimmy McGrory himself would have been proud. The replay was set for Wednesday with a tea-time kick-off and Celtic unaccountably folded to a 1-4 defeat. An unhappy season finished with Celtic drawing again with Rangers in the Glasgow Charity Cup – but going out on the toss of a coin. We couldn't even win that!

A significant event happened when Jock Stein left the Celtic Park set-up in March to become Manager of Dunfermline Athletic. His very first game saw the hitherto underperforming Pars beat Celtic en route to saving themselves from relegation. We did not realise the significance of all this until much later. We were far more concerned that the youth policy had still not delivered!

The following season 1960/61 was not the worst of the seven lean years – indeed there was a definite improvement in some areas – but it was the most frustrating. Any chances of winning the Scottish League had gone by Christmas, thanks (yet again) to inconsistent team selections and performances, but at least the club agreed that a mistake had been made when Willie Fernie was brought back. Some of us even hoped and prayed for Bobby Collins as well, but that ship had apparently sailed.

The Scottish League Cup section had seemed to be designed for no other reason than to torment Celtic. By chance, it had been drawn as an all-Glasgow section of Celtic, Rangers, Partick Thistle and Third Lanark. Celtic went to Ibrox and won 3-2 with John Hughes very impressive, and as Celtic had also beaten them at Parkhead in the Glasgow Cup, things were looking very good indeed. With two games to go in the League Cup section – and both home games against Partick Thistle and Rangers – all Celtic had to do was win one of them or draw the two of them. But this was 1960, and there seemed to be this unwritten law that Celtic must blow up on important occasions, and they duly did so, losing 1-2 on both occasions in the unforgiving rain which summed up everyone's mood. The League Cup having been exited in this manner, Celtic then lost 1-5 to Rangers in the League the following week. The good start to the season had been illusory, a dream almost. Reality hit hard.

Soon after that came the incident that frankly defies belief, but which was also typical of Celtic at that time. They had lost the Glasgow Cup final to Partick Thistle on the Monday in a disappointing performance. On the following Saturday, they were in the bus going to Airdrie when they saw young reserve goalkeeper Willie Goldie, Celtic scarf round his neck, waiting for a service bus to take him to the game. Mr Kelly stopped the bus and offered him a lift. Fair enough so far, but then once they reached Broomfield, Kelly suddenly decided that Goldie was to play instead of John Fallon! Goldie, who didn't even have his boots with him, was thunderstruck and overwhelmed. A bag of nerves, Willie conceded two goals and Celtic lost 0-2! Willie never got another game for Celtic! And what does it say about the organisation of the club?

But that was as nothing compared to the Scottish Cup final in April 1961. The final had been reached thanks to some good performances, admittedly against poor opposition in Montrose, Raith Rovers and Airdrie, but there had also been an epic couple of games against Hibs. A late equaliser at Parkhead had been followed by an even later winner at Easter Road in the replay, and there was every reason to believe that "Celtic's name was on the Cup," as the saying went.

There was the "mystic" reason, as it were, that since 1892 never had more than seven years peace time seasons passed without Celtic winning the Scottish Cup, and 1954 was now seven years away. This rubbish was peddled in newspapers and even encouraged by the club itself, with Mr Kelly often claiming that there was some sort of Providence guiding the affairs of Celtic.

There were more concrete reasons as well for believing in a Scottish Cup triumph. The forward line of Gallagher, Fernie, Hughes, Chalmers and Byrne was now doing well and producing the goods, backed up by a brilliant right-half in Pat Crerand, who was one of the best passers of a ball since Peter Wilson or Malky MacDonald.

In addition, Rangers had been removed by Motherwell, Hearts were also out, as were Dundee, Aberdeen and Hibs, and the opponents were none other than Jock Stein's Dunfermline Athletic, who had put out those traditional doughty Cup fighters St Mirren in the semi-final. There seemed to be no problem with the Pars, making their first appearance in a final, and the Celtic support were animated and enthusiastic, believing that the lean years were at an end. It was an opinion shared also by the Scottish Press.

But alas! The agonies of the disappointment of the first game, which was simply dull, were surpassed one hundredfold by the anguish of the second one. Two men, a Manager and a goalkeeper, both Celtic sympathisers in their spare time, collaborated to deny us the Scottish Cup as our feckless forwards threw it all away when we had about 95% of the play and the territorial advantage! A 0-5 hammering would have been easier to take! As it happened, Celtic pounded the King's Park goal in the first half, and the Mount Florida goal in the second, but we couldn't score. The Pars scored halfway through the second half, and then again with the last kick of the ball. The scars inflicted on those who were there or who listened to that desperately awful radio broadcast are still there over 60 years later.

Season 1961/62 saw a genuine improvement and clear signs that a good side was developing, particularly in midfield around Crerand and McNeill. Round about Christmas, there was a buoyancy that hadn't been seen for many years and there was a feeling that 1962 was to be the year. Alas, bad weather around New Year disrupted things, a few dismal draws followed and by February and March it was generally agreed that Celtic would be a good third. Yet, they beat Champions Dundee in early March and drew twice with Rangers! The problem was inconsistency, with inexplicable defeats to Falkirk, Stirling Albion and Airdrie away from home at key points of the season, and then a colossal disaster of a defeat to relegation-haunted Raith Rovers at Parkhead on the same day that Rangers won the Scottish Cup a mile away at Hampden!

These were all painful, and the season had started with a puzzling failure against St Johnstone (who would be relegated at the end of the season!) both home and away in the League Cup – the defeat at Perth being accompanied by some appalling hooliganism, a somewhat frequent leitmotif of that season with dreadful thuggery at places like Falkirk, Dundee and the culmination of it all at Ibrox (on a day when we were not playing against Rangers).

It was the Scottish Cup once again that produced anticipation and agony in equal measure. Having disposed of Cowdenbeath and Morton (both potential banana skins), Celtic then delighted their fans by coming back from the dead against both Hearts and Third Lanark to impress the rest of the country, delight the football purists and to set up a semi-final against St Mirren at Ibrox on the last day of March.

Once again, fortune seemed to be smiling on Celtic. St Mirren (although they now had Willie Fernie, released prematurely by Celtic for the second time!) were struggling against relegation and on the Monday before the game, Celtic thumped them 5-0 at Love Street in what was, for Celtic, a now meaningless League game. And yes, the serpent of complacency slithered in the door of Paradise, as we spent the rest of that week hoping that Motherwell would beat Rangers in the other semi-final, and we could face the Well at Hampden in the final.

A horror story, in some ways worse than last season's final, was about to begin. It was a bright but windy day as sometimes happens at Ibrox at the end of March with a brisk breeze blowing in from the west. Celtic won the toss, captain Dunky MacKay chose to play AGAINST the wind – and the players all fell out about it! Conventional wisdom was that you play WITH the wind because you never know what the wind will be doing in an hour's time, but Dunky seems to have made that decision on his own. A dispute is never good news, and playing against the wind, Celtic were 3-0 down by half-time!

In the catalogue of "Celtic Self-Destructions," this one is near the top, but it got worse. The fans took it for a while in surly silence in the second half, but then invaded the park in a misguided and crazy attempt to get a replay. It was never likely to succeed, the Celtic Directors, honourable men if nothing else, conceded the tie and although the players came back and Alec Byrne scored, Celtic were not only out of the Cup again, but actually very lucky not to face a ban for several years.

There were three crumbs of comfort. Dundee, not Rangers, won the Scottish League, McNeill and Crerand both played magnificently as Scotland beat England 2-0 at Hampden, and Celtic won the Glasgow Cup, beating Third Lanark in a replayed final at a virtually flooded Parkhead one Friday night in May before a low crowd. It wasn't much, but when you haven't won anything for a while, the Glasgow Cup becomes important. And so it should, for it is a fine and beautiful old trophy.

But the agony continued. If 1961 and 1962 had been frustrating, then 1963 was rock bottom. The League Cup had been another failure. It all ended with an inability to score one single goal at Tannadice Park. A perfectly legitimate goal, at least a foot over the line, had been refused, after a Dundee United player had hooked the ball clear, then Celtic pressed and pressed but squandered chance after chance. Hearts were the beneficiaries and went on to win the League Cup.

The League form was inconsistent. The first game against Rangers was lost when Pat Crerand missed a penalty and confidence plummeted. Then they regained form, thumping a couple of teams before, gallingly, blowing up against Queen of the South. And then we came up to the New Year. 1963 began as it meant to continue with a 0-4 defeat at Ibrox, but there was more to it than that, for Pat Crerand, whose heart had not been in it for a while and which certainly was not with Celtic that day, never played again, being transferred to Manchester United in the middle of the big freeze-up in February.

Pat won an English FA Cup medal that year, but the Scottish Cup final of 1963 saw Celtic supporters experience the depths of misery. An acceptable 1-1 draw in the first game against Rangers was followed by a 3-0 defeat in the replay. Celtic with an appallingly bad team selection were beaten well before half-time and the third goal saw the famous and dramatic exodus from the Celtic End as 60,000 turned their backs on Celtic in silence apart from the occasional curse of Bob Kelly and Pat Crerand.

Wise old supporters said, *"They'll come again!"* but it didn't seem likely for two reasons. One was that at the top it didn't really seem to matter. Chairman Bob Kelly did not seem to care that he was leading the club of which his father had been a founder player to disaster. It was now 75 years since that famous May night in 1888 when they played their first game, and there was nothing to celebrate. The club seemed to be finished.

The other reason was the seeming invincibility of the arrogant victors. The newspapers and the BBC certainly told us that often enough and superiority emanated in every way from the west end of Glasgow. It was as if nature had intended all this, and that there was a team destined to rule. No-one seemed to have the desire to challenge them. Celtic had actually beaten them in the Glasgow Cup in November – but had then blown up in the next round. No-one else seemed able to face Rangers and their "superior" supporters with their *"We are the people"* nonsense.

Nor did anyone seem to want to challenge their religious policy. Church of Scotland Ministers would talk in sermons about love and would do immortal memories at Burns Suppers without apparently realising that there was anything wrong with their team excluding Roman Catholics. Labour Councillors who would similarly be expected to show at least a tolerance of the religion practised by so many of Glasgow's population, failed to do so and boasted of their season tickets at Ibrox. Why did no-one think it was wrong? Why did such behaviour triumph?

The rest of 1963 saw more 0-3 beatings from Rangers, mounted police galloping up London Road to quell an anti-Kelly demonstration and more depression. A slight rallying by the end of 1963, but still a year from Hell.

More recently, 1964 had certainly been a great deal better than 1963, but still contained several major heartbreaks. There had been a creditable run in Europe for the first time, but naivety was the downfall. In the semi-final of the European Cup Winners' Cup in April, Celtic had beaten MTK of Hungary 3-0 at Parkhead and optimism was in the air that Celtic might reach the final to be played in Brussels. Sadly, the team then went to Budapest and lost 0-4, everything being blamed on faulty tactics of continuing to attack, and the referee. The referee was, by all accounts, bad...but the naivety had lain in expecting anything else!

And there had been in 1964 three heartbreaks to Rangers, all on occasions when Celtic had been expected to win. The first was

New Year's Day, the second in March a few days after an excellent result in Europe against Slovan Bratislava. We were all on the crest of a wave and expecting great things at Ibrox in the Scottish Cup quarter-final. Alas! After a reasonable first half in which one could argue that Celtic were the better side, two goals were lost either side of half-time and Celtic once again obeyed the rule that they must succumb to Rangers, whose supporters cried *"Easy! Easy!"* as Celtic caved in.

Even more painful was the Scottish League Cup final of 24 October 1964. This was a great deal worse, for Celtic had by this time beaten Rangers some seven weeks earlier at a rainy Parkhead. In addition, Rangers were going through a bad patch, and, irrationally, it was felt that as Labour had won the British General Election of nine days before, things were changing in Scottish football as well. Celtic were without Billy McNeill, but John Cushley was filling in the gap more than adequately.

Was this to be "Der Tag", when a national trophy at last returned to Parkhead after seven long, lean years like the Biblical years of famine? No. One could have written the script for it, for the game followed the familiar pattern of Celtic on top in the first half while attacking the King's Park end, but missing chances, with Jimmy Johnstone and Bobby Murdoch the major culprits, and then a more than reasonable penalty claim was turned down.

Then Rangers rallied in the second half, scored twice and although Celtic pulled one back, it was too late and once again we had to endure the sight of the Press adulating the antics of Jim Baxter with a Cup. It was just too painful, but the worst aspect of it all was that Celtic now went into freefall, and we all despaired of there ever again being a Celtic team worthy of the name. Once again, we heard the word *"finished."*

An awful two months followed. There were defeats to Kilmarnock, St Johnstone and Dundee, and then when the team seemed to have rallied a little, a defeat at home to Dunfermline on December

19 brought us back with another bump. Except, by this time, the supporters were departing in droves. They had had enough. Defeats were bad enough, but what was worse was the apparent insouciance of the Directors and Bob Kelly in particular. In mid-November they had gone into the transfer market – and bought Hugh Maxwell from Falkirk, a man about whom it was a fair bet that no Celtic supporter had ever heard of! Poor Hugh! He did score one of the fastest goals in Celtic history after about 10 seconds when his old mates came calling on November 21, but he did little else. He was an "honest journeyman" at best – possibly even a little less than that - and by the following summer, when Jock Stein was in charge, he was on his way to St Johnstone.

It was the defeat to Dunfermline (a late goal scored by one Alex Ferguson giving the Pars a 2-1 victory) which really told us that we were going nowhere. Christmas was a terrible time, with the real fear that Celtic would now never come back. The stadium was a disgrace (at both the Dunfermline game on December 19 and the Motherwell game on December 26, supporters tried to light fires to keep warm on the desolate terracings, and they had no problem finding litter and other rubbish that no-one had bothered to pick up!), the team was a shambles, there was no leadership and no prospect of any improvement. And yet there remained a huge support and plenty of money!

In the past, particularly in late summer 1963, there had been supporters' demonstrations against the Board and Mr Kelly in particular, but now in the midwinter frosty gloom of dark December 1964, no-one even bothered about Celtic. The word *"finished"* was freely used and *The Sunday Post* published a letter with a really rather brilliant analogy of the good ship SS Celtic heading towards the rocks and Captain Kelly saying that everything was all right.

Several players, notably Billy McNeill, admitted afterwards that they were thinking of a move to England next season, and Bobby Murdoch and a few others talked about emigration. Falkirk were interested in Bobby Lennox. John Hughes was greatly admired by both Newcastle United and Sunderland. Jimmy Johnstone was thinking of giving up the game altogether. There was certainly little to entice an ambitious player to stay there and it must have been an even more dreadful situation for them, because so many of them were supporters as well – but supporters of what? A team with a brilliant, glorious past, but no present. Celtic were indeed the poor team with a big support.

As always, there were ways out of the problem. Solutions presented themselves. In this case in late February 1964, Jock Stein, Manager of Dunfermline had announced that he was leaving the club at the end of the season. He had no club to go to at the moment. It was clear to anyone with half an eye to see such things that he was angling for Celtic Park. Did the Board pick up on this? Not yet. Stein was allowed to go to Hibs instead, and an opportunity had gone.

But now even the support was now clearly diminishing. Boxing Day, Saturday, 26 December 1964, saw only the real diehards there for what was now an irrelevant fixture against Motherwell. Possibly 5,000 were present at the start, and although it grew a little, the crowd never even reached the 10,000 figure which some optimistic journalists claimed. The pitch was hard, and there had been a little snow and frost. Several other games were off, but this one survived. Oddly enough it wasn't a bad game, and John Hughes wearing sandshoes scored twice, once in each half, taking them both well. It was a least a win, but it didn't disguise the problems.

The irony was that Rangers were struggling too. Their trophy-winning year of 1964 had been good, but they were now toiling, particularly after Jim Baxter had picked up a broken leg in a European game. A good Celtic team might have been able to capitalise, but as it happened, it was Hearts and Kilmarnock at the top of the League with Hibs and Dunfermline not far behind. Some said this was good for the game in Scotland. Celtic fans could not really agree and the visit to Ibrox on New Year's Day was looked upon like a visit to the dentist.

And what was going on in the rest of the world in 1964? Labour had now been in power for almost three months and had already impressed everyone by their determination and drive, as distinct from the decrepitude of the Conservatives. In the USA, Lyndon B Johnston had fended off a challenge from the dangerous Barry Goldwater in the Presidential Election but was now finding himself more and more involved in Vietnam, while the Blacks and the Civil Rights movement were beginning to cause him trouble. The Beatles were around with their *"I Feel Fine"* hit, and the health of Sir Winston Churchill (now 90) was beginning to cause concern.

But there still seemed no way out for Celtic. Wordsworth says that being young at the time of the French Revolution was *"very heaven."* Being young in these awful days was *"very hell."* Brought up on Patsy Gallacher, Jimmy McGrory, Young, Loney and Hay, Alec McNair and Jimmy Delaney, in a culturally rich childhood laced with tales of goals scored with the ball wedged between the feet of a man who somersaulted into the back of the net, brave goalkeepers killed when diving at the feet of a forward, goals scored by a man who could score a hat-trick in three minutes and another who went to Third Lanark then *"pined for home,"* I could not fault my background. But what was happening now? Would these days never come back? Were Celtic really finished?

Hogmanay was dry and not too cold, and if you weren't going out to a party or any of the "Seeing The New Year In" gatherings at the various town centres across Scotland, you had a choice between Andy Stewart (a less than closet Rangers supporter) and Duncan Macrae on the BBC or Kenneth McKellar and Francie and Josie on STV. Tomorrow of course would have the big game at Ibrox, kick off 2.00pm. Gair Henderson (often referred to unfairly as *"Gers"* Henderson because of his perceived Rangers bias) in *The Evening Times* tipped Rangers to win that one narrowly, although he didn't rule out a draw. His reasoning was that Rangers had no bad players, but Celtic simply could not be relied upon to take their chances. He was not far off the mark.

Naturally, New Year is a time to look back and to look forward. 1964 had in some ways been the most painful of all the lean years. The standard of play had possibly improved, but there were still the old failings of the forwards, and in spite of the epic win over them on September 5 in the rain, the massive inferiority complex about Rangers. 1964 soon reasserted itself. The decline had been all the more painful because we had come so close in that awful League Cup final, but then after Hampden, we had collapsed, and there now were definite clear signs that so many supporters had had enough, choosing to talk about horse-racing, wrestling (a major hit in some households on STV on a Saturday afternoon), or English football rather than the now apparently doomed green and whites. Some even expressed a preference for the other green and whites - of Edinburgh, now managed by Jock Stein.

So what would the future bring in 1965? We were not, of course, privy to what had been going on behind the scenes, but few were optimistic. All one could do was take each game as it came. New Year's Day was a Friday in 1965, and there was another game on Saturday January 2 against Clyde at Parkhead. Just what would the future bring?

On a personal note, this young schoolboy was making progress with his Latin at Forfar Academy. He recalls reading the famous line in Virgil's *Aeneid Book II* when the leader of the Trojan refugees is asked by Queen Dido of Carthage to tell her about the fall of Troy and the subsequent sufferings of the Trojans, and he says *"infandum, regina, jubes renovare dolorem,"* which means NOT *"the jujubes renew the pain of the queen's infant,"* as it was once famously translated by Billy Bunter, but *"unspeakable, oh queen, is the grief which you ask me to renew."* That was Celtic in the early 1960s – *"unspeakable grief"* – but in the same way as the

Trojans would find a promised land in Rome and become *"a nation once again,"* so did better days beckon for Celtic. It was difficult, however, to see or even envisage them in December 1964.

CHAPTER ONE

JANUARY

Ibrox and New Year's Day seldom went well together for Celtic. They had not beaten Rangers there on January 1 since 1921 when Joe Cassidy had scored a couple in a famous victory, and of course New Year's Day at Ibrox in 1943 had seen an infamous 1-8 defeat. Even though there were extenuating circumstances, like an apparently drunk referee who sent off two Celtic players for appealing for offside at one of the goals, and the undeniable fact that far more important things were happening in Africa and Stalingrad at the time, it still hurt those who had been there and found itself a place in Parkhead demonology. Just as well that the wartime Southern League was still considered to be an unofficial tournament,

History then, both distant and recent, were against Celtic on this cold but dry New Year's Day of 1965. Celtic had had a slight boost from a good 2-0 win over Motherwell on Boxing Day, but almost everyone fancied the Ibrox side. Although Celtic fans were outnumbered in the 60,000 crowd, they still made up a sizeable minority and saw a performance from them that seemed to typify their team in those days – rugged, determined and the better side for at least part of the game, but riddled with errors and folly – and once again Celtic fans despaired of their team, who would never uprise, it appeared. They did not seem to know how to win. In modern terminology, they lacked game management skills.

Promptly at 2.00pm (the earlier than normal start being preferred, so that the game would finish in daylight) Tom Wharton of

Clarkston started the game. He was one of the characters of the game, a huge man called *"Tiny"* in a figure of speech called by the learned *"antiphrasis"* (saying something which was the opposite of the truth). He was not always universally loved, but he was respected, and was famously impartial, although inclined to show off now and again.

The teams were;

Rangers: ***Ritchie, Provan and Caldow; Greig, McKinnon and Wood; Wilson, Millar, Forrest, Beck and Johnston.***

Celtic: ***Simpson, Young and Gemmell; Clark, McNeill and Kennedy; Johnstone, Murdoch, Hughes, Divers and Gallagher.***

Old Firm games are rarely classic encounters and this one certainly wasn't, but nevertheless the supporters who paid three shillings to get in were not cheated as the teams hammered into each other. Tackles were robust, and referee Wharton was hard put to keep the lid on things. Celtic, playing away from their own fans in the first half, had marginally the better of the first quarter of the game, but as was often the way of the world in those days it was Rangers who scored first. It was in the aftermath of a corner kick when Jimmy Millar headed the ball on for Jim Forrest who had beaten Billy McNeill to it. McNeill was going through a poor spell in those days – either the cause or the effect of his being unsettled. He was also still recovering from an injury. His unhappiness was obvious and spread throughout the team.

It was approaching half-time when the incident occurred for which this game is best remembered. Jimmy Johnstone had clearly been identified as a Celtic dangerman by the Rangers management and Theorelf Beck (a fair-haired Icelander whom they had signed from St Mirren and enjoyed the unlikely nickname of "Tottie") had clearly been assigned to keep an eye on him. There had been several low-level fouls on Jimmy throughout the first half, and clearly the Celtic winger was getting angry. Then Beck won the ball from Jimmy but seemed to have fouled him the process. Jimmy cracked and charged into him. Whether he punched him, elbowed him or just ran into him was a matter of some irrelevance (and the TV pictures had no obvious or conclusive evidence) – it was violent conduct, and Jimmy made no real protest. When asked his name, the story goes, Jimmy said *"Roy Rodgers."* Wharton then said, *"Well, go and join Trigger in the dressing room."* (Trigger was the famous horse of the cowboy Roy Rodgers)

It was a surreal moment. The huge Wharton, the diminutive Johnstone and Beck supine on the field. It looked like bullying, but no-one could really defend Johnstone who had fallen into the Rangers trap. It was galling, however, to see, very soon after the departure of Jimmy up the tunnel, the complete recovery of the despicable Beck who played a full part in the second half.

Oddly enough, a word of sympathy for Jim (sic) Johnstone comes from Gair Henderson in *The Evening Times*, who while agreeing that the referee could not ignore such an obvious foul, also says that several others on both sides were well worthy of the long, lonely walk as well, and he singles out Jimmy Millar and Dave Provan of Rangers, and John Hughes of Celtic who was indeed "booked" for his "clumsy" tackle.

One wonders what the half-time talk was like. Two years previously had seen the infamous argument between Sean Fallon and Pat Crerand, with Crerand apparently threatening to go home and leave Celtic with only ten men. Now as it happened, two years later, they were in a position where they were in fact reduced to ten men and were a goal behind.

But then, something odd happened, as Celtic, backed up by a defiant support who sang and clapped, and although outnumbered, were able to drown out the much larger Rangers support. *The Scottish Daily Express*, pro-Rangers as always but admiring of Celtic's pluck, talks about *"a hint of anxiety beginning to creep into the battle hymns of the Ibrox faithful,"* as Celtic, possibly in the belief that they had nothing to lose in any case, decided to *"have a go."* Wing-halves John Clark and Jim Kennedy took a grip, and the two full-backs Ian Young and Tommy Gemmell began to get the better of their direct opponents, and the Celtic fans began to believe that a miracle, or at least a respectable draw, was possible.

One has to be very suspicious about how it is more difficult to play against ten men than eleven. That is sheer rubbish normally, but then again, it depends on the quality of the ten, (May 1979 proving an egregious example) who in this case, decided that they would show the world what they could do against a team who, as later events in 1965 would prove, had peaked and who no longer warranted or deserved the adulation that they got in the Press.

One wonders how Celtic would have done if Jimmy Johnstone had remained on the field, but it is sometimes misleading to talk about Jimmy Johnstone. In 1965, Jimmy, neurotic, insecure and anything but a team man, was far from the world-beater that he became, and he possibly might not have made too much of a difference. But then we come to the moment which haunted Bobby Murdoch all the remaining 36 years of his life. We were well into the last ten minutes of the game when Celtic, now playing towards their own supporters, were awarded a penalty kick by the relentlessly fair Mr Wharton when Hughes was brought down by McKinnon.

Up lumbered Bobby, those behind the goal ready to celebrate a deserved draw and even beginning to talk about going on to win the game – but Bobby, psyched out by the occasion, blazed the ball over the bar! It was a bitter, bitter moment for Murdoch and the whole Celtic community. Perhaps, we really were, after all, not "meant" to beat Rangers. The full-time whistle came soon after, bringing with it the desolation of defeat.

New Year's Night was depressing, but we did not have a great deal of time for any prolonged introspection as there was another game on January 2, against Clyde at Celtic Park. The sparse crowd were greeted with a somewhat controversial team selection. In those days, there was no automatic suspension for the next match of a man who had been sent off and Jimmy Johnstone could have played. But he was out, and so was Bobby Murdoch, and the following day's newspapers carried pictures of them sitting unhappily in the stand. Murdoch apparently was injured, which immediately raised the question of why he was allowed to take that late penalty, (in all truth the "injury" was possibly a mental one following his miss) but that was not the main topic of conversation. It was the dropping of Jimmy Johnstone with no explanation forthcoming. Jimmy was cheered as he took his seat in the stand after loud booing of the team announcement.

The forward line thus read *Lennox, Maxwell, Hughes, Divers and Gallagher*. It did not sound a convincing one, but in four minutes, the team was handed a boost when John Hughes took advantage of a slack pass-back to crash home a fine shot. The goal was deservedly greeted with acclaim, but then after an inspired period of play on a hard and difficult pitch, Celtic began to lose out to a competent Clyde side, and it was no real surprise when Gilroy headed home a well-taken free kick with questions being asked, not for the first time, about Billy McNeill.

It was 1-1 at half-time, and a feckless second half followed with Celtic unable to take a grip on the game, *The Evening Times* reporting that *"the angry crowd kept up a continuous chorus of boos and whistles, and the feet of cold, disgruntled fans pounded on the floor of the stand."* It was a graphic description and indicated the anger and the despair of the fans. Just what was going on? More importantly was there now any way out?

The game that was due to be played against Hibs on Monday, 4 January 1965 was frozen off and frankly, this decision must have been greeted with a sigh of relief from both management and supporters. As the holiday ended, and supporters began to trickle back to their work, traditionally the lowest time of the year, the prevailing mood was depression, laced with apparent apathy and even hostility, but these latter two emotions were defence mechanisms.

It was difficult not to be angry, however, with the Chairman and the Directors whose arrogance was quite breathtaking. Because the Manager was Jimmy McGrory, little real anger was directed at him, but most supporters were, reluctantly, of the opinion that he should be replaced. The real problem of course lay higher up, and it would be hard to find a supporter who did not want the removal of Mr Kelly.

Glasgow would not have been Glasgow however without rumours. Oddly enough, some of them were correct, or at least partly so – namely that Jock Stein had been offered the job, (but had turned it down!) and that Bertie Auld was coming back to help with the coaching (in fact, Falkirk had declared an interest in Bertie). But there were also the wild ones – that someone was buying out Mr Kelly, that some of the Directors were receiving treatment in various Glasgow Nursing Homes for alcoholism, and that McNeill, Hughes and a few others were contemplating offers from Tottenham Hotspur or Newcastle United.

More mundanely, the bad weather had eased a little, and Celtic had a trip to Dundee United on Saturday. Steve Chalmers, who had been out injured (a significant injury) for over a month, was still out, but Murdoch and Johnstone were back, and Jim Brogan came in for Jim Kennedy at left-half. A striking feature of that day was the sight of half-empty supporters' buses in Gussie Park, the normal coach park. In the town itself, Taybridge Station, normally hoaching with supporters and policemen when "the Celtic" were in town, had little more traffic than the average working day. But there were still the die-hards, defiant as ever.

There was another dynamic at work here as well, and a sad one for Celtic. Dundee, with a large Irish population, had been a Celtic stronghold in years gone by, but the early 1960s had seen a slow haemorrhaging of the support of the Dundee Irish from Celtic to Dundee United. The "Tannadice Terrors" had risen rapidly since their promotion in April 1960, while Celtic were now clearly in decline. The days of Dundee United (originally called Dundee Hibernian) having *"the Celtic supporters who could not afford the train fare to Parkhead"* were over. Financed by a very successful lottery called Taypools, they were a prosperous, successful outfit, slowly taking over from Dundee FC as the predominant team in the city.

No longer were they the poor team who struggled against East Stirlingshire, Albion Rovers and Forfar Athletic. The local Press no longer patronised them with words like *"gallant"* and *"brave"* as they earned more and more column inches. In a funny, paradoxical sort of a way, they got a great boost in 1962 when Dundee won the League and then went on to have a good season in Europe. It showed that success was possible. They had now built a strange-looking stand (described as Orwellian or even Martian) which went round a corner to replace their old wooden one which creaked ominously on windy days and where one had to be very careful not to get sticks in one's bottom! Most significantly as far as Celtic were concerned, they were also slowly taking over the hearts and minds of the Dundee Irish and weaning them away from Celtic.

Recently, they had signed some Scandinavians, such as Finn Dossing and Orjan Persson, and today Dossing scored two goals past a static McNeill as United won 3-1. Celtic's goal was a good one, well-taken by John Hughes, but a perspicacious Dundee United supporter made the point that Celtic were a *"one-man forward line."* Indeed, John Hughes had hard luck with a shot that was saved by goalkeeper MacKay and another effort that hit the side net from an awkward angle. Bobby Murdoch had a good game as well, but his over-commitment to the cause led to a booking after a clumsy barge on the goalkeeper. Tommy Millar, brother of Rangers' Jimmy, scored for United near the end and made the most of it.

And so, it was another bad day for Celtic. As is often the case in life, when you need a break it is not forthcoming, and Celtic were now so far out of sight in the League race that they were struggling to get a mention in the Sunday newspapers, other than in match reports.

We always said that it could not go on…but it did. A report that Celtic were interested in Roy Vernon, Everton's Welsh International forward did not seem likely, but there seemed more credibility in another claiming they had joined the race with Falkirk for Bertie Auld, who was now keen on a return to Scotland from Birmingham City. Sean Fallon had watched him play in the English FA Cup game against West Ham United and a bid had been made. And thus it was that on Thursday, 14 January 1965, Bertie Auld returned to Celtic for a fee of £12,000, and it was also announced that he would be in the team to play Hearts on Saturday at Celtic Park.

Bertie should never have been away in the first place of course, but this was at least something to keep us happy. And yet there was a lot more to this one than met the eye. It may even have been a Stein decision, even though Jock was still Manager of Hibs. Bertie would claim afterwards that he knew that Jock was coming back, and this was the only reason he took up Celtic's offer. Otherwise, Bertie might have settled for Falkirk. It may even have been the case that Jock would not have come back unless Bertie was going to be there as well. For those who knew their New Testament, it was almost a John the Baptist moment with Bertie heralding the approach of the new Messiah. The supporters did not know all of this, of course, but perhaps the more prescient of the Press did, because hints of *"big changes"* began to appear.

The story that subsequently went the rounds was that Jock Stein had approached Mr Kelly because he wanted to talk to him. In a Glasgow restaurant (a secluded one presumably well away from the eyes of the Press), Stein had asked Kelly for advice. He said he had been approached by Wolverhampton Wanderers, an English team with a great recent past (League Champions in 1954, 1958 and 1959 and FA Cup winners in 1960) whose fortunes had taken a turn for the worse, and who wanted Stein to turn things round. *"Should I accept this job?"* Stein asked Mr Kelly. At this point,

Kelly did what he should have done years ago and offered Jock the job that he had always wanted.

We will never know how much of this story is true. Bits of it may be true. And when did this happen? It may simply be a story fabricated to fit in with the facts, but it does not really matter. The important thing was that Jock (and Bertie) came back, although we did not yet know about Jock until the end of the month.

But first there was Hearts on Saturday at Parkhead. The weather was awful, and the crowd was restricted to about 21,000 when, in normal circumstances, double that amount might have been expected. But even at 21,000, the crowd was misleading, for it contained a large support from Edinburgh, as befitted a team who were second in the League. They possibly even outnumbered the small beleaguered bunch of Celtic diehards, some of whom came along just to greet the return of Bertie Auld.

Such was the rain that some Hearts supporters dared to enter the Jungle hoping to get what little shelter one could get from that hideous cow barn with its leaky roof. This phenomenon could not possibly happen today, but in 1965 there was a certain amount of tolerance of Hearts supporters who had not yet allowed themselves to imitate the supporters of Rangers with their unpleasant chants (That all seemed to have started a year later with the transfer of Willie Wallace in December 1966). There was even a little banter between both sets of supporters, but absolutely no trouble.

Celtic's team was *Fallon, Young and Gemmell; Brogan, McNeill and Kennedy; Johnstone, Murdoch, Hughes, Gallagher and Auld*. It was actually quite an entertaining game on the heavy ground. Hearts scored first with a freak goal when the ball hit Fallon's knee and cannoned into the net after Johnny Hamilton had got the better of Jim Kennedy. Celtic equalised through Tommy Gemmell with a fine turn and shot, but Hearts were ahead again before half-time when Hamilton headed home a fine diving header.

47

The second half was characterised by more relentless rain, more incessant Celtic pressure, a running battle between Jim Kennedy and Johnny Hamilton (who hailed, apparently, from Larkhall and made no effort to hide it), a glorious chance for John Hughes which he shot straight at the goalkeeper and the referee seeming to cut the game short. Once again, Celtic supporters left a game deflated and depressed, while Hearts, when they heard the news that Dunfermline had beaten Kilmarnock, rejoiced, for they were now top of the League.

A few hurled abuse at Mr Kelly but for the rest of the severely depleted Celtic fans, there was little left to do. The gaunt features, the sullen faces, the resigned expressions all indicated rock bottom. Bertie Auld, of whom much had been expected, had failed to reignite the team – but then again, he deserved a little more than one game. Conversation on the bus back to the city centre was of Winston Churchill's deteriorating condition, English football and horse-racing. Talking about Celtic was just too painful. On the Monday, the headline in *The Glasgow Herald* was "*Troubled Times At Parkhead.*" Even that seemed liked an understatement.

No midweek football because of frost, the main topics of conversation were how long the 90-year-old warrior Sir Winston Churchill was going to last, and Labour's loss of a by-election in Leyton, something that they could ill afford with their thin majority. Saturday came round again with many postponements because of the bad weather, but Greenock, being Greenock and very wet, managed to escape the worst of the frost, and their game with Celtic was never really in much danger. The ground was naturally heavy but playable.

Morton were respectable. Last season they had won the Scottish League Second Division by some distance and were in the middle of the First Division this year, not far away from Celtic in fact! Games between Morton and Celtic had not been without trouble in the past, not least a year ago when Celtic had beaten them 3-0 in the Scottish Cup, and today, in what seemed to be a deliberate act of provocation, they came out wearing blue jerseys and orange stockings. The Evening Times tries tactfully to describe the stockings as *"tangerine"* but anyone with the slightest knowledge of the nuances of west of Scotland football knew exactly why they were wearing orange stockings.

The game was actually an all-ticket occasion following the crushing at the Scottish Cup game last year, but not all tickets had been sold. Nevertheless, there was a goodly crowd at Cappielow as Celtic ran out with two changes from last week and the team reading, *Fallon, Young and Gemmell; Brogan, McNeill and Clark; Johnstone, Murdoch, Hughes, Lennox and Auld*. Kennedy and Gallagher were the two men who were dropped.

Whether it was the sight of the orange stockings or (more likely) the influence of Bertie Auld or indeed whether it was because the players knew something that we as yet didn't, the team came out looking confident and began to play with no little skill, and the thinly populated Celtic ranks forgot the cold and reacted with enthusiasm to what they saw. They were particularly impressed by the new left wing of Lennox and Auld, with both players feeding off each other, and the more perceptive noticing a subtle change in Celtic's team formation with Auld playing slightly behind Lennox and Lennox moving out to the wing. It was no coincidence that a confusion now developed with some newspapers talking about the left wing *"Lennox and Auld"* and others talking about *"Auld and Lennox."*

Both Johnstone and Hughes, these two glorious unpredictables, were also responding to the new set-up and it was a matter of some surprise that it took 30 minutes for Celtic to take the lead, as Lennox jumped high to reach an Auld cross and head home. Then before half-time, a visionary pass from Bertie Auld was threaded through the Morton defence, and John Hughes scored Celtic's second.

The team went in at half-time to the unfamiliar noise of loud cheering from the Celtic faithful, and a new optimism from the support as the teams re-appeared. Twenty minutes into the second half, Celtic went 3-0 ahead, this time from Tommy Gemmell, who having clearly been given licence to attack, picked up a pass from Bertie Auld in the aftermath of a Jimmy Johnstone corner kick, and hammered home.

Compared with recent performances, this was dreamland, and yet Celtic's display, although impressive, was fragile. Twenty-five minutes remained, and the constant fast pace and furious commitment on the heavy pitch had taken its toll, as once again Celtic were paid back for the inadequacy of their training regime and the lack of any real strategy or "game management" skills. Too many players were simply tired. Suddenly and incredibly, within 10 minutes, Morton equalised all three goals as so many Celtic players simply disappeared out of the game, while Bertelsen, Strachan and Bertelsen (again) equalised. Quite a few Celtic players of the time will admit to the fact that the training at Parkhead wasn't very good, and that other teams always seemed to have more energy at the end of the game than Celtic did. They clearly had a point.

This was jaw-dropping, not to say heart-wrenching stuff. The euphoria of the majority of the match evaporated with astonishing suddenness – and it could have been a lot worse! Morton scored what would have been a winner, but Celtic were saved by the referee Mr Stewart of Paisley, who ruled that full-time had been reached when the ball was actually in mid-air! Morton fans obviously disagreed and one or two of them made this point somewhat strongly to the referee Mr Stewart as he left the field.

So what were we to make of all this? Celtic had still not won a game in 1965. And the collapse in the last quarter of an hour had been woeful. Yet, there was a certain something about the team that Bertie Auld had brought, and a feeling grew that something else was going to happen soon – more new players, perhaps, or even the change at the top that everyone now perceived as necessary. The Scottish Cup draw on Monday, 25 January put Celtic at the difficult ground of St Mirren on February 6. Something, we hoped, might happen before then.

There was even a school of thought that believed that it might be the best thing if Celtic went out of the Scottish Cup at an early stage. That would certainly bring a change, including perhaps even the resignation of Mr Kelly and all those who had led us into this catastrophe. Maybe a complete and total change was necessary. At this stage, Celtic were no longer going nowhere as they had been doing for the last few years – they were now going somewhere with the speed of an express train, and that was to oblivion – unless something happened!

Such extreme speculation was put on hold however, out of respect for Sir Winston Churchill, who died at the age of 90 in the early hours of Sunday, 24 January. The feelings of Celtic supporters for the old warrior were complex. On the one hand, he had been no friend of the Scottish working class and miners in particular, and he had been, directly and indirectly, responsible for some dreadful things in Ireland, but there was no denying that he had saved the world from a monstrous tyranny in the 1940s. He deserved at least respect for that. Years later, a story emerged that he had indeed offered the Six Counties to De Valera if the Irish Free State would abandon neutrality and join the war. Dev, of course, turned him down, but, if that story were true, it might have changed things considerably!

The death of Churchill and preparations for his funeral on Saturday dominated the newspapers but it did not entirely wipe out a story that had a more intimate connection with Celtic. This was that Dick Beattie, Celtic's goalkeeper in the late 1950s, was given nine months in prison for match-fixing. He was part of a gang, including a few England Internationalists, and it had been going on for some time at Portsmouth and elsewhere, but there was no evidence to connect him with any nefarious goings on at Celtic. It was nevertheless a shock and caused many people to wonder. And yet so many people loved Dick who had had his photograph taken with seven fingers in the air after the famous Scottish League Cup final, now more than seven years ago.

The weather remained cold and frozen. The lack of football encouraged the ongoing speculation about Celtic. Chairman Bob Kelly and Assistant Manager Sean Fallon had been to Ireland, apparently to look for and buy players but had returned empty-handed. To the cynics, it looked like a smokescreen or a place to hide, for Kelly was notorious for his ability to avoid trouble with some specious excuse about *"going to see the reserves"* or the vague and implausible one about *"doing something else in the interests of the club"* rather than confronting the fans. It seemed like a good trip to Sean's native land and the land of Kelly's ancestors.

The remarkable day of January 30 dawned, and Celtic's game with Aberdeen was on, as indeed was the game at Easter Road between Hibs and Rangers, although several other games were not so lucky. Celtic received a major boost with the news that Steve Chalmers, who had been out since early December, would return, and hopes were high that Celtic might deliver their first win of the calendar year of 1965 to their dispirited supporters. No-one however could possibly have come close to anticipating that remarkable scoreline today. Aberdeen had been in a steep decline since their glory days of 10 years ago, but they could always be expected to put up a fight.

But first that morning, there were the funeral obsequies in London. Churchill's favourite poem was *"Say not the Struggle Nought Availeth"* of Arthur Clough and it was read at his funeral, including the famous verse;

> And not by eastern windows only,
> When daylight comes, comes in the light,
> In front the sun climbs slow, how slowly,
> But westward, look, the land is bright!

It was a verse that was so appropriate for the dark days of 1940, and it was equally appropriate for Celtic at this critical stage of our history. We did not know it at the time, but the wheels were already, by lunchtime on that fateful day of Saturday, 30 January 1965, slowly beginning to turn in our direction.

52

The meagre crowd of 14,000 who made the way to Celtic Park that frosty afternoon were immediately struck by the heavily sanded pitch. The sand was needed in such profusion to persuade referee Mr Barclay of Kirkcaldy that play was possible. In the aftermath of the game, the *Aberdeen Press and Journal* would use words like *"unplayable"* to describe the surface, but this looks like a poor excuse. Celtic were able to play on it without any problem at all, and their supporters on the thinly populated terracings were impressed by the new-found enthusiasm for the cause, as the following eleven took the field - *Fallon, Young and Gemmell; Clark, McNeill and Brogan; Chalmers, Murdoch, Hughes, Lennox and Auld*. Aberdeen had few supporters but included three new Scandinavian players who frankly did not know what hit them.

Steve Chalmers was given a great cheer on his return from injury, but it was John "Yogi Bear" Hughes who hit all the headlines with five goals, as Auld with a penalty, and Lennox and Murdoch scored the others in an 8-0 win. Hughes, always a very good "bad weather" player, was wearing his famous "sandshoes" which he wore on frozen pitches, and for a big man, he showed a remarkable balletic splendour and ability to change pace. In a word, he was unstoppable, and it was a shame that we did not see these performances a lot more often. Each one of his goals was a classic, and the ovation accorded to him was as warm as the day was cold. It did reveal the affection in which he was held, but it was an ovation that was shared with the other members of the team. It was as if they sensed the change in the atmosphere, and that something was going to happen soon.

The walk back to Buchanan Street station that night was a pleasant one with news also filtering through that Hibs had beaten Rangers 1-0 at Easter Road in a game that had had to start a little later because of the long queues outside. It was a long time since there had been such euphoria, and that Saturday night, the rumours of changes were intensifying.

53

The Sunday newspapers that last day of January were eagerly devoured, but all that they said was that everyone at Parkhead was *"tight-lipped"* but smiled when asked about changes. One newspaper even ventured that the changes might involve a *"former Parkhead favourite"* returning, but no-one as yet mentioned the word *"Stein."* There was enough, in any case, to delight the fans in the newspapers which used extravagant words to describe Celtic's performance yesterday, lauding John Hughes naturally, but also being quite clear that the change in attitude had come about because of the return of the man from Birmingham. It was just like *"auld lang syne"* in fact, said one journalist!

The news of the appointment of Jock Stein was made on Sunday, 31 January 1965. It was a low-key announcement, and added the fact that Mr McGrory was to be appointed Public Relations Officer. McGrory was emphatically not to be sacked, and this did a great deal to enhance Mr Kelly's credit in the eyes of the supporters. It would have been a major propaganda error and a blow to any idea of "the Celtic family" to pension off Jimmy McGrory. Indeed, the "Golden Crust", only recently turned 60, still had a great deal to offer in this new post.

But the main thing was that Mr Kelly had at last admitted that he was wrong. It was not openly stated that Jock would have full say over all matters to do with team selection, but everyone realised that he would never have agreed to the job unless he were allowed to pick his own team. Initially, the terms were that Stein would stay as Manager of Hibernian until the end of the season, or until such time as Hibs managed to secure a replacement. Hibs really should have insisted on keeping Stein until the end of the season – and things might have been a lot different for them (and Celtic!), if they had – but in practice, they engaged Bob Shankly (brother of Liverpool's Bill) of Dundee in mid-February, and Stein took over at Celtic Park on March 8.

Some newspapers saw fit to make an issue that Stein was only

Celtic's fourth Manager since 1897 and the first non-Catholic. Some even, despicably, speculated whether Celtic supporters would accept him because of his ethnic origins. In so doing they revealed not only a rabble-rousing desire to cause trouble, but also a dismal ignorance of Celtic supporters. Celtic supporters never had been exclusively Catholic, and even if they had all been rigid attenders at Mass and Confession, they were far more interested in football, and a successful Celtic team. Stein was a proven leader on the field, as the events of 1953 and 1954 had proved, and Celtic supporters had seen, to their cost, that he had been a great Manager of Dunfermline in 1961. He was now to be given the chance to awaken a giant that was not so much sleeping as moribund and badly in need of resuscitation.

Oddly enough, the feeling about Stein possibly being unacceptable to the Celtic support was, or may have been, shared by Mr Kelly himself. In an interview given by Jock Stein to BBC Television long after Kelly had died, Jock gave the impression that he thought it was possible that he was not given the job in 1960 because *"as a non-Catholic, I had gone as far as I was likely to go"* with Celtic, and that was why he moved on to Dunfermline Athletic. If this was the case, it reflects very badly on the judgement of Mr Kelly and even worse on his conception of what Celtic should be.

It is of course the easiest task in the world to knock Bob Kelly (knighted as Sir Bob Kelly on New Year's Day 1969). He was leading (and in the winter of 1964/65 continuing to lead) the club to disaster. But at some point in late 1964 he suddenly seems to have realised at last that he was wrong, and that he would have to bring Stein back. How it all came about, we do not know. There is some deliberate obfuscation with stories about that meal in the restaurant and Stein first being offered the job as joint Manager with Sean Fallon, and we will never know at what stage Stein insisted on getting full say on matters of team selection, or what part, if any, Stein played in the return of Bertie Auld to Celtic when he was still Manager of Hibs! No-one is ever likely to give us the answer to such questions.

The general consensus was that Stein and Kelly met somewhere (presumably NOT in a Glasgow restaurant where they would have been recognised) on Tuesday, 12 January 1965, and that first of all Stein was offered the job of Assistant Manager to Sean Fallon. His answer was no, and then he was offered the job as Co-Manager with Sean, and the answer was still no. Stein then said he would take the job on two conditions – one was that Bertie Auld was to be brought back from Birmingham (this transfer was already beginning to happen in any case) and the other was that he (Stein) insisted on sole control of all team matters. The out-manoeuvred Kelly simply had to agree.

To what extent this is true, we do not know. Bertie Auld implied that he would never have come back if Stein was not going to be there, and how did Sean Fallon feel about all this? Certainly, in retrospect, it seems very much as if Stein's statement at the end of February 1964 that he was wanting to leave Dunfermline Athletic at the end of the season seems very much to be a *"Come and get me"* invitation, and that he only took the Hibs job when Kelly was dilatory about asking him back at that stage! We will never know.

There is one claim however that Kelly made that can easily be dismissed. This was his statement that there was some sort of "grand plan" whereby Stein in 1960 was allowed to go to Dunfermline with the deliberate idea of him coming back some day to manage Celtic once he had gained experience. This is frankly "bollocks." But it mattered not a whit now. Big Jock was back.

The issue of Stein's religion (he was not in any way a godless man but had no obvious connection with the Church of Scotland, let along the mysteries of the masonic craft as some would later claim) was probably not a serious consideration to anyone other than Mr Kelly, and even Mr Kelly changed his mind. What is absolutely certain however was that Stein totally understood the sometimes-crazy world of West of Scotland football and religion and was able to exploit it. In particular, he understood that if Rangers persisted in their absurd policy of religious discrimination, Celtic, given good management, were bound to triumph, because they could choose people of either religion, whereas Rangers restricted themselves to only half of the Scottish population!

However that may be, Kelly has to be given a great deal of credit for at least admitting that he was wrong, and from then on, relations between Stein and Kelly were nothing short of first class, both supporting each other, and as always when things at the top are good, everything else prospers as well. Mr Kelly's reformation was complete, and it could even be argued that he deserved (in so far as anyone deserves such a thing) his Knighthood in the New Year Honours of 1969. Yet, had he not made his famous and fateful decision, he might well have found himself hounded out by angry and frustrated supporters in the same way as his relatives would be in 1994. A Knighthood and Bob Kelly would not have been mentioned in the same breath by anyone in 1965.

Gair Henderson of *The Evening Times*, no great lover of either Celtic or Rangers but usually very fair about Celtic, proved himself to be extraordinarily prescient on February 1 when he detailed four reasons why he was sure that Stein would be a success at Celtic – Personality, Team Discipline, Ambition and Knowledge of the Game. Henderson himself had a great knowledge of the game and here he hit the nail on the head.

CHAPTER TWO

FEBRUARY

The cold Monday morning of 1 February 1965 saw Celtic supporters arrive at their places of work and their schools with smiles on their faces. Things had taken a decided turn for the better, and the Press were universally of the opinion that Celtic's affairs were about to take off. The Scottish Press is complex in its relationships with football teams – upbeat and even gloating when things go well, vindictive and persecuting when things are less good. And there seems to be no law against exaggeration!

Celtic supporters are usually convinced that the Scottish Press is 100% against them, and in 1965 it would have been difficult to deny that *The Scottish Daily Express*, in particular, was pro-Rangers, but they could not afford to ignore the other well-supported team either and newspaper writers are nothing if not malleable. They are also very easily influenced, not necessarily by bribery and corruption, but by the possibility of a good story. Kerry Packer, the Australian millionaire who tried to buy the sport of cricket some 12 years later, would say that *"there is a bit of the whore in everyone."* Sportswriters, sensing that Parkhead was soon going to be the centre of attraction while the influence of Ibrox was now waning, turned their attention more and more to the affairs of Celtic.

One wonders whether the events of spring 1965 might have been different if Monday, 1 February had been a milder day. The first round of the Glasgow Cup should have brought Rangers to Celtic Park that night, but Mr Weir the referee decided that the pitch was just too hard and frosty. No-one seemed to get too upset about that decision, except in Aberdeen where the supporters of the Dons (whose paranoia of "the world being against us" can often rival that of Celtic fans) argued unconvincingly that their 0-8 thrashing on Saturday was because of an unplayable pitch! And Mr Weir's decision to put off the Monday night game proved that!

But, as they say in Aberdeen, *"Ye'll nae dae!"* There was of course one key difference in that Saturday was in daylight and Monday would have been in the dark. The temperature would have been appreciably colder, and in any case, Celtic and Rangers supporters meeting each other in the dark would have caused its own problems! So the postponement of that game was greeted with very little wailing or gnashing of teeth.

The thaw arrived in time to save the Scottish Cup programme on Saturday, 6 February. Celtic were at Love Street, Paisley to play a team who had twice in recent years put them out at the semi-final stage. On the other hand, Celtic had defeated them in 1960, and more recently at Love Street in the quarter-final of 1963. But the Buddies were generally looked upon as a good Scottish Cup team, and it was far from an easy game for Celtic as they started their Scottish Cup campaign "between Managers."

The impression was that the benign Jimmy McGrory had already given up being Manager and had retired to the stand to smoke his pipe, leaving the running of the team to Sean Fallon. No-one as yet knew just exactly when Jock Stein was to arrive, but it was clear that the immediate concern and task of the players and management was to stay in the Scottish Cup, the only trophy which Celtic had a realistic chance of winning. The Scottish Cup, in times gone by looked upon as Celtic's special trophy, had not been won since 1954 (when, significantly, the captain was Jock Stein and the winning goal had been scored by Sean Fallon!) and no-one was unaware that Rangers had now overtaken Celtic's total of victories. Rangers had now won the trophy 18 times as distinct from Celtic's

17 – a side effect of the disastrous lean years of mismanagement at Celtic Park!

Tuesday, 2 February saw an upbeat report from Celtic Park to the effect that everyone was fit, and that training was going on for Saturday's Cup tie. There was even a false story leaked that Jock Stein might be at Parkhead by the end of the week. For their part, Hibs kept making optimistic noises about appointing a successor with Chairman William Harrower telling the Press that there was a short leet of three. St Mirren had taken their team down to Ayr for training purposes but kept saying that Love Street was indeed playable. In any case, by Friday the temperature had risen appreciably and the only game off was the one at Airdrie.

So it was Scottish Cup day on Saturday, something that saw a massive Celtic support mobilised for Paisley with tangible excitement clearly in the air at the prospect of the return of "Big Jock." He was the talk of everyone's conversation, and rarely had the support been in such an upbeat and animated mood. Trains, buses, motor cars all asked the questions about what "He" was going to do about the various problems that beset the club. *The Sunday Post* the following day said that "He" *"would take a hold of Celtic by the scruff of the neck and fill the terracings at the same time."* They were not wrong.

The crowd at Love Street was given as 28,300 but looked as if it were more than that. The game had to be delayed for ten minutes to allow the spectators in, and there were two audacious grabs for money at the primitive turnstiles with, in one case, a man helping himself to a handful of notes before disappearing into the crowd. In another, a man managed to steal some coins. It was clear that St Mirren were not used to such crowds.

The weather was still damp, but now and again a watery winter sun broke through, and the pitch gave no sign whatsoever of any recent frost. Celtic fielded a bubbly and unchanged team. Those who had demolished Aberdeen were given another go and were greeted with a huge roar from their resurrected, resurgent and revanchist spectators who were there in large numbers and singing all the old songs of long ago, including the *"Piling On The Agony"* song of the 7-1 game of 1957, the last time that they had won any major trophy.

The game was hard-fought in the first half and needed to be well handled by the "no nonsense" approach of Tom Wharton. Both teams missed chances, with Bobby Lennox looking sharp but John Fallon in goal being called upon to dive at the feet of St Mirren forwards more than once. Half-time was reached with no score, and Celtic fans reckoning that a replay at Celtic Park might not be the worst outcome in the world.

But Celtic went ahead within five minutes of the restart, when a Lennox shot was blocked by goalkeeper Pat Liney (who had won a League Championship medal with Dundee in 1962) but the ball rebounded to Steve Chalmers who didn't normally score many goals with his head but did so on this occasion. Celtic never looked back after this and slowly began to take control of the game with Billy McNeill, now appearing to enjoy a new lease of life following his midwinter doldrums, superb in the middle of the park, and it was no surprise when Lennox scored twice within the last 10 minutes to give Celtic a thoroughly deserved 3-0 victory, and to show the world that the corner might indeed have been turned and that here we might have a team on the march.

Gone were the sullen faces, gone were the boos and the slow handclaps and gone was the all-pervasive feeling of depression and "there's nothing we can do" attitude. The imminent arrival of Jock Stein had everything to do with this, but so too did the current presence of Bertie Auld who, as perceptive supporters noticed, was a left-winger in name only. The appropriate word was "ubiquitous," for he appeared on the right wing sometimes to allow Steve Chalmers to come into the centre as a double centre-forward with John Hughes, but he was more frequently in the midfield, dictating play and spraying passes. "Forward flexibility" had been the watchword of great Celtic teams in the past, not least the Empire Exhibition Trophy winners of 1938 and the team of all the talents of 1908, so it was a great Celtic tradition to be part of.

The interesting thing about all of this was that, effectively, apart from Bertie Auld, not very much had really changed. The man about whom all these Messianic things had been said was not here yet. And yet, things were already just so different. The psychological difference was huge. *"Sure it's a grand old team"* was now sung with gusto and even the *"lorry load of volunteers"* now seemed to approach the border town with a great deal more of a spring in their step!

Quiet confidence continued to emanate from Celtic Park throughout the next midweek. Celtic learned that they would have an early trip to Hampden in the next round of the Scottish Cup after Queen's Park defeated Dumbarton in a replay. Jimmy Johnstone was given a 14-day suspension for his ordering off in the New Year game – but that didn't seem to matter quite so much now that Steve Chalmers had returned to the outside-right spot. And, as significant as anything, an announcement was made that the old ugly Jungle was at last to be replaced by a newer and more modern structure.

It was hard to get upset about the old Jungle, which had been around since 1907. So called, it was believed, because soldiers returning from the Far East in 1945 compared it unfavourably to what they had seen in Japanese POW camps, it was an ugly structure like a huge cow barn with multiple holes in the roof, and flaky asbestos stuff descending as well. The toilet facilities could only be described as a health hazard, and how it ever passed any test by Health or Safety Inspectors remains a mystery. For a club with the wealth and support of Celtic, it was a disgrace, but here again the announcement of its demolition was another sign that a new Celtic was beginning to emerge.

The better, milder weather allowed the players to train on the pitch itself, and early in the week it was announced that it would be a same-again Celtic. It was also the same venue, for once again, Celtic were returning to Love Street, this time to play a League game. In terms of League positions, the game meant little to Celtic, but St Mirren were rather closer to the relegation zone than they would have liked to have been. It was important, however, that Celtic retained their momentum, for everyone knew that form was a temporary, transient, insubstantial and fragile thing in football. A little added spice was added to the occasion with the news that St Mirren's centre-forward was to be Pat Hughes, brother of John.

In the meantime, Rangers were wobbling and Aberdeen were in trauma. It will be remembered that there was a certain amount of moaning about the Celtic Park pitch on the day of their 0-8 hammering. There must have been something wrong with East Fife's Bayview pitch as well, for they lost 0-1 and went out of the Scottish Cup in humiliating circumstances to a Second Division club. Manager Tommy Pearson resigned a day or two later. Once again, we see the all-important element of psychology here as well. In fact, it had been the 0-8 thrashing at Celtic Park that had knocked Aberdeen out of the Scottish Cup.

The crowd for the League match was, not surprisingly, considerably down at Love Street on the Cup tie and was given as 11,000 but, once again, it looked as if there were a few more on this bright but windy day in Paisley. Certainly, Celtic fans were there in force with their banners and flags and singing their battle songs with a new fervour. They had beaten the Paisley Saints well last week in the Scottish Cup and were confidently expecting more today. They would not be disappointed, and although much was the conversation still about when Jock Stein was going to come to take over and what he was going to do when he did, there was also the phenomenon that even without Stein, a good team was beginning to develop.

A particular sustained improvement was noticed in Billy McNeill. Before the famous announcement of January 31, Billy had been lacklustre and hesitant, displaying rather too much of an ability to panic and to shout at other defenders, with his particular nadir being the Dundee United game on January 9 when Finn Dossing clearly had the better of him. Now he was far more composed, calm and totally in control of the situation. He had always had a good relationship with Stein in Jock's coaching days, as feelings of awe and hero worship dominated his thoughts. He was clearly relishing and looking forward to the opportunity to work with Jock. Indeed, the relationship between McNeill and Stein would be the anchor of Celtic's sustained success in years to come.

The more sensible supporters however, albeit equally affected by the tide of euphoria, realised that they must not as yet allow themselves to be carried away. After all, we had been there before. 1961 had seen us on the point of winning the Scottish Cup until self-destruction and over-confidence took over. We recalled the fine season of 1961/62, when we thought we were going well until we blew up against teams like Falkirk, Stirling Albion, Airdrie and Raith Rovers in the League, and that awful semi-final against St Mirren. 1962/63 saw a great autumn until suddenly Queen of the South came to Parkhead and amazed the world (and themselves) by winning, and even last year when things went so well until we met Rangers. And that was even before we started to think about the optimistic September and October of this season, when once again the spectre of Rangers and that awful League Cup final sent us spiralling downwards. We must not delude ourselves!

Today it was ex-Celt Bobby Carroll who opened the scoring for the Saints when right-back Ian Young was short with a pass-back – a rare mistake by a man who had played consistently well and tackled like a tank. By half-time however, Chalmers and Lennox had put Celtic ahead against the wind, and when the teams turned round, it was one-way traffic when Jim Brogan brought the house down with a pile driver from outside the box, then Hughes and Murdoch made it 5-1. It was a fine result, and the thing that was really so obvious to the fans was that the players were relishing the game. The sulkiness and the finger pointing at each other had now gone. They were enjoying their football, and enjoyment, of course, is a very important factor in any job, not only professional football. Bertie Auld was once again the best player on the field, and the only cause for concern was a slight injury to Bobby Murdoch who limped off before the end of the game.

On Tuesday, 16 February 1965, Hibs announced that they had appointed Bob Shankly of Dundee and brother of Liverpool's Bill as their Manager. This seemed to expedite an announcement of when Stein could come to Parkhead, but at this time of the week, Celtic were at Seamill Hydro preparing for their visit to Hampden to play Queen's Park and watched the highlights on TV of Inter Milan v Rangers at the San Siro in the European Cup quarter-final. Inter won 3-1, a scoreline which singularly failed to reduce the Celtic party to tears. Little did anyone imagine that Destiny was planning a game for Celtic against Inter Milan in little more than two years' time which would become the pinnacle of Celtic history.

But that was a long way in the future. Celtic had more immediate concerns. The game at Hampden to play the part-time amateurs of Queen's Park in the Scottish Cup was a minefield. The fact that it was at Hampden may have been significant as well. Our last visit to Hampden had been the disastrous League Cup final which had plunged the club into crisis. Rangers appeared to have a far more difficult game at Tannadice Park against Dundee United. Jock Stein's Hibs had Partick Thistle at Easter Road, and clearly the result of that game would have some bearing on the date of Stein's arrival at Celtic Park.

There was more than a hint of spring in the air as the fans made their way to Hampden Park that day of February 20. It was still a little cold, but it was bright enough with the usual swirling wind that one associated with Hampden in those days. There was a bus strike in certain parts of Scotland, so most supporters travelled to the ground on the "Blue Train" from Glasgow Central to Mount

Florida. The crowd was given as 19,000 but once again, it looked as there were a few more there than that.

It was good to be back at Hampden again. The old lady was beginning to show her age, and some of the turnstiles and fittings seemed to have been there since 1903 when it opened. On a dry day, attending Hampden was a far more pleasant experience than on a wet day, but one was still quite overwhelmed by the size of the place, something that seemed to be accentuated by the wide empty spaces in a ground that was considerably less than one quarter full. Yet these were the days in which crowds of over 100,000 were commonplace, (the Scotland v England game of last April had seen a crowd of over six figures) and world record crowds had been seen at Hampden (twice) in 1937 to see the Scotland v England International and the Scottish Cup final between Celtic and Aberdeen. The "good guys" won on both occasions, and Celtic's Jimmy Delaney played in both games! It was also the ground of Jimmy Quinn's hat trick against Rangers in 1904, Patsy Gallacher's great Cup final goal against Dundee in 1925 and the Coronation Cup final of 1953. It teemed with ghosts from Celtic's past.

Celtic surprised their supporters this day by appearing in all green. An all-green strip was not entirely unprecedented, but supporters would become more and more familiar with it in future years, as it gradually came to replace the "white with green sleeves" or "the Hibs reverse" strip as the kit to be worn when there was a colour clash. The advantage was that the numbers on the pants were slightly more easily read.

Whether it was the wind, the unfamiliar and empty stadium, a strange refereeing performance by Mr JW Paterson of Bothwell, or simply a good performance by the Spiders, who had last defeated Celtic in the Scottish Cup back in 1896, no-one knows, but Celtic disappointed their fans who had expected a barrowload of goals. Indeed, Queen's Park had their moments, and goalkeeper John Fallon was several times called upon to save the day. But round about the hour mark, Bobby Lennox scored the only goal of the game. It was a trademark Lennox goal. A defensive clearance from McNeill was not controlled by the Spiders' defence, the ball rebounded to Lennox and he ran through and scored, beating goalkeeper Bobby Clark who had already begun to impress and who would soon move to begin a professional career with Aberdeen.

Those who expected more Celtic goals were frustrated, but there was an immediate stabilising of the team, and, apart from a fine save by John Fallon near the end, there were few alarms for Celtic. It was not a classy performance, but it was a functional one, and the end result had been achieved of a place in the next round in early March. Less happily, Dundee United who had impressed quite a few people in recent months, failed to live up to expectations when Rangers appeared, and went down to the Ibrox men.

The draw for the quarter-finals was made on Monday, 22 February, and it threw up Celtic v Kilmarnock or East Fife (who had drawn at Bayview on Saturday and were due to play a replay at Rugby Park on Wednesday). There was a bit of history this season with both teams. East Fife had beaten Celtic 2-0 at Methil in the first leg of the Scottish League Cup quarter-final before succumbing to the inevitable at Parkhead in the return leg. Not that it mattered, for it was Kilmarnock who won the replay on Wednesday night.

This season's "history" between Celtic and Kilmarnock was a lot less pleasant and concerned a game at Rugby Park in the League Cup on August 29, after the section had been won. A more worldly-wise Celtic management might have put out a few reserves for this game but, not to put too fine a point on it, Celtic were what is commonly known as "kicked off the park" by a Killie side that were motivated by nothing other than spite and revenge. McNeill and Murdoch were both injured, badly in McNeill's case, and it was often felt in some Celtic circles that the loss of their captain had cost Celtic the League Cup.

There were at least four other complicating factors as well.

Ayrshire generally was looked upon as a Rangers-supporting area, Kilmarnock were managed by Willie Waddell, who had been Rangers' legendary winger in the late 1940s and early 1950s. The teams were also due to meet in the League on this coming Saturday and the Scottish Cup tie to be played the following week, March 6, would be Jimmy McGrory's last game as Manager of Celtic.

It now seemed that it was going to be Monday, 8 March that the great chain reaction was going to happen. The idea seemed to be that Jock would introduce Bob Shankly to the Hibs staff and players, then drive to Glasgow to take charge of Celtic, then Bobby Ancell of Motherwell would take Shankly's job at Dundee while Bobby Howitt would do the needful at Motherwell. It was complicated, and it would all happen after the Scottish Cup quarter-final ties. But what if there were to be a draw, necessitating a replay on the Wednesday night?

But in the meantime, there was the home League game against Kilmarnock. The reverse fixture soon after the defeat in the League Cup final had seen a severe drubbing to the tune of 5-2 as Killie took advantage of a Celtic team in the early stages of the prolonged death wish which characterised late 1964. This time, however, it was all different. The team wore their all-green strips again and came out bubbly and full of confidence. Not only that, but they got lucky and even got a break in a refereeing decision by JRP Gordon of Tayport, when he allowed a goal after John Hughes had appeared even to the Jungle and the Celtic End to have used a hand. The other goal had come from a deflection off a Chalmers shot.

It is often said that teams create their own luck, and this seems to have been an example. It would be wrong to think, however, that Celtic did not play well. They did and might even have gone further ahead. Once again, Bertie Auld was superb. Celtic also did well to rise above the rough stuff which Killie were once again prepared to dish out, especially when things seemed to be going against them.

It was actually a remarkable day in the League race, showing that the race was very open and that Celtic, if they had not sunk so low before Christmas, might well have even been in with a chance. Hibs lost to Morton, Dunfermline drew, but the major talking point was the scoreline from Tynecastle, which read Hearts 1 Dundee 7. Incredibly, Hearts still remained at the top of the League after that, but everyone now feared a late surge from Rangers to grab the title after they had scraped home, beating St Mirren 1-0.

And so ended the month of February. The lengthening day had not yet been accompanied by any obvious or sustained improvement in the weather. Indeed, the bad weather had returned with frost, and even a few blizzards. At Parkhead, things remained upbeat, and once again Bob Kelly showed a new, refreshing and virtually unprecedented sense of being able to grasp the realities of the current situation by feeding the Press more details of a projected super stadium. He had, of course, talked about this many times before, and while all this was to be welcomed, nevertheless the priority remained the need to get a good team on the park. Supporters normally come to see a good team, not an impressive new stand…but they now by the mid 1960s (such had been the rise in expectations) wanted to be able to watch their team in comfort, and Scottish football had been slow to understand that.

CHAPTER THREE

MARCH

The month opened with the news that a new Manager had been appointed at Aberdeen. Curiously, it was an almost exact parallel with what had happened at Celtic precisely a month earlier with the appointment made on the last day of the month, but the announcement not made until the day afterwards, Monday, 1 March. The new Manager of the Dons was Eddie Turnbull, who had done so well with Queen's Park, as Celtic had found out when they met them on February 20.

Eddie was of course a well-known figure in Hibs and Scottish history, a member of the "Famous Five" of *Smith, Johnstone, Reilly, Turnbull and Ormond*. He had served in the Second World War in the Royal Navy, being part of the Arctic convoys to Russia, so he was tough. Indeed, he was well known for his abrasive approach to footballing matters. Rumour had it that he and Jock Stein were not good friends.

He would have a tough job at Aberdeen, a team which had under-performed dreadfully since winning the League and the League Cup ten years earlier in 1955. Yet, they had a huge latent support in an area of Scotland which they had more or less all to themselves, and there were distinct parallels with Celtic in this respect, in that they had a captive audience. There really was no excuse for such appalling mediocrity in the North-East of Scotland any more than there was in the East End of Glasgow. With both clubs soon to be under new management, an improvement was looked for. And an improvement came.

At Celtic Park, things remained quiet during the first week in March. There was little doubt that Bertie Auld had made a great difference to the team, not least because of the effect that he had on Bobby Lennox, who was now clearly thriving in his new role on the left wing, where he was able to exploit his speed. On the right wing, Steve Chalmers, now recovered from injury, was also doing well, being preferred to the talented, precocious, quixotic and unstable Jimmy Johnstone, but, more than that, there was an optimistic buzz about the place that there had not been for some time. Billy McNeill after his appalling midwinter was now back, obviously in charge and relishing his job as captain.

Everyone was aware of just how important the forthcoming Cup tie against Kilmarnock was going to be, but the focus of attention of the general Scottish footballing public was diverted to two other things. One was the weather. Snow, ice and frost had made a late return, imperilling quite a few football fixtures, especially the European Cup quarter-final match at Ibrox where Rangers were 1-3 down to Inter Milan from the first leg.

No matter how many Celtic supporters say things like *"I don't care about THEM,"* the fact remains that in the context of Glasgow, how Rangers do is of vital importance to Celtic, and vice versa. Feigned insouciance simply does not work, and in any case, the media attention would always make sure that no-one ever has the slightest chance of forgetting what is happening on the other side of the city. And those who go around saying *"I am not a Rangers supporter, but it would be a good thing for Scottish football if they did well in Europe"* are usually laughed at for telling lies. The game was under a little doubt for a spell, but *"money talked louder than snow"* and the game went ahead in difficult, but still playable conditions on Wednesday, 3 March 1965.

Rangers were beginning to struggle. Baxter had been out since December, and tonight they disappointed their fans by failing to reduce the leeway on Inter. The Scottish Press unanimously condemned the negative tactics of Inter Milan. This did not so much defend Rangers as reveal their own Scottish naivety. Did they honestly expect Helenio Herrera to do anything else? Kenneth Wolstenholme, doing the TV commentary for the BBC highlights programme, kept telling the viewers that there was a chap in the stand shouting *"This is easy, Rangers!"* It was anything but. It was a disgruntled Rangers support that left Ibrox that night, and there was the undeniable and uncomfortable feeling among them that, with the recent developments at Celtic Park, their number was up.

Jock Stein inspired fear in them, a fear and a complex that they never got over. Not only was he soon to appear at the home of their rivals, but even before that, Rangers had to face him in another guise, as Manager of Hibs in the Scottish Cup at Easter Road on Saturday. Defeats in football are usually infectious in that one leads to another (and didn't Celtic fans just know that?). Would the dispirited and under-pressure Rangers now crack and go out of the Scottish Cup as well as the European Cup?

But so to the remarkable and dramatic day of Saturday, 6 March 1965. There is seldom any doubt about the contention that Jimmy McGrory was one of Celtic's best-ever players, if not THE best with 550 goals enough to win most arguments. His record speaks for itself. As a Manager over the 20 years from 1945 until 1965, however, his record, although not without some spectacular successes, was disappointing, and season 1964/65 would be his last as Manager for the man who never lost his dignity or gentlemanly demeanour. He was, quite simply, too nice a man to be a football Manager.

His fate was probably sealed at the League Cup Final on 24 October 1964, when Celtic were the better team against Rangers but failed to take their chances in the first half while a clinical Rangers team grabbed their opportunities in the second half. The depression that followed this disastrous disappointment saw many more defeats over midwinter 1964/65, as we have seen. The form was so poor, and supporters were departing in such large numbers, that a change at the top was inevitable, even at a team like Celtic which had no great reputation for sacking Managers.

Before the change could be implemented, however, Celtic had a Scottish Cup quarter-final. They had to win this game, or at least avoid defeat and get a replay, otherwise Stein would arrive to a dead season. The opponents were Kilmarnock, possibly appropriate because Kilmarnock were the only other club where Jimmy McGrory had been Manager, in the few seasons before the Second World War. But there was more to this game than that. Kilmarnock and Celtic had some recent history with the events of that awful day at Rugby Park in which they *"shared a rough house"* (as the newspapers had tactfully put it) still in the memory of everyone.

We have mentioned the Hibs v Rangers game but the other two Scottish Cup quarter-final ties that day were interesting as well – Motherwell v Hearts and Dunfermline v Stirling Albion. All four games survived the weather, a thaw having arrived just in time overnight to dispel the frost which had enveloped Scotland for a few days, and which caused the postponement of a few League games. It was actually a bright sunny but rather chilly day, typical of the early Scottish spring.

The Scottish League was this year a very open one. Celtic were out of it, of course, but so too, it was beginning to appear, were Rangers, who had had a very poor January and February, and at the moment both Edinburgh teams along with Dunfermline Athletic and Kilmarnock were in with a chance. Very few, however, of the 47,000 crowd who turned up at Celtic Park that day would have predicted that they were about to see a game between the Scottish League Champions and the Scottish Cup winners of 1965. A great deal of water was to flow under the bridge before these two things happened.

Celtic appeared in their "Hibs reverse" strip of white jerseys and green sleeves. It was not a bad strip (although, naturally, inferior to the green and white horizontal stripes) and it was a shame that this handsome combination of colours would never again be seen (This game would turn out to be the last-ever time that Celtic would wear this strip). Already they had appeared in an all-green strip against Queen's Park at Hampden, and then again against Kilmarnock in the League game, and the all-green kit would now become the "second" strip. The teams for the last game of Jimmy McGrory's managerial reign at Celtic were;

Celtic:

Fallon, Young and Gemmell; Clark, McNeill and Brogan; Chalmers, Murdoch, Hughes, Lennox and Auld.

Kilmarnock:

Forsyth, King and Watson; Murray, McGrory and Beattie; Brown, McInally, Hamilton, McFadzean and McIlroy.

The referee was Hugh Phillips of Wishaw, not always a popular man with some Celtic supporters but generally regarded by the Press as one of the best referees in Scotland, and indeed in Europe where he had fulfilled a few appointments. He would have a good game that day, keeping the lid on a pot that could have on several occasions boiled over.

The sun was out, but it was still cold, and the pitch was a little on the hard side. Kilmarnock came out in all-blue jerseys and many people in the crowd and the Press Box wondered whether Killie had changed from their normal vertical stripes in order to make a point to Celtic. Often referred to as the *"poor man's Rangers"* in Ayrshire, this change of strip did little to dispel that impression. It will be recalled that some six weeks earlier Morton had appeared similarly clad.

Parkhead was busier than normal with the *"Celtic, Cha! Cha! Cha!"* much in evidence. This was a *"Cel-Tic"* chant followed by three handclaps. It varied with *"Sure its's a grand old team" and "It was on a dreary New Year's Eve"* reverberating around the stadium as Celtic started playing towards the Rangers End of the ground and soon asserted some sort of command. Half-time saw Celtic one up and the goal came in the 16th minute as a result of a ploy which Celtic had developed recently, the brainchild, one assumes, of Bertie Auld, now revelling in his "midfield general" role.

It consisted of Bertie standing on the other side of the goal when a corner kick was taken on the right, and Steve Chalmers doing likewise when it was on the left. The corner kick would then be floated over the heads of everyone, and as the defence momentarily relaxed, the ball would then come back in immediately from the other side. It did not always work, but it did this time. Chalmers took the kick, the ball soared over the heads of everyone until it came to the lurking Auld who immediately hammered it back in to find the head of the elastic Lennox, who was not always famous for scoring goals with his head, but he did this time.

Celtic had a few more chances before half-time but 1-0 it was when the players retired. The interval was spent with the crowd in rare good humour and everyone talking in upbeat fashion of Jock Stein's imminent arrival and the changes he was going to make, the players he was going to buy etc. But everyone knew that there was still a job to do here, for Kilmarnock were not going to give in easily. However, with Celtic now attacking the Railway End (with its roof that only came halfway down the terracing!) where most supporters congregated, optimism was in the air.

Bobby Murdoch brought out a great save from Scotland goalkeeper Campbell Forsyth, Kilmarnock counter-attacked and the play raged back and forward until almost the hour mark, when both sides scored within a minute. Jackie McInally (the man with the fine Celtic surname and the father of future Celtic player Alan) scored first-time when he had been left unmarked. Almost immediately, Bertie Auld scored for Celtic, when a free-kick on the right taken by John Clark found Bobby Lennox who prodded it on to Auld who got there just before Forsyth did, and the banners and scarves went up again to scatter the despondency of losing an equaliser and to signal that Celtic were back in the lead.

This being Jimmy McGrory's last day in charge, it was fitting that John Hughes would score a goal that was so like those that Jimmy scored 30 years previously. Hughes was a big man, and on this occasion, he soared like a bird to connect with a cross from the ubiquitously diligent Bertie Auld. Funnily enough, John's direct opponent that day was called McGrory as well – this was Jackie, a great centre-half for Killie for many years but no relation to the mighty Jimmy now sitting in the stand, smiling, puffing on his pipe and delighted to see his team 3-1 ahead.

But Killie were not finished yet, and within the last 15 minutes McInally scored again in a goalmouth scramble and the latter stages of the game saw both teams unlucky not to score. But McNeill was superb for Celtic, and Mr Phillips' whistle sounded with Celtic 3-2 winners. Jimmy McGrory thus finished his tenure as Manager with a win. He would now hand over the team to incoming Manager Jock Stein in good "nick" and feeling confident about itself.

McGrory permitted himself a smile. His 20-year tenure had not been without its successes but really only one League title (1954) in two decades is indefensible for a club of Celtic's size and status. But it was all about today for Jimmy as he accepted the congratulations of his Kilmarnock counterparts, and it got even better. Across in Edinburgh, Rangers and Hibs had been drawing 1-1 but a rumour spread that Hibs had scored a late winner – but then again, there always are such rumours! However, the TV in the Boardroom confirmed that Willie Hamilton had scored a late goal for Hibs – a lucky header, but a winner nevertheless, and Rangers were now out of the Scottish Cup and the European Cup in the same week. Those who tell you that this had nothing to do with Celtic and the improved situation at Parkhead, are telling lies.

It was often said that Jock Stein won the 1965 Scottish Cup for Celtic with his last act for Hibs. This is of course a rather simplistic way of putting it, but there is little doubt that the removal of

Rangers did help matters for Celtic. That day also saw Dunfermline beat Stirling Albion 2-0 – no surprise there – but also the Scottish Cup downfall of the strong going Hearts to Motherwell – something that also planted all sorts of seeds of doubt at Tynecastle as far as the League was concerned. All in all, Jimmy McGrory's last day as Manager was not a bad one!

It was not, of course, Jimmy's last day at Celtic Park. Nothing like it! He was kept on as Public Relations Officer. This role involved issuing Press Releases, welcoming guests and opposition Directors to the Boardroom, visiting supporters' clubs and generally acting in the role now fulfilled by an Ambassador. It was a job to which the gentlemanly Jimmy was clearly suited, and he performed these duties well in spite of failing health (he suffered a heart attack in 1968) until he finally retired in 1979. Jock Stein always called him *"Boss"* and told the players to do the same.

Sunday, 7 March 1965 was one of those days when one just felt that the millennium had indeed arrived. There was a great deal to be happy about – a good win over Kilmarnock in the Scottish Cup, Rangers and Hearts now out of the Scottish Cup and the new Manager to arrive on Tuesday. The weather was clearly improving as well with the snow steadily melting, and it was understandable that, along with spring in the air, there was a spring in the step of Celtic players and supporters. And oh! What a difference a year makes! A year ago, Celtic, having impressed in midweek, blew up at Ibrox in the Scottish Cup and lost, fecklessly, 0-2.

Monday brought news that Celtic would play Motherwell in the Scottish Cup semi-final at Hampden on March 27. This was possibly the best draw because Motherwell were currently managerless as Bobby Ancell was still in the throes of departure to Dundee. In the other semi-final, the two current form teams of Scotland, Dunfermline and Hibs faced each other. Both had some fine players – but one of them would have to go out. The draw also raised the interesting possibility of an all-Stein Scottish Cup final, as it were, between Celtic and Hibs. (He had also of course had a considerable influence over Dunfermline!) But that was way in the future.

More immediately, next midweek (March 17 at Hampden) Celtic had three players chosen to play in the Scottish League International against the English League, including the obvious one of Bertie Auld, who had dominated the Scottish scene since his return six short weeks ago. John Hughes was also chosen, as indeed was Billy McNeill whose form had picked up since the dark days of the New Year.

It was on Tuesday, 9 March 1965 at 9.30am (according to *The Evening Times* of that day) that Jock Stein took over at Celtic Park. The journalist Peter Hendry claims that he asked Bob Kelly the direct question *"Will Jock Stein pick the team?"* and the answer was *"Jock is in complete charge."* This was basically what Celtic supporters were wanting to hear. There would be no more foolish interfering with team selections, no more players being picked or dropped on the whim of a man who didn't really know all that much about football, and there would be a football strategy in place. Stein was formally introduced to the Celtic squad at Barrowfield Park training ground that day, and the new era had begun. The sun was shining, and that was appropriate. *"Westward, look, the land is bright!"*

In a totally bizarre coincidence, *The Glasgow Herald* that morning in its Business section carries an advertisement for the selling of shares in a business of John G Stein and Company Limited, Manufacturers of Refractories. It had nothing to do with our Jock of course, but it must have worried a few supporters of Rangers and others that he was taking over other aspects of life as well! Indeed, his name would seldom be out of the newspapers from now on – a deliberate piece of massage and manipulation by Jock Stein who "made the newspapers support Celtic!"

Stein's first task was to choose a team for the visit to Airdrie on Wednesday night. It was a meaningless League match as far as

Celtic were concerned against the apparently doomed Broomfield side. Nevertheless, Celtic supporters descended there en masse to see an unchanged side win their seventh game in a row by beating the luckless Diamonds 6-0 and Bertie Auld scored five of them, John Hughes scoring the other. Conditions were far from ideal on a soft, boggy pitch, but some of the play was absolutely sparkling with all the players keen to show their new Manager how good they were.

In the case of Bertie Auld, there was no need, but some others were not so sure of their place in the team, especially as new Managers often bring in new players. Tommy Gemmell told the story years later of how he had heard that Jock Stein liked to see attacking full-backs. Tommy forged up the left wing as often as he could that night (the poverty of the opposition allowed him to do so with impunity) trying to show off. Stein congratulated the team, smiling at everyone, but then in private growled to Gemmell afterwards, *"Remember your job is as a defender!"* It was as well that Gemmell did not always heed that advice in future years, for Gemmell's attacking play was a feature of Celtic and produced many goals, not least a rather famous one in Lisbon!

A plan for a new League set-up was introduced this week, consisting of three divisions instead of two. As it was, with the First Division of 18 and the Second Division of 19 (a crazy number in any case, necessitating one team having a week off every Saturday!), life was unwieldy and there were too many games with nothing at stake, particularly near the end of the season. The Press tried manfully every season to persuade everyone to get excited about whether a team was going to be eighth rather than ninth, but the public were not interested. Change was required, but there were also selfish interests at stake, and the plan would duly be shelved to become the national bore when the football on the field got stale. Eventually, ten years later, change would come.

But for Celtic fans, there was now the chance to welcome Jock Stein to Celtic Park for his first home game. It was against St Johnstone. It turned out to be a damp squib in more ways than one. In the first place, rain of the steady, relentless Glasgow kind reduced the crowd to 18,000 according to what Celtic said, although in fact there seemed, as always, to be a few more than that. But it meant that the crowd were packed in the inadequate Jungle, and in the limited shelter at the Railway End, while the Rangers End was almost completely bereft of spectators. The rain did ease a little later on in the afternoon, but it was still a dismal day.

And dismal was the word for the performance of the team, who lost their first game for a couple of months to St Johnstone, a team who were not as yet entirely clear of the relegation zone in spite of having beaten Celtic 3-0 at Perth in November. This had been in the middle of the "freefall" spell in the wake of the League Cup final in that dark hour of Celtic's history. Today, St Johnstone had clearly settled for a draw. These "parking of the team bus" tactics were, of course, nothing new in the context of away teams at Parkhead, but Celtic really have to know how to break them down. Today, everything failed. Whether it was because the players were trying too hard to impress the new Manager, or whether too many players simply had an off day we cannot be sure, but St Johnstone resisted the pressure, scored in a breakaway at a key time, then resisted more pressure (of the hysterical rather than the thought-out variety) to earn a 1-0 victory which was as important to them as their famous 2-1 Parkhead victory in February 1936, which put that great Celtic team out of the Scottish Cup.

The matchday programme was impressive and clear, with Jock Stein saying categorically, *"I have been handed the reins of management and I alone have to do the driving. For the playing side, team picking, tactics, coaching and scouting, I have full responsibility."* Well, that was clear at least! Half-time came with Celtic well on top but never really coming very close to opening the scoring as the St Johnstone defending was crisp and competent. The goalkeeping of McVittie was first class, with a particularly good save from a Chalmers shot from 18 yards which even elicited a murmur of approval from the frustrated faithful.

Early in the second half, St Johnstone went ahead with a fine drive from the edge of the penalty area. This caused Celtic to redouble their efforts, and then John Hughes scored only to have the score chalked off for a foul on a defender. It was a marginal decision, but the referee was Bobby Davidson of Airdrie, never exactly the darling of Celtic Park. In this case, however, he was probably right.

In any case, one of the first things that Jock Stein would tell his players was never to rely on a refereeing decision. Make sure that you are 5-0 up, then a refereeing decision will not matter. This was clearly not happening here, as the forwards simply failed to deliver. A token of what was to come, however, was seen in Billy McNeill's willingness to join in the attacks, particularly for corner kicks. Once or twice, he had bad luck.

But the man of the moment was St Johnstone's goalkeeper Mike McVittie, who time and time again defied the Celtic forwards. Frustration grew, but then in the very last minute, Celtic were awarded a penalty kick when Bobby Murdoch was brought down. At least, Celtic would get a draw, it was felt, but sadly the new talisman Bertie Auld proved that he was only human after all when he had his penalty kick saved by McVittie. The full-time whistle went soon afterwards, and the Perth Saints had recorded their first ever "double" over Celtic by beating them home and away in the League. It was a depressing experience, although the game itself didn't really matter and in any case, a boost was given with the news that Aberdeen had beaten Rangers, seriously impairing what little chance the Ibrox side had of winning the League.

Jock Stein was not all that unhappy, at least on the surface. He told the BBC radio and television people after the game, *"I see now why I am here!"* and vowed that he would work to solve the deficiencies of the team. What he said to his players in the dressing-room after that in private, we do not know, but we can adduce that from this game at least two positives emerged.

One was the deployment of Billy McNeill as an attacking centre-half. There was nothing new about this, of course, for famous centre-halves in the past like Willie Loney and Willie Lyon could join the attack on occasion, but Stein realised that McNeill with his unparalleled skill in the air could be a great asset to the attack on days like this when goals were hard to come by. There was now an aerial presence at corner kicks.

The other was an equally important decision (indeed, the crucial one for the next few years) concerning Bobby Murdoch. Bobby was a talented player but had had a poor game today. Many of the support (not least a popular and well-read fanzine called The Shamrock) had wondered whether Murdoch might not be a better player further back, where he could dominate the midfield, and have the ball in front of him oftener, rather than be in a position where the ball was coming to him from behind. Today had proved the point. Too often, Murdoch had appeared clumsy and awkward, and not really showing his tremendous ball-winning talents and his passing ability. Maybe a change of position was in order. He had played once or twice at right-half if injuries to other players had compelled him to do so, but he had never played there for any length of time.

Generally speaking, Stein realised that he had time on his side. The Scottish League had been lost and so these games could be used for experiments. He was determined to give everyone a chance, to try a few experiments. The game that he really had to win was Motherwell at Hampden on March 27 in the Scottish Cup semi-final. Other games, and there were still seven League games to go, were of lesser importance. But, as it is Celtic we are talking about, the support demanded victories.

The next game was Dundee at Dens Park on March 20. Games between these two teams in the early sixties were invariably close fought and good games to watch, even though Celtic had often found it very difficult to get a win there. This one would prove to be no exception, but before that happened, there was the Scottish League v English League game at Hampden Park on the Wednesday night.

There were 38,409 spectators at Hampden and they saw a 2-2 draw. Celtic had four players in the Scottish side – McNeill, Chalmers, Auld and Hughes, Chalmers being a late addition. Celtic supporters often argued among themselves about the value of John Hughes, and he similarly split opinions in the Scottish ranks on this occasion. He scored the two goals, but Raymond Jacobs in *The Glasgow Herald* has this to say, *"Hughes carried the attack on his ample shoulders excitingly in the first half, when he at times stampeded the English defence with long boring runs. In the second half, however, there seemed to be nothing left in the horse (sic) and it is doubtful whether he is ready yet for higher status."*

This seems to be quite a valid point about John. The word *"boring"* is presumably used in the sense of "boring a hole" rather than "boring people to tears," and Raymond Jacobs seems to have hit the nail on the head by saying that John Hughes was infuriatingly inconsistent and could not be relied upon to last a whole game at his brilliant best, let alone string together a run of fine performances. Many Celtic supporters said exactly the same thing and would say that one of Stein's tasks would have to be to persuade Hughes to play brilliantly all the time. The talent was certainly there.

And so it was the road and the miles to Dundee on Saturday. The weather was bright and sharp, although still a little chilly, but a big crowd assembled. 15,000 was a good crowd for a game which did not really mean very much for either side. Dundee were clearly past their peak of 1962 when they (deservedly) won the Scottish League then reached the semi-final of the European Cup in 1963, but then they had shot themselves spectacularly in the foot by selling Ian Ure and Alan Gilzean. Yet they still had many good players, particularly the very talented Charlie Cooke, whom they had brought in from Aberdeen, and a few others like Andy Penman, Kenny Cameron and Hugh Robertson.

Stein made a few changes to the Celtic team. It was the first time that the team had been changed since January and it read *Fallon,*

Young and Kennedy; Murdoch, McNeill and Clark; Johnstone, Chalmers, Hughes, Lennox and Auld. Tommy Gemmell, having made his point about attacking full backs, was given a rest in favour of Jim Kennedy; Jim Brogan, who hadn't really done anything wrong, was dropped in favour of Stein's iconoclastic but nevertheless popular and inspirational move of bringing Murdoch to the right half position, and Jimmy Johnstone was given his first game in the team under Jock Stein.

The relationship between "Wee Jimmy" and "Big Jock" would be complex over the next ten years. Each was exactly what the other one wasn't – a talented but neurotic and insecure player on the one hand, and a stern, strict but not always unbending Manager on the other. Each needed the other in a way. Stein's ambition to make Celtic the greatest team on earth was not likely to happen without the man who, on his day, could be the best player around, and Johnstone needed the firm hand of Stein to keep him in line. Jimmy's escapades and Jock's reactions were almost stereotypes sometimes and provided a long-running Scottish soap opera with many episodes. Stein would say in future years that one of his greatest achievements was keeping Jimmy Johnstone in the game longer than might otherwise have been the case.

The story goes about how a few months before, when Stein was still Manager of Hibs, he was at Celtic Park for a reserve match in which Jimmy was playing. They met in the toilet after the game, both acknowledged each other's presence, then Jock stared at him and said, *"What are you doing here?"* The socially inept Jimmy was tongue-tied as Jock thundered *"You're far too good a player to be in the reserves!"* Now, Jimmy, still in disgrace after his encounter with Tottie Beck on New Year's Day and his consequent suspension, was being given his chance to play on the right wing, with Steve Chalmers moved to inside right to allow Bobby Murdoch to move to midfield.

Did Stein's changes work at Dens Park? The answer would have to be *"Not Proven."* It was fast, open football in the tradition of these two teams and the final score was 3-3. Johnstone certainly proved his point. He scored a good goal when curiously left unmarked by the Dundee defence, and another goal came after a fine move involving Murdoch and Johnstone found Lennox. Lennox had a fine game and had scored in the first minute as well. The bad news was that the attacking Celtic were leaving too many gaps at the back with McNeill returning to his hesitant, indecisive, careless ways which we all thought he had left behind when Stein arrived, and Bobby Murdoch had the misfortune to score an own goal when a fierce drive hit his foot and was diverted past his goalkeeper John Fallon.

Celtic had been 3-1 up, and then Dundee had equalised. This in some ways looked like a defeat to some of the downhearted support, but on the other hand, there were many good things on view as well. The left-wing combination of Lennox and Auld was consistently good, Murdoch's play at right-half deserved at least another try; Ian Young was good at right-back, and John Fallon, although occasionally unorthodox in his goalkeeping methods, had some good saves as well. Everyone agreed, however, that it was a good football match, and that there was still a great deal to come from Celtic this season. Rangers played out a feeble draw against Kilmarnock at Ibrox, but Hearts and Hibs both won, creating the premature impression that the League flag could be returning to Edinburgh for the first time since 1960.

The next game was hard on the heels of this one. It was against Hibs at Celtic Park. It was a game postponed from the winter and both teams agreed to play it on the Monday night of March 22, for they were both involved in Scottish Cup semi-finals on Saturday. It was a game full of ironies, for had it been played when it was originally scheduled, Jock Stein would have been the Manager of Hibs rather than Celtic. As it was, it was a crucial game for Hibs, who needed to win if they were to maintain their title challenge. For Celtic, it was less important. There were places available for next year's Inter Cities' Fairs Cup, but it was possibly true to say that these considerations were of less importance than the need to get on form for the ensuing semi-final against Motherwell.

Circumstances played a part in Celtic's team selection. Jimmy Johnstone failed a fitness test and Stein decided to put Chalmers on the right wing and Murdoch back at inside-right for this one game, while bringing back Jim Brogan. Jim Kennedy retained his place at left-back at the expense of Tommy Gemmell. Bertie Auld was also out with a slight injury and Stein did not risk him, giving Hugh Maxwell a rare start at inside-left. The weather was not pleasant with a lot of rain which kept turning to sleet. It meant that the pitch was heavy and not really conducive to good football. Considering that it was a rainy Monday night, the crowd of 19,000 was a very good one indeed.

It was a curious, unbalanced sort of game with all the action in the first half. It was 4-2 for Hibs at half-time, and that was how it stayed all through the second half. Hibs successful defenders in that second half were men with Celtic connections, one in the past and one in the future – John McNamee who had had to leave Celtic Park because he had no hope of replacing McNeill and Pat Stanton who spent many years with Hibs and won very little, but then signed for Celtic late in his career and won a League and Cup double in 1976/77! These two kept such a stranglehold over the centre of the field that the Celtic forwards were compelled to shoot from ridiculous angles and distances, to the disgust of the bedraggled Celtic support, some of them now beginning to realise just how inadequate "the Jungle" was for sheltering supporters!

The first half had at least provided quite a lot of action for the fans, but it was at the wrong end. Neil Martin took advantage of McNeill - who was clearly going through another crisis of confidence - and scored a hat-trick, while the other Hibs goal was scored by the unfortunate Ian Young, who dived in an attempt to clear and scored what would, in another context, really have to be classed a brilliant goal. That was hard luck. When 3-0 down, Celtic pulled one back from a Lennox rebound off the goalkeeper's chest, and then just before half-time, the same player scored another to make it 4-2.

Many of the goals from both sides came from defensive and goalkeeping errors, but there could be no denying that Hibs were a class outfit and looking at this stage good for a Scottish League and Cup double. They were now only one point short of leaders Hearts, but their Scottish Cup rivals Dunfermline Athletic had a remarkable night, beating the now doomed Third Lanark 8-0 at East End Park.

For Celtic, it was a sobering night. The one thing that it did was clear up any arguments about who was the better left back – Tommy Gemmell was restored on Saturday – and it did seem that Bobby Murdoch played better in the midfield than in the forward line. It was now quite obvious if it had not been before, that Hugh Maxwell was little more than an honest journeyman, if that. Allied to that, it was equally plain that there could be no Celtic revival without Bertie Auld. Apparently, Stein remained calm and pointed out gently that the way that Hibs had played was the way that he wanted Celtic to play. He said he would work to achieve that end and joked about how he now had a 100% record of losing at Celtic Park!

This result did little to calm the nerves of the support as they approached the semi-final. Rational analysis would have to say that if Hibs were to meet Celtic in the Scottish Cup final, there could really only be one winner. But Hibs were up against Dunfermline Athletic, who of course had won the trophy in 1961 when Jock Stein was their Manager. It was funny how that name kept occurring in discussions about the Scottish Cup!

The only team that Stein had had no direct connection with was Motherwell. Their Manager was Bobby Ancell, one time of Dundee as a player and soon to go back to them as Manager. They were no great side as far as League form was concerned this year – they would have been on the fringes of relegation if that issue had not been so clear cut – but they were a team that could never be written off. They were a team whom the kind critics described as *"experienced"* and the unkind ones described as *"old."* Their star forward was Joe McBride, a man of many clubs, who was now with Motherwell and scoring goals for them – but it was no secret that he wanted to go to Celtic, nor was there the slightest doubt that Stein admired him and would do so all the more after this particular game.

Stein had a full squad available to him with Bertie Auld recovered from his injury (if he ever had one in the first place) and Jimmy Johnstone also back in contention. This time, Jock sprung a slight surprise by giving a game to Charlie Gallagher – his first game under Stein – and dropping Steve Chalmers, while restoring Murdoch to the right-half position. Thus, in conditions which *The Evening Times* describes as *"grey skies, a smirr of rain and a high wind,"* the following teams took the field on Saturday, 27 March 1965 before a crowd of 52,000;

Celtic:

Fallon, Young and Gemmell; Murdoch, McNeill and Clark; Johnstone, Gallagher, Hughes, Lennox and Auld.

Motherwell:

Wyllie, Thomson and R McCallum; Murray, Delaney and W McCallum; Lindsay, McCann, McBride, Weir and Hunter.

Referee: ***AJF Webster, Falkirk***

McNeill lost the toss and Celtic had to play against the wind, defending the King's Park goal in the first half. The wind was strong and capricious, and thus it was that the Celtic fans in that King's Park end (traditionally the Celtic End) had a great view of Motherwell's two first-half goals. Young had already chested a ball down on the line to prevent Motherwell going ahead before they actually opened the scoring. It was another McNeill nightmare as he failed to clear a ball properly in the centre of the field, McBride picked it up, ran past McNeill and fired in a shot which Fallon managed to half stop but could not prevent from rolling into the net.

It was no more than Motherwell deserved, and for a long time Celtic struggled to get back into this game. When they did score, it was a little fortuitous when goalkeeper Wyllie failed to hold a Johnstone cross and the ball rebounded to Lennox who didn't really hit it cleanly enough and a defender almost managed to clear his lines but only diverted the ball into the roof of the net.

Those in the Celtic End breathed a sigh of relief, but they were only on level terms momentarily, for a few minutes later in the aftermath of a corner kick, the unmarked McBride shot with a left foot drive, the ball rebounded off Fallon's chest, and McBride made no mistake with his second effort. Once again depression descended on the Celtic End, and this time it lasted until half-time with Motherwell clearly the better team and deserving of their lead.

But there were still 45 minutes to go, and this time Celtic would have the benefit of the strong wind, which was showing no sign of abating. The intermittent rain made life unpleasant for the spectators (Hampden in 1965 had no shelter whatsoever, apart from the two stands, which even in 1965 were beginning to show their age) and the wind was making the playing of good football quite difficult, even for the team playing with the wind. It would be up to Celtic's ball players – Gallagher and Auld - to hold the ball, because it was not a good day for John Hughes, who could play brilliantly in other forms of bad weather, particularly a frozen pitch or heavy muddy ground, but not the wind.

The wind made it impossible to hear what the public address system was saying, but those of us who had that still fairly new invention called a transistor radio were able to tell everyone that Dunfermline were beating Hibs 1-0 in the other semi-final at Tynecastle. This was looked upon as a bit of a surprise, given Hibs' fine performance on Monday night at Parkhead, but as here at Hampden, there was still a long way to go. *"Jock Stein will have something up his sleeve for the last 10 minutes,"* my companion told me.

There were three crucial refereeing decisions in the second half. One was in the very first minute, when Jimmy Johnstone was sent sprawling inside the box. Incredibly, no penalty was given for that; the second was on the hour mark, when Bertie Auld beat three men and was then brought down. No argument this time. It was a penalty. Bertie then, ball under his arm, walked to place the ball on the penalty spot – no easy task in the wind – and then duly scored to make the score 2-2. The third decision was in the last minute, when the ubiquitous Auld scored from a Johnstone pass what looked to those of us behind that goal to be a good goal but was chalked off for offside. It was possibly Johnstone who was offside rather than Auld himself. TV pictures that night were not totally conclusive, but in any case, a draw it was and the replay arranged for Wednesday, 31 March at 7.30 pm.

Celtic had indeed played a great deal better in the second half with the wind behind them. Murdoch had come more into his own, Gemmell had had a few surging runs forward, and we had seen a few of Gallagher's fine passes. Auld had orchestrated it all, and possibly Celtic had done enough to deserve to win, but 2-2 was the score. Newspaper reports mention the increasing tendency for McNeill to come forward for corner kicks and free kicks, saying things like *"McNeill, of all people..."* and *"even McNeill,"* as if this was a new Celtic secret weapon. So indeed it was, and it was soon to be unleashed to devastating effect.

The evening papers told us that Dunfermline had indeed defeated Hibs 2-0. Hibs were no great Scottish Cup team, having last won the trophy in 1902, but they were still a good bet for the League. Dunfermline, now managed by Willie Cunningham, were no bad team, however, and would be difficult opponents, but there were those who felt that Celtic's name was already on the Cup, for in two key games – Hibs v Rangers and Hibs v Dunfermline, the lesser team had won. But before anyone could think about Dunfermline, there was still Motherwell to beat in the replay.

To his credit, Stein refused to blame it all on the wind, and more or less admitted what all supporters believed, namely that it had been a sub-standard performance from Celtic. Jimmy Johnstone had picked up a thigh knock, from which he seemed to be recovering. There had been a school of thought that felt that if Jimmy played, Steve Chalmers could be moved to the centre-forward position to allow John Hughes to go to the left wing. The snag was that this would mean disturbing the left wing of Lennox and Auld, which was currently very successful. In the event, whether because he had not yet recovered from his injury or whether for tactical reasons, Jimmy didn't play, and Steve Chalmers lined up on the right wing.

In the meantime, Motherwell had changed Manager and were now led by Bobby Howitt. Bobby Ancell had gone to Dundee as part of the chain reaction which followed Jock Stein's arrival at Celtic Park. Bob Shankly had replaced Stein at Hibs, and Ancell had replaced Shankly at Dundee. Howitt would do well at Motherwell but to take on Celtic in a semi-final replay for his first game was a big ask.

Celtic had not done well in recent years in Wednesday night replays at Hampden. Three Scottish Cup finals had been lost in 1955, 1961 and 1963 and two semi-finals in 1957 and 1960, but nevertheless the smart money was on Celtic, who would have their huge support behind them, and the conditions would be much calmer and more conducive to good football. Although they themselves were playing a very important League game against Hibs at Easter Road that night, Dunfermline Athletic were represented at the game, for they now awaited the winners.

The teams were:

Celtic:

Fallon, Young and Gemmell; Murdoch, McNeill and Clark; Chalmers, Gallagher, Hughes, Lennox and Auld.

Motherwell:

Wyllie, Thomson and R McCallum; Murray, Delaney and W McCallum; Carlyle, McCann, McBride, Weir and Lindsay.

Referee: *AJF Webster, Falkirk*

It was a game that Celtic won easily and with style. The crowd was 58,959, an improvement (incredibly) from Saturday and something that said a great deal about the weather and the improved transport facilities now that dual carriageways and motorways were beginning to make their appearance in Scotland, and which facilitated transport to night games. The fans that night saw possibly the first indication of the truly great side that Celtic were to become.

In the first place, Billy McNeill was much improved, dominating proceedings and managing his side with aplomb. And this was also the night that Bobby Murdoch emerged as a right-half, silencing all possible doubters as he won the ball in midfield, distributed it with accuracy and polish and turned defence into attack just like he was turning on a switch. It was the first of many occasions that the press would say “world class” in the context of Bobby Murdoch.

Playing towards the Mount Florida end, Hughes had already scored a goal which was mysteriously disallowed for offside. It was a shot which touched the goalkeeper, hit the bar, crossed the line then came out for Lennox to tap the ball in. There was no way that this goal should not have been allowed to stand. First, it definitely crossed the line before it came out to Lennox, and even if Lennox was standing in an offside position, he was not offside, for the ball had touched goalkeeper Wyllie. This was a clear injustice which, added to the disallowing of the goal late on Saturday, was causing the crowd to mutter, but then Chalmers put Celtic ahead when he breasted in an Auld corner kick.

The 1-0 lead was scant reward for Celtic's efforts, but in the second half when Murdoch and Auld really got going, Celtic pressed almost constantly after a slightly hesitant start in which Motherwell came as close as they were ever likely to score against a now solid Celtic defence, with McNeill radiating confidence and the two full-backs Young and Gemmell tackling like tigers. Halfway through the second half, Celtic went two up when goalkeeper Wyllie, who had hitherto had a good, albeit lucky, game in the Motherwell goal, dropped a high ball and Hughes took full advantage. Five minutes after that, Lennox killed Motherwell's fast vanishing hopes when he ran on to a long ball and squeezed the ball under Wyllie's diving body. The game finished with Celtic well on top, and the large crowd dispersing happily to their cars, buses and railway stations, talking happily about the good days that had returned to Celtic Park.

The month of March thus ended with Celtic fans in a rare state of euphoria that it would have been hard to imagine at the beginning of the year. At long last, a good Manager had been appointed, and the team had responded to this with the fans similarly beginning to enjoy life and looking forward to the Scottish Cup final against Dunfermline on April 24. Dunfermline were good, but that night they had lost to Hibs in the League, (having beaten them in the Cup on Saturday!) something that seemed to suggest that they were not invulnerable. And what a remarkable man Jock Stein was! Could he achieve a double of Celtic winning the Scottish Cup, and Hibs, the team he had managed until early March winning the Scottish League? Such thoughts exercised the minds of Celtic fans as the trains rolled home that pleasant spring night as March gave way to April.

CHAPTER FOUR

APRIL

Celtic thus entered the month of April 1965 on a high. The performance on Wednesday night against Motherwell showed that they had a team capable of winning the Scottish Cup, even though the League performances had not been very good. The problem was inconsistency. It was generally reckoned that on a good day they could beat Dunfermline Athletic in the Final; on a bad day, one would have to fancy the Pars. Five League games remained to be played – against Third Lanark and Partick Thistle at home, and away to Hibs, Falkirk and Dunfermline.

First up was Third Lanark on Saturday, 3 April. It turned out, although no-one knew it at the time (however much the prescient might have suspected), to be the last game that these two teams would ever play against each other. The 3rd Lanarkshire Rifle Volunteers were founder members of the SFA in 1873, had played a long and glorious part in Scottish football history, but had now fallen on hard times. There were two main causes for this – one was the depopulation of Glasgow in what was called the "Glasgow overspill," whereby people and families were moving to places like East Kilbride and Cumbernauld, but the other was, as later became apparent, internal corruption within the club. Good teams were dismantled, and players transferred for money which was not re-invested. In early April 1965 by the time that this game was played, they were already relegated to the Second Division and after two years of failing to rally in the lower reaches, they would go out of existence in 1967.

There was not really very much at stake in this match, and the low crowd of 14,000 reflected that. Arguably, they saw Celtic playing one of their worst games, even in this dreadful League season. Those who had spent all their money attending both the semi-final and its replay and could not afford a third trip to Glasgow, or who had decided to spend the Spring Holiday weekend elsewhere did not miss much. Third Lanark, themselves virtually bereft of supporters by now, were given a sympathetic cheer when they came out. They were not without Celtic connections. They were led by Dunky MacKay, an old Celtic favourite who had possibly been unfortunate in the time that he was at Celtic Park. Thirds also had at inside-right Mike Jackson, another of the "promising" Celts who had not quite made it in the early 1960s, and their goalkeeper was Evan Williams, who would one day come to Celtic and play in the 1970 European Cup final. Their Manager was no less a person than Bobby Evans, still a Celtic legend.

Celtic were given a huge welcome for the game that they had played in midweek to get them to the Scottish Cup final, but the cheers, after a period of silence, soon turned to groans as the heroes of Wednesday night failed to live up to their billing. Celtic fans, never the most patient of people, were not slow to turn on their players, particularly the forwards who were disjointed and whose shooting was poor. Well before half time, Chalmers, Hughes and Auld all received a "round of the guns" from the supporters for their feckless finishing, and the slow handclap so prominent at Celtic Park in the dark days of midwinter but now not normally heard so often, made an unwelcome re-appearance. It seemed a little unfair.

Possibly the fact that Jock Stein was not there, off on an undisclosed scouting mission in England, was significant. But presumably Sean Fallon made his feelings plain at half-time, for the team perked up their ideas a little in the second half, but still without being able to score. The crowd were beginning to go home muttering about *"You never get two good games in a row with them"* when within the last ten minutes, Chalmers made some ground and crossed to Hughes, who shot, and the ball took a wicked deflection off Dunky MacKay to get the better of Evan Williams. The goal at least raised some sort of a cheer, but it was frankly an awful game. Although Jock Stein wasn't there, it was his first victory at Parkhead as Manager!

It was thus a very sad end to a rivalry which had lasted the whole 77 years of Celtic's history. The clubs had shared, among others, Tom Maley, Johnny Campbell, Tommy McInally and Ronnie Simpson, and Third Lanark had been the opponents in Celtic's first-ever Scottish Cup final in 1889. Leaving aside the Celtic connections, there had been men like Jimmy Brownlie, Jimmy Mason and Jimmy Carabine, all of whom had graced a Scotland shirt with distinction. Their disappearance from the scene in 1967 was a source of great sadness for all of Scottish football, and of course, their ground, Cathkin Park, had been originally called Hampden, and had been the scene of Scotland Internationals and Scottish Cup finals, notably Celtic's second Scottish Cup win in 1899 when they beat Rangers 2-0.

April 3 was a good day for everyone in the League race except Hibs. They went down 1-2 at Dens Park, Dundee in a result that was rich in irony, because Bob Shankly had just moved from Dundee to Hibs, and was roundly booed by Dundee fans with short memories. Hearts beat St Johnstone, and Kilmarnock and Dunfermline also won. This meant that with three games to go, Hearts were now three points ahead of both Hibs and Kilmarnock and five ahead of Dunfermline, although the Pars had a game in hand. Something rather remarkable, it seemed, would have to happen before Hearts would lose the League. But something rather remarkable did indeed occur, as we shall see.

In 1965, the Scotland v England game was a big thing, and April 10 was the day of the International at Wembley. This particular game was one that everyone spoke about, and those who could afford it and who were lucky enough to have contacts to provide tickets, would go on the biennial pilgrimage to London. It was all about drink, of course, and having a good time, but it was a rich experience to dress up in tartan, get the train on Friday night and come back, usually a physical wreck with exhaustion and crapulence, sometime on Sunday afternoon without having been to bed since Thursday night. There was an added edge that year, for Scotland had won in 1962, 1963 and 1964 and a win in 1965 would be four-in-a-row, not unprecedented, but last done in the early 1880s. And all that as well as the imminence of the World Cup to be held in England in 1966!

So the main talk in the newspapers would be about injuries to players, and how to avoid them. Billy McNeill, who had now recovered from his bad patch at the turn of the year, was chosen to play with several other Celtic players on the fringes. Unlike modern times, when International players are wrapped in cotton wool, quite a few players were involved in midweek fixtures, in McNeill's case against Hibs at Easter Road on Wednesday, 7 April.

Once again, it was a game that did not really mean very much to Celtic other than in Stein's plans to find a settled team for the Scottish Cup final, but for Hibs, it represented their last chance to get back into the League race. Bob Shankly was not off to the best of starts. Indeed, he never really settled and would have been far better off staying with Dundee. He had beaten Celtic at Parkhead a fortnight ago, but then had lost a semi-final to Dunfermline and disappointed the supporters by a narrow defeat to Dundee. Tonight, he blew up spectacularly against Celtic and finished Hibs season there and then.

Jock Stein, booed and jeered at by Hibs fans as he got off the Celtic bus for his perceived desertion of them, kept the same Celtic team as had limped to victory over Third Lanark. This performance, however, was crisp and efficient, in particular a devastating spell of three minutes towards the end of the first half in which Auld, Chalmers and Murdoch scored past a bewildered Hibs defence to put Celtic 3-0 ahead at half-time. Auld then scored in the second half, and poor Hibs even missed a penalty when Neil Martin shot weakly at John Fallon.

1965 opens for Celtic with the traditional Ne'erday fixture with Rangers, this time around played at Ibrox.

Top: Billy McNeill shakes hands with Rangers skipper Eric Caldow before kick-off, as referee Tom 'Tiny' Wharton looks on, then watches as Ronnie Simpson deals with a Rangers attack.

Bottom: Billy clears the danger from Ibrox duo Jimmy Millar and Jim Forrest. Forrest was on target as Rangers won 1-0.

Two appointments in early 1965 which changed the course of Celtic's history forever.
Bertie Auld leaves Birmingham City to sign for Celtic for a second time on 14 January 1965.

Page 19 DAILY RECORD, Monday, February 1, 1965

Celtic make Jock new manager

'Jock Stein will be in full charge of the team. He will make the other appointments he wants at the club. He will be the boss'... Celtic chairman Bob Kelly.

STEIN WILL BE THE BOSS

By JIM RODGER and TOM NICHOLSON

JOCK STEIN

JOCK STEIN IS THE NEW MANAGER OF CELTIC AND HE WILL BE THE BOSS.

McGrory gets a key job in new set-up

No contract

Great wish

Don't blame the snow, Rangers!

By WAVERLEY

Wingers neglected

Millar, Bock fail

Struggles

JOHN'S FIVE HIS BEST EVER

Celtic announce that Jock Stein will be leaving Hibernian to take over at Parkhead.

The legendary 'white sannie' match of 30 January 1965. John 'Yogi' Hughes scores five of Celtic's eight goals in an 8-0 rout over Aberdeen at an icy Parkhead.

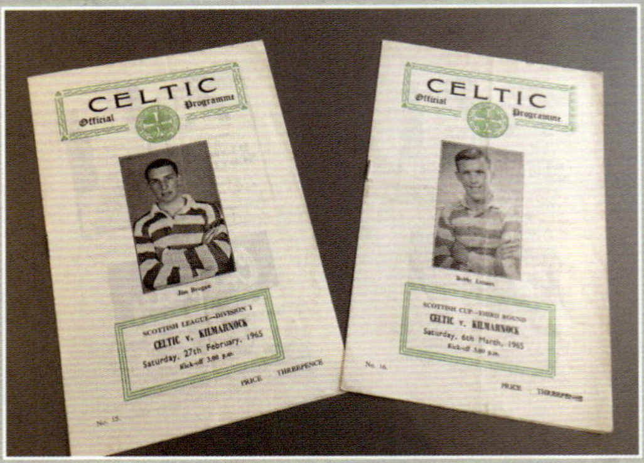

It might not look like it but these two photographs featuring Bobby Lennox are taken just seven days apart and both feature matches against Kilmarnock at Celtic Park, despite the different kits.

Top photo is from the League match of 27 February 1965, which Celts won 2-0. Kilmarnock would then drop just one point from their final eight games to clinch their only Scottish title to date.

Bottom image is from the Scottish Cup quarter-final clash between the clubs which Celtic won 3-2. This was Jimmy McGrory's final game in charge of the club and was also the last time the Shamrock strip was worn.

An unforgettable era is about to begin at Celtic Park as Jock Stein becomes the fourth manager of the club, having accepted the offer from chairman Bob Kelly. The Glasgow Cup is prominent in the bottom image, the last trophy won by Jimmy McGrory as Celtic manager and the first by Billy McNeill as club captain. The St Mungo Cup, won by Jimmy's Celtic team in August 1951, is also displayed on the left of that photograph.

He's home! Jock Stein is back at Paradise.

Jock begins his new job by overseeing a training session at Barrowfield on 9 March 1965. Players from left to right are (Back) John Hughes, Stevie Chalmers, Ian Young, Bertie Auld, Billy McNeill and (Front) Bobby Lennox, Tommy Gemmell, Bobby Murdoch and John Fallon.

Jock and his new backroom team are photographed in the dugout at Broomfield the following night. From left to right are Neil Mochan (Trainer), Bob Rooney (Physio), Jock and Sean Fallon (Assistant Manager). Bertie Auld scored five goals as the new era commenced with a 6-0 thrashing of Airdrieonians

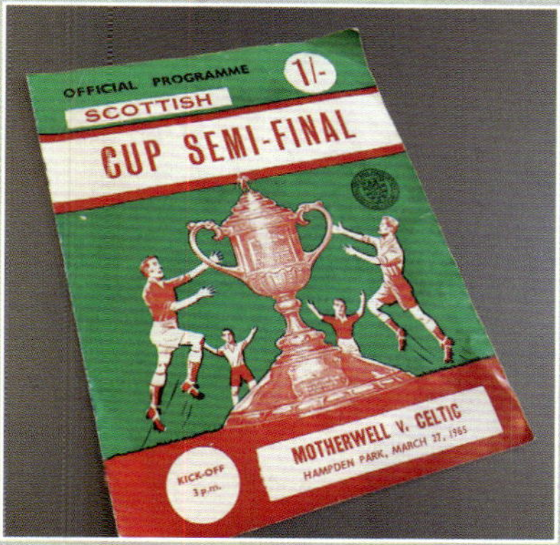

Top left: Bertie Auld equalises for Celtic in the Scottish Cup semi-final against Motherwell at Hampden on 31 March 1965

Top right: Stevie Chalmers chests the ball home to give Celtic the lead in the 3-0 replay win four days later. John Hughes and Bobby Lennox added further goals.

Bottom: Stevie is again in the thick of the action three days later against Third Lanark at Celtic Park, with future Celtic goalkeeper Evan Williams and Bobby Lennox also challenging for the ball. A late own goal from former Celtic captain Dunky MacKay gave Celts a victory in what was the last-ever match between the clubs.

Skippers Jim McLean of Dunfermline Athletic and Billy McNeill of Celtic carry out their preliminary duties ahead of the 1965 Scottish Cup final under the watchful eye of referee Hugh Phillips.

Bertie Auld times his leap to perfection to beat Dunfermline defender Willie Callaghan to the rebound from Charlie Gallagher's spectacular long-range drive and level things at 1-1 in the Scottish Cup final.
A happy Bertie is then joined in the net by a leaping Stevie Chalmers with Tommy Gemmell looking on.

The goals which finally settled the destination of the 1965 Scottish Cup and ended the long wait for major silverware at Celtic Park.

Top left: Bertie Auld drills the ball past Dunfermline goalkeeper Jim Herriot for his second equaliser of the afternoon, early in the second half. Future Celt Tom Callaghan looks on in dismay. Top right: There's no doubt how acrobatic Celtic goalkeeper John Fallon feels about Billy McNeill's winning goal! Bottom: Celtic skipper Billy McNeill leaps majestically to meet Charlie Gallagher's perfect corner-kick and powers his header into the net to win the Scottish Cup.

Scenes of Celtic joy and jubilation as the inquest begins amongst the Dunfermline defence.

Stevie Chalmers and Bobby Lennox are first to congratulate Billy McNeill on his late winner and they are quickly joined by Bertie Auld and John Hughes.

An embrace for Billy McNeill from Celtic physio Bob Rooney as the full-time whistle blows at Hampden.

The first of many for Celtic's most celebrated manager and captain partnership! Manager Jock Stein hugs his skipper Billy McNeill as he leaves the Hampden pitch, with Charlie Gallagher and Bobby Lennox also feeling rather pleased with life.

There's no feeling quite like it!

Billy McNeill holds the Scottish Cup aloft at Hampden and the celebrations can begin on the Hampden pitch.

That winning feeling! Billy McNeill celebrates with teammates John Clark, Tommy Gemmell, John Hughes, Ian Young and Bobby Lennox outside Hampden then poses with Jock Stein and Bob Kelly.

The Celt c team bus is engulfed by thousands of fans as it makes its way from Hampden.

Jubilant Celtic supporters outside Glasgow's Central Hotel demand the appearance of the team with the Scottish Cup.

The cup-winning Celtic team pictured with the trophy ahead of the Glasgow Cup first-round clash with Rangers at Celtic Park on 30 April 1965. Celtic won 2-1 on the night.

Billy McNeill. Scotland's Player of the Year 1964/65

Man-of-the-match was undeniably Bobby Murdoch, who shone like a beacon throughout with even the Hibs fans compelled to give a ripple of applause for some of his inch-perfect passes. There wasn't a huge Celtic support there that night, but those who were there would talk about this night as the start of something big. For Hibs fans, it was the start of a feeling of real bitterness and jealousy of Celtic. This had always been a recurrent theme, but now it intensified. Had their Directors held on to Jock Stein until the end of the season, they might have won both the Scottish League and the Scottish Cup, (and certainly the way they played against Celtic in March was impressive) but they had now blown up. Indeed, the spring "blow up" of Hibs became a regular and almost predictable pattern in future years.

It was probably after this game that Stein decided that the winners at Easter Road viz. *Fallon, Young and Gemmell; Murdoch, McNeill and Clark; Chalmers, Gallagher, Hughes, Lennox and Auld* would be the team for the Cup final, but that was still more than two weeks away and a great deal had yet to happen. For the moment, Celtic were shelved in favour of the England v Scotland International at Wembley.

It was an awful game. Billy McNeill was the only Celt playing and he was the captain. The rest of the team was made up of another four Home Scots – Alex Hamilton of Dundee and John Greig, Willie Henderson and Davie Wilson of Rangers – and six Anglo Scots – Bill Brown of Tottenham Hotspur, Pat Crerand and Denis Law of Manchester United, Bobby Collins of Leeds United, Ian St John of Liverpool and Eddie McCreadie of Chelsea. Frankly, there was enough talent to win quite a few games of football, but for some reason they misfired. Two goals down, they then pulled one back, then England had two players injured (no substitutes in 1965 so they were down to nine men) and although Scotland drew level, they could not force a win over an England defence which deserved all the accolades of *"heroic"* that were poured upon it.

Fingers were pointed at the Scottish forward line of *Henderson,*

Collins, St John, Law and Wilson for their inept and insipid performance. Collins, released by Celtic as long ago as 1958 (!) looked out of his depth, Law gave one of his most infuriating performances and the Press were uniformly amazed at how such a prolific goal-scorer for Manchester United could be so woeful for Scotland with some journalists flabbergasted at how the inside-left took throw-ins on the right side of the field! St John never got going, (and did not endear himself to anyone by talking to the Press and trying to blame it all on John Hughes of Celtic, who was not even playing!) and there was a distinct lack of sparkle from either of the Rangers wingers. The whole team were described by *The Glasgow Herald* as *"bedraggled and shamefaced"* as they traipsed from the field and Manager Ian McColl was much lambasted for his inability to seize the opportunity. But the blame has to be shared, and it was worrying, because World Cup qualifiers were appearing. It was also clear that McColl's heart was no longer in the job and he left soon after to join Sunderland, something that had a few implications for Jock Stein and Celtic.

But the major disappointment for the whole nation, and for captain McNeill in particular, had to be set aside, for the climax to the domestic season was fast approaching. While mighty events were taking place at Wembley, only a few Scottish games were played but one of them was the highly significant one at Tannadice Park where Hearts drew 1-1 with Dundee United. Finn Dossing for Dundee United and Willie Wallace of Hearts were the scorers, and, on the surface, it looked like a reasonable result for the Edinburgh men. In fact, it would cost them the League, but at the moment they were two points ahead of Kilmarnock with two games to go. Dunfermline also won, beating Third Lanark 2-1 at an almost deserted Cathkin Park. They were four points behind Hearts, but had a game in hand, so a League and Cup double was by no means out of the question for the Pars.

Billy McNeill only travelled as far north as Nottingham from Wembley to meet his Celtic teammates, who were playing Nottingham Forest on Monday, 12 April in a testimonial for a player called Bob McKinlay.

The team lost 0-2 but played well. McNeill and Clark played only in the first half and were replaced by Cushley and O'Neill, while Jimmy Johnstone got a game as well. Celtic's performance was much appreciated by the Midlands crowd which included about 3,000 Celtic fans now resident in England, and Jock Stein said that he had learned a great deal as they headed home. A defeat in a friendly is not necessarily a bad thing, as long as one can learn from it.

There then followed a mockery of a game at Falkirk at Brockville in the Scottish League on the Wednesday night. The weather was appalling with wind and rain, a crowd of 3,356 appeared (possibly the lowest-ever crowd in peace time between these two clubs), Celtic were without McNeill, Clark and Chalmers and lost 6-2 on a barely playable pitch. Celtic were overrun in the first half with John Cushley, usually an adequate deputy for McNeill, having one of his worst-ever games for the club and were down 5-1 at one point with Falkirk looking set for more. But things stabilised and 6-2 was the final score. Bertie Auld scored twice (once with a penalty) for Celtic on a night that everyone who was there would try to forget.

Of more significance was Dunfermline's 3-1 win over Rangers at East End Park in similar conditions. Dunfermline were now level with Kilmarnock, both two points behind Hearts and with two games to play. Thus, Saturday, 17 April was a crucial one in the League race. Hearts might have won the League that day, but although they won well, so too did Kilmarnock, but Dunfermline were effectively eliminated by only being able to draw against St Johnstone, their only goal coming from Alex Ferguson. It was a huge disappointment for their supporters

Celtic played another terrible game this Easter Saturday. They lost 1-2 to Partick Thistle, now managed by ex-Ranger Willie Thornton, at Celtic Park before 8,000 fans who were not so much angry as apathetic. Frankly, there were better things to do that miserable Saturday afternoon, and this was only the hard core of the support who had appeared. Stein dropped Tommy Gemmell in favour of

Jim Kennedy, and Charlie Gallagher in favour of Jimmy Johnstone in a forward line which read *Johnstone, Lennox, Chalmers, Auld and Hughes*. If this was Stein giving Kennedy and Johnstone a last chance to book a Cup final place, they failed to grasp it. The first half was goalless, then Partick Thistle scored twice in the second half and most of the crowd were on the way home, leaving the ground to the small knot of Thistle supporters who had seldom had a moment like this. Then Steve Chalmers headed home a goal from a Bertie Auld corner to make the final score 1-2.

It was painful, but what was perhaps as significant as anything was the message in the matchday programme (usually a bland and simplistic organ of communication of the *"We are looking forward to a good game today"* variety) from Jock Stein who said categorically, *"This will not make pleasant reading – it is not intended to do so. Our own staff of players have had their chance – there can be no justified complaints if we seek to strengthen our team. And that is going to be done, irrespective of what happens within the next week or so. Time and time again this season the team has shown great promise...it is difficult to understand how a team can play so well as Celtic did against Hibernian when we won 4-0 and be so disappointing against Third Lanark and Falkirk."*

This message, quoted in *The Evening Times*, was clearly a threat to the players and a promise to the fans that there were going to be changes. Whether it was wise to be so candid and brutal in the programme (where it was grasped and seized upon by an eager Press) is open to question, but it certainly did not take a trick this particular game, which saw the meagre crowd depart, thoroughly apprehensive of what was going to happen in the game that really mattered - next Saturday, the Scottish Cup final against Dunfermline Athletic. On the other hand, it was a promise that things in the long term, were going to get better.

But yet there was a glimmer or two of hope for the immediate future as well. Clearly Jim Kennedy, only a year ago playing for Scotland, was on his way out. Others like Hugh Maxwell and John Divers had not even been given a chance, but the main question seemed to centre on Jimmy Johnstone. Very popular with the fans and capable of some amazing trickery, wee Jimmy had nevertheless failed to deliver in the games that he had played under Jock Stein and seemed to be suffering from a crisis in confidence. He was believed to be frightened of "Big Jock" and was even contemplating, it was said, giving up the game altogether.

But whatever the make-up of the team was going to be, there was the undeniable factor that Celtic playing in a Scottish Cup final before 100,000 fans was a totally different matter from a meaningless end-of-season League game at a desolate Parkhead before a tenth of that amount. And meaningless? Yes, the Parkhead game was indeed that, but one particular game played that afternoon was anything but. This was the Dunfermline Athletic v St Johnstone game, where Dunfermline who NEEDED to win, failed to do so. Celtic did not NEED to beat Partick Thistle, but Dunfermline had to win against St Johnstone to stay in the League race and could only draw. It was a significant point in the propaganda battle. Would they similarly under-perform in the Scottish Cup final?

The dynamics of the football mindset are difficult to understand, but it is often true that if a team is going for a double, and they lose out on one trophy, they will then go on and lose the other one as well, because defeat and victories are "infectious" in that one often leads to another. Already this year, Hibs had "blown up," losing the semi-final to Dunfermline Athletic and then crucial League games to Dundee and Celtic. And although it was many years in the future, 1986 would show Hearts collapsing in front of Albert Kidd one week, and then to Aberdeen in the Scottish Cup final the following week. Football is a game played in the mind as well as on the football field!

The results this weekend meant that Hearts looked likely to win the Scottish League this year. Their final game this season was at home to Kilmarnock, their closest challengers. They were two points ahead of Willie Waddell's men, but under the difficult to understand system of not goal DIFFERENCE, but goal AVERAGE (goals for were divided by goals against), it meant that if Kilmarnock could win 2-0 at Tynecastle on the last day of the season, the same day as the Scottish Cup final, they would pip the Jam Tarts for the Championship. This, frankly, did not look likely, but in football…you never know!

The build up to the Cup final is often a vital time. Both teams had something to pick themselves up from after last Saturday's disappointments. Dunfermline were now out of the League race and Celtic's performance had been truly abysmal with Jock Stein's timeous statement about the need to clear things out and his promises to bring in new players not missing anyone and hitting the wall. It was clear, however, that this was a decision for the future. At the moment, hardly anything in the whole world was more important than Saturday's Scottish Cup final. For those in school, the "Highers" and "O" Grade exams were beginning. These were crucial, life-defining moments to so many people – but the Scottish Cup final was more so!

Jock Stein decided to take his squad of 14 to Largs on the Ayrshire coast from the Tuesday to the Thursday for light training before returning to Glasgow for a final training session on Friday. The 14 chosen were *John Fallon, Ian Young, Tommy Gemmell, Jim Kennedy, Willie O'Neill, Bobby Murdoch, Billy McNeilll, John Clark, Jimmy Johnstone, Steve Chalmers, Charlie Gallagher, John Hughes, Bertie Auld and Bobby Lennox*. The squad surprises us from a modern perspective. In the first place, there are three left-backs in Gemmell, Kennedy and O'Neill, more than sufficient presumably but enough to lead to some speculation that one of them might be deployed as a left-half, allowing John Clark to play at right-half and then Bobby Murdoch could return to the forward line. Speculation along these lines (and it did appear in certain areas of the Press) clearly did not understand Stein's major positive move so far, namely the transformation of Bobby Murdoch from an ordinary to average inside-forward to a world class right-half.

But there was also no reserve goalkeeper. John Fallon thus went to Largs knowing that, barring injury, he was in the Scottish Cup final team. Ronnie Simpson was left behind at Celtic Park – he had only been brought in as a cover for injuries in September 1964 – and not for the first time, people began to speculate that Ronnie's long and distinguished career, which had included two English FA Cup-winner's medals with Newcastle United away back in 1952 and 1955 was coming to an end. But it was not as simple as all that. Stein, never a great understander of goalkeepers, did not at this stage seem to rate Ronnie Simpson very highly. Indeed, it had been Stein when Manager of Hibs who had decided to transfer Ronnie to Celtic. But one thing was clear, and that was that John Fallon, that likeable redhead, would be in the goal at Hampden on Saturday.

There were others left behind at Parkhead for whom the exit door now seemed to opening; Hugh Maxwell, bought last November from Falkirk and who had never impressed apart from a brilliant early goal against his old club; John Divers, potentially a great player but always a little slow and who did not always give the impression of being too keen to get involved; Jim Brogan, whose time might yet come, it was felt, and John Cushley, who had performed adequately when McNeill was injured, but was never really likely to replace him.

Press releases from Largs emphasised that this was no strenuous training session. Phrases like *"toning up"* and *"relaxation"* were used. Indeed, the players at this stage of the season did not really need to be worked hard, and it was felt that a couple of days away from home and a break from training routines with different food would do them a great deal of good and would encourage team spirit and camaraderie. It was an old ploy of Willie Maley's and had brought the players and the club great benefits. Bertie Auld in The Scottish Football Book 11 tells how a photograph appeared of him wearing football boots on one of the greens of a golf course – but the studs had been removed!

What was a surprise was the public announcement as early as 11.00am on the Wednesday of Saturday's team. Jimmy Johnstone, Willie O'Neill and Jim Kennedy were the unlucky ones, and thus the team was *Fallon, Young and Gemmell; Murdoch, McNeill and Clark; Chalmers, Gallagher, Hughes, Lennox and Auld*. It was, in fact, the team who had produced the two best performances since Stein's arrival, namely against Motherwell in the semi-final replay and Hibs in the 4-0 win at Easter Road.

The announcement, made in bright pleasant spring sunshine as the players had a light training session at the Inverclyde Recreation Centre (to which they walked from their hotel!), was designed to remove all the harmful speculation in the Press and elsewhere. There were those who deplored the dropping of Jimmy Johnstone, but then again, Jimmy, although immensely talented, did not always produce the goods and it was felt that Steve Chalmers was a safer option. Chairman Bob Kelly, it was said, approached Jock Stein and queried his deployment of Murdoch as a right-half. Stein smiled respectfully to his Chairman but said that Saturday would show what a great right-half Bobby Murdoch was.

The team returned to Glasgow on Thursday at lunchtime, relaxed and fit, while on the same day news broke of a considerably less happy football club's trip. Eight Chelsea players were sent home from their Blackpool hotel by Manager Tommy Docherty. They included Scotsmen George Graham and Eddie McCreadie, and although no great details were issued, the Press talked about "incidents" at the Blackpool hotel. It is not difficult to work out that this had something to do with alcohol and possibly some less than totally respectable Blackpool ladies, but it was a brave action for Docherty to take considering that his team, already winners of the League Cup, were still in with a chance of the English League, won this year in the event by Manchester United.

Friday passed uneventfully. Dunfermline did not yet name their team, but their Provost - the curiously named James Forker - announced plans for welcoming home his triumphant heroes, and the local MP

Adam Hunter announced that he was having his "surgery" early on Saturday morning so that he could get to Hampden. Meanwhile, Gair Henderson of *The Evening Times* revealed his skill at prophecy. He stated *"Dunfermline's Cup"* and *"Hearts' Flag"* because the Fifers were *"Ahead in Team Work"* and *"Hearts won't slip now."* Gair Henderson was a fine football writer; Cassandra, (the daughter of the King of Troy who was always correct in her prophecies) he was not.

And so the day dawned. It was a bright, pleasant spring day, but it was not like any other spring day. Was this to be the day of deliverance, or was it to join the previous four Scottish Cup finals in its crushing disappointment? It was probably the case that Dunfermline were the better side – their League position certainly indicated that – but on the other hand, as the perspicacious Celtic supporters kept pointing out – they could not win last week against St Johnstone when they had to win to keep themselves in the League race. Yet their men were all fit today and in Willie Cunningham they had an able Manager and tactician. They still had two men left from their win in 1961 – Alex Smith and Harry Melrose, whereas Celtic had five in Billy McNeill, John Clark, Charlie Gallagher, John Hughes and Steve Chalmers. But of course, the key thing was that Jock Stein had changed sides.

The journey to Glasgow for supporters that bright Saturday morning was animated with a surprising amount of conversation about who was going to win the League, rather than the Cup. There was still in 1965 among Celtic supporters a general respect (not exactly love or affection, however) for Hearts and a general dislike of Kilmarnock, who wore blue, were managed by Willie Waddell and had *"kicked Billy and Boaby aff the park"* that awful day last August at Rugby Park. So if Hearts won, drew or even lost 0-1 today, they would win the League and that would not necessarily be the worst outcome in the world. *"Ah dinnae like them, mind, but at least they are no' Rangers!"* Pleasure was then expressed at the almost total collapse of Rangers this season.

It was immediately obvious in the streets of Glasgow that morning as one disembarked at Buchanan Street railway station that there was a special atmosphere in the air. Lewis's Polytechnic was full of green and white scarves, tammies and favours, and fewer black and white ones. But it was friendly with loads of banter. There are some teams' supporters with whom Celtic fans get on well and Dunfermline were one of them. Old grannies decked in the black and white were seen to put arms round wee Celtic boys, asking where they came from and what was their favourite TV programme, did they like the Beatles and of course the vital question of *"Who was going to win today?"* Old Celtic supporters told younger Pars ones that they remembered Peter Wilson becoming Dunfermline's manager before the war. The young Dunfermline boys were impressed, but clearly did not have a clue who Peter Wilson was.

Lunch was consumed but not always digested. Such were the nerves and the excitement of the day. The lunchtime edition of *The Evening Citizen* was reassuring. *"Even if, by some unkind quirk of fate, the Cup is not wearing green and white ribbons tonight, things will soon change at Parkhead,"* but the focus was all on today. At Central Station, awaiting the Blue Train (they might have changed the colour for one day!), we saw women with shopping, young men with cricket bats (they were getting a good day for the start of the season) and other people wandering around aimlessly as people sometimes do at railway stations, looking perhaps for friends of the opposite sex who had failed to appear, but the largest proportion of the crowd wore green and white.

The destination was Mount Florida. If the opposition had been Rangers, we would never have dared to take that train, for Mount Florida was at the western or "Rangers" end of Hampden. It would have had to be King's Park, but that was not a problem today. A well-dressed man, a pleasant faced but somewhat apprehensive woman, and two wee boys with black and white Dunfermline Athletic scarves got on. It was clearly their first time at Hampden.

A group of beery green and whites came on and the Pars family feared the worst. But one of the Celtic chaps with few teeth bent down and said to one of the youngsters, *"And what's your name?"* Before we knew where we were, the conversation was all about holidays in Fife, "my granny came frae a place called Cairneyhill (dae ye ken it?)" and *"I hope we get a good gemme the day."* The wee boys grew in confidence, said they didn't like Rangers, and the father told everyone that he knew the Callaghan brothers who were playing for Dunfermline today. He also said that in their spare time, the brothers were Celtic daft – but that was hardly a great secret. A few other Celtic fans started singing a song which had a bad word or two in it – and one of the Celtic fans shouted *"Hey! Cut it oot! There's a wuman here wi twa young laddies!"* His moral stance was somewhat undermined by the fact that some other women, dressed in green, were joining in the blasphemous and obscene singing, but it was a brave effort.

Meanwhile, the mother was being relentlessly chatted up by a Celtic fan who was not unattractive but clearly past the first flush of youth. We got all the usual Glasgow dance hall chat-up patter about her hairstyle and *"I wish I'd met you before he did"* jabbing his thumb at the now totally relaxed and smiling father. Not only that, but *"the next time we're in Dunfermline, ah'm comin' roon tae your hoose for a cup o' tea."* The precocious older boy, clearly an expert in such matters, then said that Celtic would be at East End Park on Wednesday night – providing of course, that today was not a draw. There was then a general feeling expressed that today might well be a draw *"like the lest time, aw' for anither big gate."*

The train, which had seemed to be saying *"Cel-tic"* repeatedly on its whistle, arrived at Mount Florida. The Dunfermline family were all wished well, the mother by no means discouraging of a wee kiss from the Celtic charmer, and the two wee boys were clearly in awe of Celtic supporters at their best, and repeated their feelings about not liking Rangers, while adding Falkirk and Raith Rovers to their list of un-favourite football teams.

It was great to walk up to Hampden Park in the dry on a fine day. No mud, no urine and your shoes unsullied. That old North Stand was showing its age, though, wasn't it? But five shillings (no Boys Gate) was the price for admission to the Celtic End – that massive area of terracing which had seen so much action in Scottish football history and was destined to see a great deal more today.

Two things struck me about the view from the top of the Celtic End, and they were to do with what was happening away from the pitch. One was the amount of "dead body" fans who had not managed to get into the ground in a totally vertical position and had collapsed through the sheer amount of drink that they had consumed! They were laid out gently but thankfully by their friends on the banking at the back of the terracing, and lay there, presumably, for the duration of the game! I counted about 12 such people and wondered how it was possible for anyone to get themselves more or less comatose with drink on a day like this! And what would have happened to them if it had been raining?

And the other thing I saw was a sight that excited both pity and envy. Behind Hampden at the Celtic End in 1965 were allotments for those of the horticultural persuasion. I looked down and I saw a man who was planting potatoes, or whatever one does with allotments. My contempt for this man – how could anyone work in a garden a hundred yards away from this? – soon changed to jealousy when I considered the state I was in, quivering like a jelly, perpetually needing the toilet and finding it difficult to resist the temptation to be sick. This man on the other hand, with his braces holding up his trousers and his old jacket and bonnet hanging from a post, was working away in total relaxation although it must have been difficult with all the noise around him.

But now the ground was filling up. We knew that the crowd becomes less condensed the further down you go, and the late arrivals are often crushed so we tried to descend the mighty terracing which was becoming more congested by the minute. A group with no scruples pushed its way through singing the song about the lorry load of volunteers who approached the border town on New Year's Eve eight years ago. We grabbed a hold of one of their flags, followed them down and got a good view.

The tension was palpable. Apparently, the radio at lunchtime had mentioned a rumour about an unexpected injury in the Celtic camp. This was discussed at length, but when the team was announced it was as expected. I had a look at the supporters near me – some clearly veterans of the Cup finals of Jimmy McGrory and Patsy Gallacher, many now approaching middle age who recalled Charlie Tully, many like me who had not yet had any clear recollection of them ever having won anything, and some even younger. There were men and women - the women often more garishly dressed in green than the men, again some old, some young, some trying to look younger than they were – but everything had this in common – the stress and pressure on their faces. *"We'll forgive everything, Cellic, everything, if ye's jist win the day."* There had indeed been an awful lot to forgive.

The Evening Times reports some strange behaviour by the Dunfermline Manager Willie Cunningham. The team bus arrived well over an hour before kick-off and the party of 16 players were all hustled into the away dressing-room (Celtic had won the toss for the home dressing-room, apparently) and stayed there until they emerged down the tunnel at 2.55pm. The Directors went upstairs for their refreshments with their Celtic counterparts, but the players were nowhere to be seen.

Just what was behind this, we cannot tell. Maybe Cunningham had not yet finalised his team selection; maybe he just did not want them talking to the Press; maybe he did not want them to see the massive Celtic support, which was building up, but in any case, their players were deprived of their walk on the Hampden turf.

No-one would have thought it significant at the time, but Pars' centre-forward Alex Ferguson was dropped, presumably being blamed for Dunfermline's inability to beat St Johnstone last weekend. It must have been a major blow for the youngster, whose playing career in

Scottish football did not always enjoy the best of luck nor the greatest success. The team chosen, however, was the team that had beaten Rangers some ten days ago, and it was clearly this one on whom Dunfermline placed their major hopes for success.

Celtic on the other hand, their team having been picked and briefed, were able to have a short stroll on the pitch. It was not the habit in those days to have a warm-up on the pitch as they do now, and they were all in civvies as they waved to the crowd, giving the impression of being totally relaxed, a relaxation that presumably they did not feel.

The teams that appeared were as follows;

Celtic:

Fallon, Young and Gemmell; Murdoch, McNeill and Clark; Chalmers, Gallagher, Hughes, Lennox and Auld.

Dunfermline Athletic:

Herriot, W Callaghan and Lunn; Thomson, McLean and T Callaghan, Edwards, Smith, McLaughlin, Melrose and Sinclair.

Referee: ***Mr H Phillips, Wishaw.***

McNeill won the toss and elected to play towards the King's Park end. The actual 90 minutes are of course well reported in contemporary newspapers and are available on YouTube, but they do not begin to convey the sheer emotion involved on that day. The standard of football by both sides was amazingly high considering all that was involved, and the Celtic performance, particularly in that second half was such that quite a lot of Celtic supporters given to mysticism wondered whether it was all "meant." One recalls the statement of the Second World War veteran who had played his part in the liberation of Italy, as well as other great Celtic triumphs involving Jimmy McGrory and Patsy Gallacher in the past who stated quite calmly in reference to the events of 24 April 1965 that he had *"never seen anything like that!"* Frankly, money could not buy the memories that day produced.

But to the game itself. It started briskly and Celtic playing with the wind had the better of the opening exchanges. Dunfermline's centre-half Jim McLean was warned for a rough tackle and then John Hughes had a good run. One or two shots went wide or high, and it was clear that nerves, as one would expect in a Scottish Cup final, were playing a part. We also knew that there was a long way to go. It would be nice to take a lead, but we also knew that it wouldn't necessarily decide the issue.

In the event, it was Dunfermline up at the distant end who scored first. It came from a throw-in which Thomson then hit up the field to Sinclair who knocked the ball on to Harry Melrose who in turn hooked the ball into the roof of the net. It was a well-taken goal, but it could easily have been prevented with a little more concentration. The knots of Dunfermline supporters (Celtic supporters would have outnumbered them by about 20 to 1 at a conservative estimate) cheered their early lead, but for Celtic supporters, that sinking feeling, that all too familiar emotion in the early to mid 1960s, began to manifest itself once more.

We were aware that there were still about 75 minutes to go, and that there really was plenty of time, but we were also aware that the loss of a second goal could effectively kill the contest. Funnily enough, that loss of the goal seemed to settle the Celtic players, but the equaliser when it came was an unusual and dramatic one. It came originally from the boot of Charlie Gallagher, who picked up a pass from John Clark in the middle of the Dunfermline half, made a few yards and shot for goal. Those of us clustered behind that goal had a brief moment of seeing the ball heading towards us, and we were all set to cheer a great goal, but the cheers turned to anguish as the ball hit the bar and soared up into the air. It might have soared out of play for a goal kick, but here the capricious wind played its part, for the ball went straight up into the air, and the ever-alert Bertie Auld took his opportunity to get there before any of the Dunfermline defenders.

Thus, Celtic were back on level terms as that terracing behind him erupted into ecstasy.

That was in the 30th minute and Bertie had to be disentangled from the netting, just like Patsy Gallacher in his great Cup final moment of 40 years earlier. Now we felt that we might get somewhere. We might now be able to even get ahead before half-time, but sadly it was not to work out like that, for it was Dunfermline who scored again just before the interval. Young was adjudged to have fouled Sinclair a few yards outside the penalty box. It looked like a fair challenge from the far end, but Mr Phillips was in no doubt. It was a dangerous position, and the Celtic defence lined up to face what they thought was going to be a shot from Melrose.

But Melrose tapped the ball to John McLaughlin, and at that very point the public address system started to make a pointless announcement about something to do with the imminence of half-time. No-one will ever know what it was all about, for McLaughlin hammered home a fine shot. To what extent Celtic were put off by that announcement we will never know – they certainly never complained about it after the game – but those around me in the Celtic End were convinced that it was a distraction, and the more paranoid thought it was all deliberate!

Half-time came soon afterwards with the Pars all cock-a-hoop at their team going in 2-1 up at the break. The Celtic community was stilled. We had been built up and now we had been knocked down again. There remained another 45 minutes of course, but it was still a depressing experience. Jim Farrell, the Celtic Director (and father-in-law of Jim Craig) tells the story about how he was on his way to the Directors' Lounge along with Mrs Stein. She was of a different religious persuasion to her husband and tended towards Rome rather than 121 George Street, Edinburgh. She said as a joke to Mr Farrell that a prayer to St Anthony might be no bad thing. St Anthony, apparently, had jurisdiction over things that were lost, (like a house key or a wallet, for example) but might yet be still found. Celtic were like that at the moment, thought Mrs Stein.

Far away from such theological and celestial speculations, more concerned with the mundane and the pressing, we on the East Terracing made a big mistake. We decided to go to the toilet. Quite a few men did not bother about such niceties, and simply did the necessary where they were, but we were of a decent family and made our way to the none too hygienic toilets. One had to climb the huge terracing and descend the steps at the back to try to get there. It was a crush, but we managed it. The problem, however, was then that we could not get back in. It would remind the learned of Virgil's Aeneid, when Aeneas was told that there was no problem getting down to the Underworld. The problem was getting back! *"Hic labor, hoc opus est!"* We certainly could not get back to our old places and were condemned to watch the second half from the top of the terracing where heads and other things got in our way.

It was not entirely without its advantages. One certainly got a fine panoramic view of the distant proceedings, both of the ground and the surrounding streets, and the amount of the "out of the game" drunks still lying on the banking. The allotment gardener was still there with a spade and a wheelbarrow, and once again, I envied him. No-one was bothering him; he was not bothering anyone, although he cannot but have been aware of the passion, the drama and the noise going on not all that far away from him. Maybe he had a transistor radio with him.

But we still had the problem of seeing the game. Celtic equalised through Bertie Auld (who else?) after a fine one-two with Bobby Lennox, but our view of it was obscured by heads. We came out of the terracing and walked along the path at the back before we eventually managed to get a reasonable view of the action holding on to the post numbered "25" at the very back of the terracing. Beside us stood a black man – not all that usual in 1965 Glasgow – a refined, soft-spoken gentleman, and a few youngsters, and we actually had a good view once the crowd settled down. We saw Fallon's great save from Alex Edwards, which seemed to have got behind him, and we saw Clark getting something stuck up his nose after a facial knock, and we saw the battle raging.

Dunfermline used the wind rather badly, often over-kicking the ball and putting it too far ahead of their forwards, while Celtic played more sensibly against the wind, keeping the ball low and with Auld and Murdoch in the middle of the field spreading passes to Chalmers, Hughes and Lennox. Celtic were having more of the play, but if someone had offered a 2-2 draw and a replay on Wednesday night, I probably would have taken it – such had been the gut-rending emotion of it all. Once again, I thought with envy of the gardener planting his potatoes and of my mother, who was no great football fan and was often amazed by the intensity of it all, quietly making her tea and listening to the radio commentary, more concerned about whether her wee boy would get home safely rather than who was to win the 1965 Scottish Cup!

But then Celtic won a corner on the left after a run by Bobby Lennox. Across trotted the ever-reliable Charlie Gallagher to take it. One of the things that we had noticed since Jock Stein's arrival in 1965 had been the increasing frequency with which Billy McNeill would go up for a corner kick. The Pars defence was not as prepared for it as they should have been, and Billy rose majestically to head home that magnificent iconic goal that changed everything.

I have no clear recollections of the goal, although I do remember thinking that it might have been Tommy Gemmell who scored (same colour of hair and I was, after all, about 250 yards away!) but the veteran beside me kept saying *"Billy McNeill! Billy McNeill! Billy McNeill!"* as we were engulfed in a tidal wave of celebration, scarves waving and people hugging you and jumping on top of you.

But there were still nine minutes to go. If I have no distinct recollections of the actual goal, I can recall with vivid clarity the last nine minutes. Flags waving all around the ground, a growing swell of noise, smiles, cheers but with myself holding on to the gangway 25's post and unashamedly praying to God, whether he was a Catholic or a Protestant, to let us win today. Surely, we could not be denied now! But 10 years ago, Celtic had been 1-0 up in a Scottish Cup final against Clyde and had lost a last-minute equaliser from a corner kick. This kept going through my mind, as no doubt it did through the thoughts of so many people – possibly even Jock Stein who played in that game. They were perhaps better at hiding their emotions than I was but were undergoing all the agony just the same. Those who tried to tell me after the event *"Ah knew we were OK when Billy scored"* are, frankly, liars. Still more hideously wrong was the fatuous statement *"It's just a fitba match!"* We still had these minutes to see out.

Bertie Auld did not seem to be worried though. He took his time, pretending to trip over a pile of police coats placed too close to the pitch, and generally clowning. In truth, Dunfermline seldom got over the halfway line in those last desperate minutes. I kept watching the linesmen. I knew that linesman signalled to the referee about how long to go, usually with their fingers against their black uniform and I kept looking for that. Eventually, I decided that there was no point in looking at anyone other than referee Hugh Phillips, and so I watched him obsessively as Celtic retained possession. Eventually he turned and pointed to the pavilion, and the immediate impression was of everything going up – players arms in triumph, flags, scarves and people – youngsters lifted up by their parents, arms in the air – and everything was green and white.

And everything rose metaphorically as well. There was the glint of silver in the South Stand. This was what it had all been about – the Scottish Cup, and we had won something at last!

Tears welled up unashamedly, as the green and white figures appeared to collect the trophy, and out they came to get their photographs taken. Oddly enough, my feelings were for Dunfermline Athletic as much as anything else – a good team and their supporters were a decent bunch, and we knew what they were going through – and I joined in the polite applause for the Pars. But everything around me was going crazy, and I was particularly careful not to fall down the terracing stairs as the triumphant Celtic crowd swept out. There was no point in getting killed NOW!

The images remain – the seller of *"The Shamrock"* magazine *"the long downtrodden man"* as we called him, with a grin on his face instead of the hunted, persecuted look of before, and then the sight of a middle-aged, middle-class man, well-dressed with a tie and a soft hat and possibly a banker or a teacher during the week. He had collapsed over a hedge. He was not in any way under the influence of alcohol, nor did he wear any club colour. Nor did he use any foul language as he looked at me and a few other bystanders and said with all sincerity and in measured tones, *"I couldn't have taken it if we'd lost the day!"* And the two young teenage girls clad in green and white and singing – not *The Celtic Song*, nor *Sean South of Garryowen* but the Beatles *"She Loves You! Yeah! Yeah! Yeah!"* Incongruous, but there is nothing logical about ecstasy!

A few Pars fans were about, clearly disappointed but nothing nasty about them. Handshakes were exchanged and smiles and *"We will see you on Wednesday,"* a reference to the League game scheduled for that night, and one of them with a transistor radio told me that Kilmarnock had won 2-0 at Tynecastle. The implications of that one didn't sink in until later, such was the all-consuming rapture of the moment.

The train from Mount Florida to Glasgow Central was noisy and overcrowded, dangerously so in fact but no-one cared. It was then, however, that real fear took over me that this might all be some sort of a dream and that I was going to wake up! Various thoughts of existentialist philosophy coursed through my mind, but they were soon driven out by the words of *"the dreary New Year's Eve"* and *"sworn to be free."* If I was going to wake up, so too would thousands of others!

But I didn't waken up, and we got home by about 10.00pm after an idyllic and triumphant journey. The green and whites had returned. Parkhead was Paradise once more. Sunday was spent talking about nothing else, and the whole world had changed. Rangers supporters and Hearts supporters avoided me – Hearts in particular, for that day was the start of untold miseries for them, but Rangers supporters as well knew that the game was up. Jim Baxter, their hero of the past few years, was beginning to play up and cause trouble again. Celtic's success was one of those things that did not apparently have any direct connection with Baxter – but we all knew that it did. It was almost as if a switch had been pressed and for the next decade, with a very occasional exception, everything would run in favour of Celtic. The world had indeed changed.

It was like what Churchill said. *"Before Alamein, we never had a victory. After Alamein we never had a defeat."* It was apparently based on something that Pitt the Elder had said of the Seven Years War, and it wasn't 100% literally true – but it was close enough. We felt similarly about Saturday, 24 April 1965. For the next ten years our defeats would be rare, and our successes would be repeated and indeed expected.

Newspapers were devoured, because the Scottish Press, often accused of being irredeemably anti-Celtic and pro-Rangers, in fact now showed its true colours. The true colours were, for crude circulation reasons, the colours of the winners of the most recent trophy, and for a few days we had little other than how good Celtic were and how good they were going to be. Rangers paid the price for mediocrity – neglect and indifference. The restrained *Glasgow Herald* contents itself by saying *"Celtic's Barren Years End"* and *"Determination Wins Out"* but it also describes as *"like a bad dream"* that bleak day last October when Rangers showed off the League Cup, and the Celtic End was totally deserted. The Press had not been slow to latch on to the hysterical adulation of Jim Baxter and Rangers that day, but the boot was well and truly on the other foot now, while *The Scottish Daily Express*, usually very pro-Rangers, has to talk about this *"not being the Hampden Roar"* but rather the releasing of the deep-seated emotion of so many years in the wilderness, and yes, signalling that Parkhead was indeed Paradise once more.

In *The Evening Times*, Gair Henderson said that this game was the Celtic equivalent of 1928. In that year, Rangers had won the Scottish Cup after an interval of 25 years and then went on to win the trophy another five times before the Second World War. It was not perhaps an analogy that Celtic fans would have necessarily identified with, but things had now changed course, and possibly Gair Henderson was correct. He felt that this was just the breakthrough that Celtic were needing, and that they would now go on to win a great deal more. In this he was very perceptive. He also, more mundanely, gave a great deal of credit to John Hughes who kept moving about from wing to wing taking Dunfermline's centre-half Jim McLean with him and thus leaving a hole in the middle of their defence for Bertie Auld to exploit.

Speaking of Bertie, the late Charlie Gallagher told a story about what happened in the dressing-room after the game. Everyone was naturally on a high, but Auld recalled an occasion in the past when Jock Stein had apparently expressed reservations about playing him and Gallagher in the same team because they were *"too similar"* in their contribution to the team. Bertie came up to Charlie and told him to put his medal round his neck and come with him to see the Boss. The shy Gallagher was reluctant at first, but Auld had no such inhibitions and persuaded him to come with him. *"Hey, Boss,"* said the intrepid Bertie, *"Ah thought you once said that we couldnae play together in the same team? The SFA seem tae disagree with that - they've just gi'en us a medal each!"* Jock looked the pair of them up and down - and smiled.

The season was not, of course, finished. The Summer Cup, won last year by Jock Stein's Hibs, would begin on Saturday. Both Celtic and Rangers (they often worked together in spite of what the supporters might have thought) once again declined to enter, but there was still the Glasgow Cup to be played with Celtic and Rangers facing each other at Parkhead on the night of Friday, 30 April, arranged for that night, tactfully, to avoid a fixture clash with the start of the Summer Cup.

In addition, there was still that League game to be played, ironically enough against Dunfermline Athletic at East End Park on Wednesday, 28 April. A decent enough crowd of disappointed Pars fans turned up, and they had to listen to the Celtic fans in unaccustomed gloating mood about Saturday. There was little, however, for Celtic fans to be happy about in tonight's performance. Stein rested Young (who had actually, so "high" was he, volunteered to play for the reserves at Aberdeen on Monday night!), Auld, Gallagher and Chalmers. Murdoch was back in the inside-right position, and he was less of a success than he had been on Saturday. The team read *Fallon, Gemmell and O'Neill; Brogan, McNeill and Clark; Johnstone, Murdoch, Hughes, Maxwell and Lennox.*

It was a game marked by careless football by a team no longer under any great pressure. The luckless Hugh Maxwell missed a penalty kick, John Clark scored an own goal, John Fallon had a shocker in goal and the only goal that Celtic got was a deflection. For Dunfermline, Alex Ferguson, dropped for the Scottish Cup final and clearly with a point to make to Manager Willie Cunningham, had a good game and led his line well as Dunfermline won 5-1. They were given a generous ovation at the end by their fans and indeed the magnanimous Celtic ones as well. Indeed, it was probably their best-ever season. Coming second in one major competition and third in another may have been a disappointment to their fans, but it was hardly a disgrace for a provincial side and Stein went out of his way to be gracious to them in his after-match comments. He could afford to be! Indeed, he himself was responsible for so much of their success and still had so many friends in the "auld grey toon."

Of far greater significance to Celtic fans, however, was the Glasgow Cup, in particular the first-round tie to be played at Parkhead against Rangers on Friday night. 41,000 were there to see this rather remarkable game in which it was now clear that the roles had been reversed from a few years ago. So often in the past had Celtic played brilliantly against Rangers and had nothing to show for it. Tonight was the absolute opposite, with Celtic winning without playing well, but enjoying that elusive but absolutely necessary quality called luck. At one point, Rangers were reduced to nine men through injury, (but they were able to bring one back) and had a great deal of the play, but Celtic still won 2-1. It was as if the scales of fortune had turned and that Nemesis was out to make Rangers supporters pay for their previous arrogance.

That it was Celtic who felt themselves now to be the predominant team in Glasgow was indicated by the elaborate amount of time taken to photograph the team with the Scottish Cup in front of the Rangers fans in their part of the enclosure. Anyone who does not believe that this was a triumphalist attempt to put Rangers in their place is not living in the real world, and the players were cheered to the echo by the Celtic fans. Celtic's team was the Cup-winning side, and Rangers were represented by *Martin, Provan and Caldow; Hynd, McKinnon and Greig; Henderson, Wood, McLean, Brand and Wilson.*

Rangers, without Baxter, were like a dog with no teeth, but they also had dreadful luck with Roger Hynd having to retire, Norrie Martin the goalkeeper having to change places with Davie Provan after he hurt his hand and George McLean also injured with a damaged hand. McLean was able to return but Hynd stayed off. Bob Rooney, Celtic's trainer even earned himself a reluctant round of applause from the Rangers fans when he ran on to the field to attend to goalkeeper Martin, as Rangers' trainer Davie Kinnear was busy in the dressing-room attending to Hynd, who had apparently broken his ankle.

Amazingly, Rangers held out for about three quarters of the game, and then, even more astonishingly, they went ahead when Willie Henderson looked as if he was about to cross but shot instead with his left foot and scored! Celtic now rallied and equalised through Auld with a shot that a specialist goalkeeper would have saved, and then 10 minutes from time Chalmers scored with a rebound from a Gemmell drive. Eleven men then held out against ten, and Celtic had beaten Rangers, but it would have had to have been a very hard-hearted Celtic fan who did not feel a pang of sympathy for Rangers that night. Life does indeed kick you when you are down, even if you are Rangers. But Celtic fans could now afford to be magnanimous.

The month of April, however, ended on a sombre note for some 20 young Celtic players. They were released. There had been a playing staff of 50 which was considered, rightly, to be far too unwieldy. In conjunction with that, it was decided that the Celtic 3rd XI team, which played in the Combined Reserve League, would be disbanded. Streamlining seemed to be the order of the day but more substantial changes were looked for with new players arriving and a few others heading through the exit gate.

The 41,000 who headed home that night also reckoned that Rangers, whose season was now over, would fight back next year, but that Celtic still had the Glasgow Cup to play for. The thought of winning two Cups in the one year was an attractive one. It reminded one of what they said about Glasgow buses. You went for a long time without seeing one, but then two arrive at once! April 1965, a momentous and pivotal month in the history of the club, now gracefully and gently yielded to May, and the heavenly bliss of last Saturday continued… for all eternity, it seemed.

CHAPTER FIVE

MAY

Saturday, 1 May 1965 saw bright and breezy weather in Scotland, wet and dismal weather in England. Celtic were still on a high after the events of a week ago, which had been enhanced a little by last night's Glasgow Cup win over Rangers, even though Celtic's greatest supporters had to admit that they were lucky, on this occasion, to get the better of their old rivals. But, as supporters kept telling each other, it all proved one of the truisms of human life, let alone Scottish football, that when you are on top and don't really need any breaks, that is when you get them. On the other hand, when you desperately need a lucky break, that's when it doesn't happen. Rangers had had every conceivable break for many years, but the tide had now turned last week with Billy McNeill's headed goal. Even God now seemed to be supporting Celtic!

It was, in fact, Rangers' worst League season for more than 20 years. They had won the Scottish League Cup, but that was all. Both clubs would be expected to buy a player or two over the summer, but Celtic could now buy from a position of strength, whereas Rangers now had the look of desperation all over them. They had been toppled. And the body language of both players and supporters tended to confirm that!

The English FA Cup final was dull, mirroring the weather, until it suddenly perked up in extra-time. The protagonists were Liverpool and Leeds United, appropriately in terms of Roses, Liverpool in the all-red of Lancashire and Leeds in the all-white of Yorkshire. Bobby Collins, that Celtic veteran of the 1950s, was now the captain of Leeds United, and it was strange on TV screens that night to see the diminutive figure of "the wee barra" alongside the huge bulk of Ron Yeats, one time of Dundee United, as they shook hands at the start. Collins' second appearance at Wembley within a month was no more successful than his first, for Leeds came off second best, losing 1-2 to Liverpool after extra-time. It was, amazingly, Liverpool's first ever capture of the FA Cup. Manchester United had won the English League that year.

The Summer Cup saw good wins for Hibs and Dundee United in their respective city derbies over Hearts and Dundee, but Celtic were more concerned about the Glasgow Cup. Their win over Rangers had earned them a game against Clyde at Parkhead on the Monday night of May 3 in the semi-final. 12,500 appeared to see a comfortable win for Celtic. John Hughes was out with a stomach upset, so Steve Chalmers came into the centre and Jimmy Johnstone played on the right wing. The first two goals were headers from Bertie Auld and Billy McNeill, and the third was a clinical finish by Bobby Lennox. Johnstone entertained the crowd but had a propensity to *"try to beat one man too many"* as *The Glasgow Herald* put it.

So Celtic were into another Cup final, this time against Queen's Park at Hampden the next week, but that was not the main talking point among Celtic fans the following evening. Celtic had called a Press Conference on Tuesday morning. Everyone had assumed there was going to be an announcement of a new signing for next season, or possibly more details about the new "Jungle" that was about to be built, but no-one could possibly have predicted what was going to be announced.

In a world first (as far as anyone could tell), Celtic were going to start a newspaper next season to be called *The Celtic View*. It was immediately clear that Jock Stein was very much involved in this, for he believed that the media must be massaged. In Scotland, that was not an easy task for a Celtic Manager, but now he had his own newspaper. The voice of Celtic would be heard loud and clear all over Scotland and the world, and Stein's old colleague John McPhail would be heavily involved in this. There would seldom be a dull moment at Parkhead.

The idea that the Press and the media in Scotland was anti-Celtic was deep-rooted in the Celtic psyche. A detached analysis would have to conclude that this was not 100% true, although the Glasgow dailies did devote an awful lot of their pages to Rangers. In like manner, the BBC radio and TV programmes seemed to spend more time talking about Rangers than anyone else, and presenter Peter Thomson was so blatantly pro-Rangers that he was called *"Blue Peter"* and it was often said that you could tell by the expression on his face (before he said anything!) whether Rangers had won or not. It was rumoured too that the BBC were not guilty of employing a huge number of Roman Catholics, whereas STV tended more to the rebel cause.

However that may be, this was Celtic's determination to fight back. Not only was it Stein's intention to give the Press enough to talk about Celtic, he now had his own instrument as well with which to do something about it. Not for him was *"the world's against us"* moan. If it were so, he was going to do something about it.

Stein would have a similar attitude towards referees. He was not immune to the belief that the "referees are against Celtic" view could be justified but took the view (correctly) that refereeing decisions can only matter in tight games. Therefore, if you are 5-0 up, and the referee gives a dodgy penalty against you, then it doesn't really matter, does it?

The Glasgow Cup Final had to be delayed until Tuesday, 11 May because on the evening of Saturday, 8 May, Scotland had an

International friendly against Spain at Hampden. McNeill and Hughes were playing and 60,000 attended but they saw a dreadful game in which there was very little football of any quality, but rather too much emphasis on going for the man rather than the ball. International football should be a spectacle, and one recalled a similar game three years previously which had to be abandoned because of the attitude and behaviour of the Austrian players. This time things were different, with Scotland just as much to blame as the Spaniards. Billy McNeill earned a little praise for his attempts to calm everyone down, but it was a game that very few people came out of with any credit, and the 0-0 scoreline is in itself an eloquent testimony as to how good the actual football was.

Meanwhile, the rest of the Celtic players kept training for the Glasgow Cup final against Queen's Park. The Scottish Cup-winning team was given another go, and a crowd of 17,051 at Hampden saw a very one-sided Cup final. Lennox scored in 10 seconds, after Gallagher had set him up from the kick-off, then again a quarter of an hour later, and then Auld, Chalmers and Murdoch made it five without reply. Granted the opposition was not great and the weather was dismal but nevertheless Celtic had now won two Cups in the one season! The Glasgow Cup, rich in tradition (it was older than the Scottish League for example) and once able to attract crowds of 80,000, had seen better days but it was still worth having.

Stories went around that on the day the Glasgow Cup was brought into the Celtic Boardroom, the Scottish Cup which had been suffering from feelings of loneliness and isolation in her unfamiliar surroundings suddenly burst into song with *"Take My Hand, I'm A Stranger In Paradise,"* a song which had been very popular since making its first appearance in the musical *"Kismet"* in 1953.

Less happy news came in an injury to Billy McNeill which threatened his participation in the two World Cup qualifiers later in the month, and also in the suspension of John Hughes for 14 days at the start of the new season. It seemed a little draconian, and it was looked upon as even hypocritical when the SFA allowed him to return to the Scotland training camp so that he could play in the World Cup qualifying games! And then the following day two things happened which seemed, on the surface, to have little to do with Celtic, but which nevertheless affected them intimately. One was that Liverpool failed to reach the final of the European Cup, which meant that still no British team had as yet won that Cup, and the other was the resignation of Scotland Manager Ian McColl.

Certainly, no one linked the Inter Milan v Liverpool result with Celtic, but Celtic were immediately linked, albeit indirectly, to the Scotland job when it was announced that Jock Stein had agreed to take interim charge of Scotland for the two qualifying games against Poland and Finland at the end of the month. McColl was interested in the manager's job at Sunderland and had, in any case, shown signs of getting fed up with the International role, particularly after the piles of criticism heaped on him after the Wembley failure. Stein's acceptance of the Scotland job did not, at this stage, seem to be any great threat to Celtic and their supporters, for it was stipulated that this was a temporary appointment.

In any case, there were no domestic fixtures at this time, and it could only be beneficial for Stein to pick up a little more experience. Stein, always a patriotic Scotsman, clearly relished the challenge and there was indeed a large groundswell of opinion which wanted Scotland to do well. Next year's World Cup finals would be held in England, and it would clearly be possible for Scottish supporters to go to see games and support their team.

It was possibly a good thing as well for Celtic to be seen to be supplying Scotland's Manager. Celtic's relationship with Scotland was always complex. Celtic Park had been built in the 1890s for no other reason than to house the Scotland v England International. On the other hand, it was sometimes very difficult to persuade

Celtic supporters that the SFA were not institutionally against them. The fact that Jimmy McGrory had never been given the opportunity to play for Scotland at Wembley was a particular bone of contention, when he always did well at Hampden! Now it was hard to sustain any belief in the hypothesis of discrimination when Celtic's Manager was also the Manager of Scotland!

The first game of Scotland's section had already been played back in October 1964 when, a few days before the dreadful Celtic v Rangers League Cup final which had caused such distress, Scotland beat Finland 3-1. Scotland were now to play Poland and Finland in away fixtures before Poland would come to Hampden in October, Italy in November and then Scotland would go to Italy in December. This qualifying group is a story in itself and is virtually a microcosm of what Scotland is all about with tears of joy and tears of chagrin, a fair amount of self-destruction and certainly the opportunity to blame it all on the English.

Scotland had arrived at their destination in Poland on Friday, 21 May 1965. They discovered, to their horror, that what had been portrayed as a five-star hotel was little other than a youth hostel with minimal facilities and many having to share bedrooms. Oh dear! The poor things! There was little point in complaining, for this was Eastern Europe in the 1960s which had made little economic progress since the war in which Poland had swapped the tyranny of Nazi Germany for the tyranny of the Soviet Union. Indeed, the tyranny of the USSR was everywhere, and this particular game was under the control (if that is the right word) of a Russian referee whose decisions were sometimes eccentric.

The game on Sunday, 23 May in the dismal Polish mining town of Chorzow was watched by about 80,000 spectators in torrential rain but many of the supporters found the conditions so uncomfortable that they went home at half-time. There was little shelter and little good football, but Scotland did well to get a 1-1 draw with a second-half goal from Denis Law. Law had seldom shown his club form when playing for Scotland, but he did on this occasion and those journalists who stressed that Denis showed his class "at last" also hinted that the reason was that he was now under the guidance of the stern Jock Stein for whom he had the utmost respect, and who would stand for no temperamental nonsense.

Scotland's team was *Brown, Hamilton and McCreadie; Greig, McNeill and Crerand; Henderson, Collins, Martin, Law, and Hughes.* Poland scored early in the second half, Scotland equalised in the 75th minute, and began to look as if they might snatch a winner when something amazing, tragic, funny, ridiculous and typically Scottish occurred.

For reasons that defy rational explanation, the game was not on television. Given the amount of Scottish fans who were fascinated by this game, it betrays a breathtaking arrogance, and can really only be put down to the old Scottish Calvinistic tenets of *"make them pay"* and *"don't let them enjoy themselves."* But it was on BBC Radio - at least the second half was from 6.55 until 7.45 that Sunday evening. The commentary was reasonably good, the game was definitely exciting and the commentator, Douglas Lowe, was becoming more and more interested in the possibilities of John Hughes, revelling as always in the wet conditions, pulling off what would have been one of Scotland' best-ever victories.

Indeed, John was charging down the left wing on one of his forays with about five minutes to go when the radio coverage of the game quietly faded out and we heard the Kelvinside accent of a polite young woman telling us that it was time to listen to a religious broadcast! It was a Service from the Buccleuch and Greyfriars Free Kirk in Edinburgh, at the start of their General Assembly. Some of the religious people had themselves been very angry because of football being on at all on a Sunday (the 11th Commandment once again in the Scottish Presbyterian bible of *"thou shall not enjoy thyself!"*) and they were not very likely to agree to a wait of five minutes until full-time.

But we still did not know the score! Phone calls of protests rained into the BBC, but to no avail. It was well over an hour later on a news broadcast programme that it was confirmed that the game had indeed ended 1-1. It was a very respectable result and Scotland now had reason to be optimistic about qualification for England's World Cup in 1966. The Celtic players had acquitted themselves well, as indeed had interim Manager Jock Stein who now had to lead the squad to what on paper at least seemed an easier fixture – Finland in Helsinki.

But before this could happen, Celtic (or what was left of the squad) played in a friendly match against FC Austria in Vienna. The purpose in arranging this rather strange fixture seems to have been to allow ex Tottenham Hotspur centre-forward Bobby Smith to have a trial for the Austrian side. The game did not attract a huge crowd to the massive Prater Stadium and Celtic, without the Scotland players and also Bobby Murdoch who was left behind to have a minor operation to his ankle in Glasgow, lost 0-1. The team was *Fallon, Young, and Gemmell; Clark, Cushley and O'Neill; Johnstone, Maxwell, Chalmers, Lennox and Auld* and John Divers was given a game in place of Hugh Maxwell at half-time. The general opinion was that, in spite of the 0-1 defeat, Celtic played well with Cushley in particular having a good game. The team stayed on in Vienna for a few nights before returning home. It was a pleasant, although slightly pointless, end to the season.

The world had also been enthralled with the World Heavyweight Boxing championship bout between Cassius Clay (or Muhammad Ali as he now called himself) and Sonny Liston at Lewiston, Maine, but those who stayed up to watch it could have gone to their beds quite soon, for they contest lasted less than one round and Clay knocked him out. Naturally, there were allegations of a fix, but such things are hardly unusual in the world of boxing.

Also, back in Scotland, moves were gathering pace for Celtic to sign Joe McBride of Motherwell. It was no great secret where Joe wanted to go and he had turned down a few offers from other clubs, notably Dunfermline. He stayed loyal to Motherwell for they were still in the Summer Cup where they had reached the final against Dundee United, but negotiations were at an advanced stage while Celtic were in Austria and Scotland in Finland.

The facilities in the Finnish capital of Helsinki were chalk and cheese compared with the depressing surroundings of Poland. For the game on Thursday, 27 May, Stein made two changes. To the distress of some Celtic fans, he dropped John Hughes on the grounds that this was a dry and bumpy pitch, and that Hughes was a far better player on wet grounds. He also introduced Willie Hamilton of Hibs, and Bobby Collins was also dropped.

Willie Hamilton was of course well known to Stein, and the story goes that one day at training at Parkhead, some of his players (clearly fishing for compliments) asked Jock who was the best player he had ever worked with. The answer was not *"Jimmy Johnstone"* or *"Billy McNeill"* or *"Bobby Murdoch,"* all of whom would have had a fair claim, one would have thought, but *"Willie Hamilton."* Stein had been able to bring out the best of Hamilton at Easter Road, but Willie was sadly of the mould of so many Scottish football players who could not always free themselves of the temptations of alcohol. It was certainly noticeable that the teetotal Stein made no attempt to bring him to Celtic Park, no matter how highly he rated him at Hibs.

But he did give Hamilton a Scottish cap here – his one and only Scottish cap – and it has to be said that Willie did not shine this afternoon in Helsinki. Scotland won 2-1, which has to go down as a success, even though the Press are fairly unanimous in failing to become over-enthused about the standard of football. Finland scored first, then Denis Law missed a penalty for Scotland before Davie Wilson equalised late in the first half. John Greig then made it 2-1 early in the second half, and that was how it stayed, with Scotland keeping control of the game.

Thus ended, as we thought, Stein's spell of Manager of Scotland. He had been more than a success – a win and a draw away from home has to be highly regarded in International football, and with three games left, two of which were at home, Scotland's chances of qualification had to be highly rated. The snag was that two of the games were against Italy, home and away! And so Scotland came back. Everything at the moment was looking good. On the same night that Scotland had beaten Finland, Inter Milan had beaten Benfica to retain the European Cup. It would be nice to think that someday a Scottish side could win that trophy! It wasn't likely, but everyone had a right to dream!

CHAPTER SIX

JUNE

The month of June is usually a very quiet one in Scottish football. 1965 was not a World Cup year, and there was no tour of America or Canada (occasions which are usually only very intermittently interesting, to put it mildly) so Celtic supporters did little other than sit back and savour the events of the last year. A few played golf, tennis, cricket or bowls and those who followed these sports did so with lightness in their heart and with peace in their souls, reflecting how quiet and relaxing these pastimes could be in direct contrast to the winter passion, and in particular the recurring drama of April 24. Those who were there talked about it endlessly, and those who weren't there, wished they had been, and in some cases pretended that they had been. Money could not buy a day like that!

It was also such a contrast to the grim old summers of 1963 and 1964. What a pleasure it now was to set the jack, to face fast bowling, to drive down the fairway without "the dark anguish of the soul!" In tennis, the Umpire's call of *"Thirty-All"* very soon became *"Bertie Auld."* Introverted, neurotic supporters now became cheerful people with jokes and laughter and characterised by a constant desire to talk about recent events in the world of football. There was now no need to change the subject when football was mentioned. Life had changed and changed utterly.

Even religion was smiled at and laughed about. A TV advertisement for Heinz Baked Beans involved a song *"A thousand housewives every day, pick up a can of beans and say, Beans Mean Heinz."*

This was changed to *"A thousand Catholics every day, throw their rosary beads away, Stein, Stein, Stein,"* as if the new leader of the Celtic religion was the messianic Stein! Even a few priests were known to laugh at this!

But one could not rest on one's laurels for ever. The future had to be faced as well. Not for a long time had supporters looked forward to the start of the season with statements like *"eight weeks come Saturday"* and how the fixtures would *"soon be out."* The Scottish League was now identified as a priority. It was astonishing to reflect that in the 11 years since 1954, Celtic had never won the League, and in those lean years, they had not even come second, apart from in 1955 when a good Aberdeen side beat Celtic. Since then, Rangers, Hearts, Dundee and now Kilmarnock had won the title, but such had been the ineptitude at Celtic Park that Celtic were classed among the "also rans." Not only that, but before 1954 we had to go back to the grim days of 1938 with Hitler, Chamberlain and Munich holding the floor before we would find a Celtic team which had won the League. The League Championship was all about consistency. We had to become Champions of Scotland. That would be Stein's aim, we reflected during all these pleasant summer months.

On Saturday, 5 June 1965, Joe McBride signed for Celtic from Motherwell for £22,500. This came as no great surprise, and Stein even showed Motherwell and their supporters the courtesy of waiting until they had won the Summer Cup on Wednesday, 2 June before he moved for Joe. Motherwell duly won the trophy at Tannadice Park, although most of the work had been done in the first leg at Fir Park. Motherwell had done themselves proud with players like the veteran John Martis, Pat Delaney - son of Celtic's Jimmy of long ago, and a young goalkeeper called Peter McCloy.

But Joe McBride's heart was set on Celtic. He was of course "Celtic daft," as befitted a man born on 10 June 1938, the very day that Celtic won the Empire Exhibition Trophy, and he was always happy to tell the story of the Scottish Cup semi-final in late March, when during a break in play, Bertie Auld had come up to him, pointed to all the green and white scarves all around the stadium and said *"Joe, dae ye no' want tae be a pairt o a this?"* The reply ran along the lines of *"Aye, but no' jist noo."* But now Joe had his wish.

If Celtic and their fans had any reservations about Joe, it was the fact that he had played for so many clubs. Apart from Motherwell, he had already turned out for Kilmarnock, Wolves (briefly), Luton Town and Partick Thistle. His forays in England had not been successful but he was certainly a proven goalscorer, as Celtic knew from that Scottish Cup semi-final where it might just have all gone wrong for them.

He would certainly get an immediate taste of the action in August it was felt, for John Hughes had been suspended for 14 days from the start of the season as a result of several misdemeanours, and Celtic had been placed in a very difficult League Cup section of both Dundee teams and, of all people, Motherwell! The fixtures were now awaited with bated breath!

Another forward departed. This was the unfortunate Hugh Maxwell on his way to St Johnstone. An earnest and decent player for other clubs, notably Falkirk, Hugh was quite simply not up to Celtic standards. He had only been with the club since November and had played only twice for Stein, and the club lost on both occasions. Bertie Auld later said that Hugh was too frail to make the grade with Celtic. He joined St Johnstone for a knock-down price.

Wednesday, 17 June saw a statement from Willie Allan of the SFA, and it would be fair to say that well-written, anodyne and carefully phrased though it was, it caused a few eyebrows to rise in Celtic households. It concerned the game in Scotland's World Cup group between Finland and Italy and it ran *"Mr Stein will attend the match between Finland and Italy on Wednesday on behalf of the SFA. His mission should not be regarded as having any significance in relationship to any appointment to the vacant post of team manager."*

Celtic supporters worried about this. There was always the possibility, however remote and unlikely, in that bright summer of 1965 with a glorious future beckoning for Celtic, that Jock might be offered the Scotland job on a full-time basis. There were even those, such is the Celtic paranoia, who felt that Rangers were using their influence on the SFA to prevent Stein continuing as Manager of Celtic! Stein was of course a great Scottish patriot. He had never been good enough to win a Scottish cap himself (he did win a Scottish League cap) and was always keen to advance Scotland's role in the world.

He would, of course, be Manager of Scotland on a part-time basis while still managing Celtic in the autumn. Even this would cause a few ripples in Celtic hearts. Celtic had to be a full-time job! Nothing must be allowed to distract from this mission! On the other hand, there was a counter argument. Where could there be a better job than Manager of Scotland to watch players and assess tactics if Celtic were going to advance in Europe? As long as everyone understood that the job was to be part-time and temporary, there would be no problem.

It was a subject well discussed, as indeed was a strange friendly game organised between Hearts and Kilmarnock in which there was to be no offside! Substitutes were to be allowed, and at half-time the rules were to be changed with lines drawn from the penalty box to the touchline, and a player could only be offside if he were in front of that line (This law would get an airing in the Scottish League Cup in 1973 and 1974). The "no offside" game ended up 7-0 for Hearts (some revenge for the events at the same ground on April 24, perhaps!) but the crowd was small, and although there were quite a few VIPs there to see the experiment, little more was heard of the idea – although it did fill the newspaper columns in the quiet summer months.

Willie Waddell was still in charge of Kilmarnock, but he had now decided to leave Rugby Park in the flush of victory, now that he had at last won the League for them. Those of us with an eye to see such matters were under no doubt that he was now after the Rangers job in order to challenge his old rival Jock Stein. That would eventually happen, but in the meantime, he had to be content with writing for *The Scottish Daily Express*. Ex-Celt Malky MacDonald was now to be the Manager of Kilmarnock for the new season.

For older Celts, there was major cause of sadness on June 23. At Robroyston Hospital, one of the greatest Celts of all time, Jimmy "Napoleon" McMenemy, died at the age of 85. He had been a key player in the legendary Celtic teams before World War I and had come back as trainer to play his part in the success of the team of the late 1930s. Although in failing health, he had been until recently a regular attender at Celtic Park, and it was good that he had lived long enough to see the return of the Scottish Cup in 1965, for he himself had won the trophy in 1904, 1907, 1908, 1911, 1912 and 1914 with Celtic and in 1921 with Partick Thistle. He had been called Napoleon either because of a facial resemblance to the famous Corsican or because of his ability to play football strategy in the way that Bonaparte plotted military tactics. His death was very sad, and it left only Joe Dodds and Davie McLean of Maley's great side still alive. Like so many other famous Celts, Napoleon was buried in Dalbeth Cemetery about half a mile up London Road from where he created so much glory.

His death, so sad, was another poignant reminder, at least to the older members of the support, that Celtic had enjoyed great days in the past, and that perhaps, the great days were about to return. Those who went misty-eyed on family occasions, or even just on an ordinary Saturday night at the recollection of *Bennett, McMenemy, Quinn, Somers and Hamilton,* could now be answered with *Chalmers, Gallagher, Hughes, Lennox and Auld* by the eager youngsters who often nourished secret feelings of jealousy that their own childhood had been scarred by under-performance - whereas Grandad had been so lucky. He had of course been less lucky with wars and poverty, but now in this new age, things were looking up in every respect.

Glasgow and Scotland were busy and vibrant. The slums were being demolished and those houses which still had an outside toilet to be shared with other families were now disappearing. It was a mammoth task, but it was now clearly happening. Healthcare was improving, motorways were planned and being built, and The Beatles and others were hammering home the message that young people did matter. It was their time, and it also seemed the time of Celtic. On the day of the Scottish Cup final, I had bought out of Lewis's Polytechnic in Argyle Street the record of Glen Daly singing *"Kelly, The Boy From Killan."* The lyrics talked about *"goodly news"* and *"a hymn for the dawn of the free."* That was so appropriate for the balmy days of Summer 1965.

Fixtures for the new season in the 1960s were usually issued on a Saturday in time for the evening newspapers, and this year it was June 26 which saw the League and the League Cup fixtures appearing. We were due to open the season at Tannadice Park on Saturday, 14 August against Dundee United, and by an odd quirk, we were back at the same ground to open the League season on Wednesday, 25 August. In these days, in the League Cup section, three games were played on Saturday, Wednesday, Saturday and before the fixtures were reversed, a League game was played on the Wednesday. By sheer chance, it was Dundee United again, and then United would go to Parkhead on the Saturday. We would see a lot of the Tannadice Terrors in the early weeks of the season.

Other fixtures were eagerly devoured – Rangers on September 18 and New Year's Day, Morton at Celtic Park on Christmas Day and then we finished off the season with them on April 30, Aberdeen on January 15 at Pittodrie and other such occasions so that trips could be arranged. No season, of course, ever works out like that because of postponements and other competitions, but at least it was a template, and it encouraged the view that the eagerly awaited new season was just round the corner. And August 14 being the start of the season, it was now just seven weeks away!

"Where would McBride fit in?" Obviously, as John Hughes was suspended for the initial part of the season, he would be in the centre, but what about afterwards? *"Will Jock sign anybody else?" "Will Murdoch stay at right-half?" "What about wee Jimmy Johnstone?" "Will John Fallon be good enough, or what about that old guy Ronnie Simpson?" "And what about the new newspaper – The Celtic View?" "Jock Stein's goin' tae hae the best team in Britain!" "Whit dae ye think?"*

All these questions were discussed at length and with animation during these long summer evenings. *"Impatient for the coming fight,"* in the words of *The Soldiers' Song*. We were all that. Holidays were an irrelevance. We needed the fitba' back. The contrast between 1965 and previous summers was quite stark.

CHAPTER SEVEN

JULY

The players reported back for training on Monday, 19 July 1965, the first full day of the Glasgow Fair. Because of the pruning of the playing staff in the spring, there were only 19 full-timers and nine part-timers. Beneath all the bonhomie and *"Good to be back"* sort of stuff, there was a certain amount of apprehension for the new season, but also excitement for what lay in store with the new Boss. A lot had happened since early March when Jock Stein took over, but that was only four months ago, and the players didn't really know him, even though he had gone out of his way to be nice to them, and indeed to everyone.

July, before the season starts, is usually the time when training is at its hardest. With the best will in the world, quite a few players take it rather too easy at the end of the season and they often return a little overweight and in less than the peak of condition. More than that, they are not mentally attuned in that they have not been thinking about football. The start of the training often comes as a rude awakening. This year however it would be different.

There was a game scheduled for July 28 against Motherwell in the Isle of Man. Before that, Jock Stein, giving an example of how well he knew how to manipulate the media, leaked two stories to help them out at a quiet footballing time. One concerned two young Brazilians, Ayrton Ignacio and Marco di Souza, who were coming to Celtic Park for training and assessment. To what extent they were ever likely to be offered contracts or to what extent it was merely a publicity stunt, we do not know but it did galvanise the support who felt that anyone who was a Brazilian was bound to be a good football player!

The other was the first of Stein's many Open Days for the Press. There had been a tendency in the past to keep the Press at arm's length, but long ago Maley had realised the value of massaging them, and Stein now followed this example. Pictures appeared in newspapers of players literally "jumping through hoops" (Jock made jokes about how it was all about winning more penalties!) and jumping up to head balloons on things that looked like gallows, while Jock talked amiably and genially to all the Pressmen, even those who had upset him in his previous incarnations of being Manager of Dunfermline or Hibs! Coffee and biscuits were available, the weather was good, and players too were encouraged to talk to the Press.

There was another spin-off about all this as well. The players all trained hard, and because the training was carried out with initiative and imagination by Neil Mochan and Bob Rooney, the players began to enjoy it. Previously the training had not been very good with poor training gear and it normally consisted of little more than running round the track. Now there was an emphasis on ball skills, passing and team games, and training stopped being a chore and more like a pleasure in the company of friends. Inevitably, in all groups, there will be personality clashes, but Stein and McNeill now worked to minimise such things. It was important to "love" each other!

No-one was more aware of all this than new signing Joe McBride. Joe was on record as saying that he *"couldn't wait to get into training in the morning,"* so much did he enjoy being there and how pleasant training was. Normally, training in his previous clubs had been a drudge. Now it was fun! He was where he wanted to be.

The game against Motherwell on the Isle of Man was a low-key start to the season. It was played at King George V Park at Douglas in aid of handicapped children. It looked like an excellent fundraiser for a worthy cause because it was the second week of the Glasgow Fair and the Isle of Man was always a popular holiday spot for Scottish people. The only problems were torrential rain, not a great deal of shelter for the supporters, and an attendance of fewer than 3,000 people!

It was not exactly a needle game, for both teams travelled on the same plane and sat talking amiably to each other. Motherwell of course were still basking on their Summer Cup success in the same way as Celtic were still glowing about the Scottish Cup. Their relationships were very much intertwined at this point after the semi-final, the McBride transfer and the fact that they would be in the same League Cup section. Under new Manager Bobby Howitt, Motherwell felt they might be going places as well.

The game was in many ways, other than merely the weather, an anti-climax. It ended 1-1 and Celtic were possibly lucky to get a draw. Bobby Murdoch was left behind in Glasgow because he was not yet fully fit after his foot operation, and the team was a strange one of *Fallon, Young and Gemmell; Clark, McNeill and O'Neill; Hughes, Johnstone, McBride, Lennox and Auld.* Poor Joe McBride lasted 10 minutes on his Celtic debut before having to retire after a clash of heads with John Martis and he was replaced by Steve Chalmers. The unremitting rain made it a poor game, but Motherwell scored halfway through the second half and looked likely winners until Chalmers grabbed a late and not entirely deserved equaliser. Bertie Auld was also injured and replaced by John Divers, and all in all, it was not a great start to the season. But it was only a pre-season friendly. Such games are not important other than in how they highlight specific strengths and weaknesses.

A slow start to the season is not necessarily a bad thing. It is what is happening behind the scenes that is important. Stein was shrewd enough to talk to all his backroom staff - Fallon, Mochan, Steele and others, to cultivate all his contacts in the complex world of junior football and to keep the newspapers on his side. He would also have his own plans for his own newspaper, *The Celtic View*. It is never easy to launch a new newspaper, but this was the ideal time to do it.

CHAPTER EIGHT

AUGUST

August 1965 saw exciting times at Celtic Park as the new season approached. There was *The Celtic View* to be launched on Wednesday, 11 August. It was the first newspaper of its kind in the world and was the brainchild of Jack McGinn. Jock Stein himself wrote regularly for it (and he himself clearly did the writing; he did not employ a "ghost") as well as a journalist called "Kerrydale," widely believed to be John McPhail. It sold well and remains a valuable source of detail for the club at this period.

Before the season itself was due to start on August 14 at Tannadice Park, Celtic had arranged another two pre-season friendlies. One was against Shamrock Rovers in Dublin, and the other was a far more loaded affair against Sunderland at Roker Park. Sunderland had of course two new boys this season – Manager Ian McColl, ex-Scotland Manager and ex-Rangers player, and Jim Baxter who had now caused enough trouble at Ibrox to encourage the club to let him go, especially after this April when the club failed to land any silverware following their rather lucky capture of the League Cup in October 1964. As long as they were winning, the Ibrox establishment were prepared to tolerate some bad behaviour, but now that Celtic had risen, and Baxter had in any case broken his leg thereby limiting his efficiency, he was allowed to go.

The Dalymount Park game on Tuesday, 3 August against Shamrock Rovers was as one-sided as the 7-0 scoreline would have suggested, as a crowd of 10,000 (already sympathetic to Celtic, one suspects) stood in wonder and awe at the football produced by this Celtic side. The Shamrock Rovers players (some of whom asked the Celtic players for their autographs after the game!) were simply torn apart in this fine display of attacking football. Murdoch was back at right-half, and that made a huge difference to the team of *Fallon, Young and Gemmell; Murdoch, McNeill and Clark; Johnstone, Gallagher, McBride, Lennox and Hughes*. Steve Chalmers was given a game for Charlie Gallagher in the second half, but Bertie Auld was left in Scotland to recover from an injury sustained against Motherwell on the Isle of Man.

Celtic began the way they meant to continue and might have reached double figures if they had really tried. McBride scored a hat-trick, Lennox two and Hughes and Gallagher one each. They thoroughly deserved their standing ovation at the end of the game from the Glasgow people on holiday and those people of Dublin who support Celtic – which is of course virtually everybody! Much was made of the fact that Shamrock Rovers were part-timers, but they had won the Irish Cup and Celtic had come a cropper against part-time opposition quite a few times before in the past. Jock Stein went out of his way to suggest that Shamrock Rovers still were worthy opposition, and to wish them well for the coming season.

In any case, no-one could have complained about the poor quality of the opposition in the next game – against Sunderland at Roker Park. This was a tremendous 5-0 win which at a stroke silenced all those (in Scotland and England) who disparaged the Scottish League and said patronising things about how Celtic would do well to avoid relegation in the English First Division. The English League was much vaunted in both England and Scotland with Saturday lunchtime TV programmes showing the highlights of last week's English games and creating an erroneous impression among the naïve (and there were many) that English football was nothing other than great goals!

The game could only be described as a "hammering," with goals from Lennox, Murdoch, McBride and two from Hughes at the end. Jim Baxter, frankly, looked lost and out of his depth, even at one point being hit by an orange (!) thrown from the crowd, and the Mackems of Sunderland looked shattered as Celtic were in total control from beginning to end. Harry Hood, one time of Clyde and who would one day join Celtic, must have wondered what he was doing in Sunderland when he might have already been a Celtic player.

The teams were

Sunderland:

McLaughlan, Parke and Ashurst; Harvey, Hurley and McNab; Hellawell, Hood, Sharkey, Baxter and Mulhall.

Celtic:

Fallon, Young and Gemmell; Murdoch, McNeill and Clark; Johnstone, Gallagher, McBride, Lennox and Hughes.

Referee: *Mr T McKitterick*

On the field, there was nothing wrong with Celtic's performance. Jock Stein said reflectively, *"There was pleasing teamwork and a great deal of profitable individual quality. We were not flattered by the 5-0 margin. All the training and talking of the past weeks is being justified."* But then he added, as a caveat for those who were getting carried away with themselves, *"We are not a great team, but we are a team of great promise. There will be no let-up in our efforts, however, to become a great team."* A pre-season friendly is of course just that. It means nothing.

Off the field, however, the name of Celtic was once more dragged into the gutter by moronic fans whose behaviour was savage and a disgrace before the game, during the game and after the game. We have said how Jim Baxter was hit by an orange and was jeered off the park. That was bad enough, but it did not stop there. There is little point in saying that Sunderland fans were just as bad. That was true, and there were even some Newcastle fans who joined in on the side of the Celtic fans, while Sunderland supporters (including some who had never been to Scotland in their lives) decided to support Rangers, even to the extent of waving blue flags and scarves!

But it was an awful display of Celtic fans who frankly could not cope with the strong drink after a long bus journey. Windows were smashed, people were terrorised, and things like park benches and bus shelters were vandalised, with even several attempts made to rob pubs and shops! This could not possibly be condoned, and Jock Stein was not slow to make his feelings known in quotes to newspapers. Not the least of his many fine achievements was to be his success in tidying up the support. It would take a long time, but he would succeed.

Meanwhile, Celtic announced that Jock Stein could become available to manage Scotland for the length of time that they were in the World Cup but stressed that his Celtic commitment had to come first. Not all supporters, given their innate suspicion of the SFA which they tended to equate (wrongly) with Rangers, were happy about this, but it was a sign of Celtic being seen to be reasonable, and once again an attempt to catch the middle ground of Scottish public opinion while leaving their enemies with nothing to complain about. As in the 1890s, when Celtic Park was built to accommodate the huge crowds that came to see Scotland v England games, Celtic were once again identifying with Scotland and cutting the ground from under the feet of those who accused Celtic and their supporters of being alien.

This was announced in the first edition of *The Celtic View* on August 11. A picture of the Cup-winners was printed on page one with the Scottish Cup proudly displayed. The newspaper radiated confidence with a picture of other trophies won by Celtic. It told us that Billy McNeill had won the *"Player Of The Year,"* that Steve Chalmers had had a good round of golf in Dublin, that ex-Celt John McAlindon was the floodlight technician at Celtic Park and the only Englishman employed by Celtic, and that George Connelly a talented ball player from Fife had joined the club. It was all upbeat, optimistic stuff.

And so as the new season dawned, Celtic appeared to be in good shape. The defence was steady, and Murdoch had proved beyond any doubt that right-half was his position. As far as the forward line was concerned, although John Hughes would be suspended for the first few games, there were still another six top quality forwards from which Stein could choose – Chalmers, Gallagher, Johnstone, Auld, Lennox and now McBride. It was a happy position to be in.

The Monday night of August 9 saw an astonishing crowd of 18,000 at Celtic Park to see a Trial match! They had been lured there to see the new Brazilians in action, but unfortunately a last-minute hitch in administration (an excuse not universally believed) rendered this impossible. Nevertheless, they saw some good football played by most of the first team and the youngsters and left happily. On Wednesday, Jock Stein, Manager of Celtic and Scotland, became Manager of Glasgow as well, when a Glasgow select took on Tommy Docherty's impressive young Chelsea side at Hampden Park. It was not one of Jock's happier occasions for the hybrid collection of Glaswegians (artificially balanced with four players from both Celtic and Rangers, two from Clyde and one from Partick Thistle all playing in Scotland jerseys) went down 0-3 to a lively Chelsea side. 36,000 fans were not impressed, nor did the experimental rule of only being offside in your penalty area and its lateral extension seem to make any difference.

All this of course was of little importance in comparison to the "road and the miles" journey to Dundee on Saturday, 14 August 1965. Dundee United, managed by Jerry Kerr, were one of the success stories of Scottish football in the early 1960s with their strange new stand which turned a corner and their infusion of quality Scandinavian blood. They were financed in part by a very successful lottery called Taypools, and it was clear that they were in the First Division to stay. With a small but eager and predominantly young support, they were always a tough nut to crack, especially at Tannadice.

Dundee was a difficult city to understand, and Dundee United's support was complex. United had been founded in 1909 as Dundee Hibernian, wore green jerseys and were unashamedly Irish. But in 1923, just as the Irish troubles were dying down, they moved away from their Irish origins and called themselves Dundee United, also changing their strips from green to black and white. A few decades later, they would further distance themselves from their Irish origins by going to the other extreme and changing to orange! The Dundee Irish were sympathetic to Dundee United even in their many bad days, but as United were not very good and struggled to get out of the Second Division, they retained their main allegiance to Celtic. Sometimes this was put to the test, however. A Scottish Cup tie in 1949 when Second Division Dundee United removed an awful Celtic team from the Scottish Cup made them wonder!

That, however, was an isolated occasion, and the 1950s saw Dundee United revert to under-performance and the perception that they were the poor man's team of the city. But United's promotion in 1960 coincided with Celtic's mediocrity at that time, and things began to change. There was a slow, but not total, movement of the Dundee Irish towards Dundee United. Indeed, games between United and Celtic were as much for the heart and soul of the Dundee Irish as anything else.

Surprisingly, the game on August 14 was not all-ticket and seldom had Dundee seen quite so many Celtic fans as it did that hot, sunny day at Tannadice Park. In addition to the suspended Hughes, Celtic were also without Joe McBride who had been injured against Sunderland and thus the forward line read *Johnstone, Gallagher, Chalmers, Lennox and Auld*.

Unusually for the times, Celtic came out to do a warm-up before the start of the game wearing all-green jerseys. They then returned to the pavilion and re-emerged wearing the green and white hoops, while Dundee United appeared in all-black! It was an even game, and Celtic were a little unfortunate to lose 1-2. Possibly the key joust of the day was Billy McNeill losing out to Finn Dossing, the Danish centre-forward of United who often seemed to get the better of him. Dundee United's first goal was scored by ex-Celt Bobby Carroll, who had now joined the Tannadice men from St Mirren. Bertie Auld equalised with a diving header but in so doing, he overstretched himself and was off the field injured when Dundee United scored their winning goal a minute or two later through Dennis Gillespie. From then on it was all action but United held out with Celtic clearly missing their strike force up front of John Hughes and Joe McBride. Chalmers was ineffective, and Gallagher's contribution was minimal.

It was a sobering experience for Celtic, but hardly disastrous – a defeat in the first game of a nine-month season gives plenty of time to recover! - and although these things shouldn't be important, the fact that Rangers also lost today made everyone a little happier on the way home! It did show, however, that success this year was not going to be easy. Scotland was fortunate to have many good teams in those boom years of the mid 1960s, and Dundee United were one of them. In the other game of the section, Motherwell beat Dundee 1-0 at Fir Park, and Wednesday night would bring Motherwell to Celtic Park while the two Dundee teams met at Dens Park.

The second edition of *The Celtic View* was a lot less bland and anodyne than the first one had been. Its headline was *"Bid To Eliminate Hooliganism"* and made clear the determination of the club not to tolerate anything which would besmirch the good name of the club, as had happened on the two recent trips to Sunderland and Dundee. The Dundee United game had not seen as much sustained thuggery as the Sunderland one, but there had still been enough. The influence of teetotaller Stein in all this was seen in the comment that *"too many supporters' buses leave from public houses."*

McBride was still not fit to play against his old teammates in the Motherwell game, but Stein sprung a real surprise when he dropped Charlie Gallagher and brought in John Divers. John, son of a former Celtic player of the same name, had never really impressed Jock Stein up till now. Indeed, he had not yet played a first-team game under Stein. He was in danger of becoming the forgotten man of Celtic Park and he must have wondered about his future at the club. However, even those who wondered about the motivation and the speed of John never doubted his footballing ability, particularly in passing, and tonight he was given a game for the club to the surprise and wonderment of the 30,000 crowd. This forward line thus read *Johnstone, Divers, Chalmers, Lennox and Auld*.

It was not a great game, with Celtic clearly aware that another defeat after Saturday would probably deal a fatal blow to their League Cup hopes. The game was one of attrition, particularly in the first half, but in the second half Celtic began to open out a little more and Jimmy Johnstone began to get the better of the Motherwell left-back. It was from a pass from Johnstone that Divers slammed in the only goal of the game. It was a win but still not scintillating stuff in a game played in quite dark conditions, for two of Celtic's floodlight pylons seemed to be out of action! Either that or Celtic were just being mean! The failure of the Parkhead floodlights may well, however, have put an idea or two into Celtic heads about floodlights, and how it was possible to make a political point about the lighting of grounds. We shall observe the results.

Celtic 1 Motherwell 0 was, however, a victory and the fact that the Dundee derby turned out to be a goalless draw meant that Celtic had gained a point on Dundee United. As important as anything else that day, however, was the behaviour of the fans. Had they read the announcement in *The Celtic View* that Celtic were launching a major initiative to attack hooliganism? Appeals were made to the rest of the support to make it obvious that bad behaviour was not to be tolerated, and tonight behaviour was impeccable. Mind you, a home game on a Wednesday night is a different matter altogether from a booze-fuelled away day. But the main topic of interest over the next week was to be Saturday's game against Dundee at Celtic Park, a game that potentially called into question the whole validity of the Stein revolution.

Saturday, 21 August was a very bad day for Celtic. The supporters who had disgraced themselves at Tannadice last week were still being dealt with at Dundee Police Court (they were mainly the ones who had failed to turn up on the Monday) and fines were being disbursed by Bailie WP Roberts, while a few more got themselves arrested at Parkhead today – unusually, for behaviour at Parkhead itself was normally very good. That was bad, but worse was the game itself. It was Joe McBride's first appearance in a green and white jersey in Scotland, and it would have to be said that it was a failure. John Divers was retained at inside-right, and McBride took the place of Chalmers. 35,000 appeared and everyone left the ground regretting the absence of John Hughes.

It was a complacent Celtic at Parkhead performance of which we had seen rather too many in the past few years. Celtic were well on top in the first half but could not score against a well-organised Dundee defence in which Alex Hamilton the Scotland right-back was absolutely outstanding. Then Celtic in the second half, attacking the traditional Celtic End, upped a gear or two, continued to have bad luck in front of goal, and then when they got a little too desperate, Dundee struck – twice. The first goal by Kenny Cameron had an element of luck about it with a rebound, and then a deflection which gave Fallon little chance, even though John did manage to turn and get a hand to it, but the second goal was a good one when Cameron got the better of Gemmell and scored into the roof of the net.

The second goal went in just as a shower of rain came on (it had been a good day up till then) and there was something very symbolic about that. There was no comeback for Celtic after that, and Dundee finished well on top in front of a half-empty Parkhead which was not so much angry as stunned. There may have been some excuse for last week at Tannadice, but this one imperilled qualification to the extent that many supporters would have been prepared to write them off there and then. Dundee United thumped Motherwell 4-1 and now had five points, Dundee had three and Celtic and Motherwell two. Even at this stage, Celtic could not now catch Dundee United on their own (2 points for a win) and needed help from Dundee and Motherwell while winning their remaining three games. This did not seem likely.

The fact that Rangers also lost again (to Aberdeen this time) did not really seem to be relevant tonight as we travelled home that fine summer evening. But in the same way that the city of Dundee had caused all the problems, it was the same city that provided the solution. By some odd quirk, the first League fixture was at Tannadice Park against Dundee United on the Wednesday, 25 August. There were those who argued that this was not a good idea, and it would have been far better to put Celtic against a team who were not in their League Cup section, but in the event, it turned out to be absolutely brilliant for Celtic. There are some games that are pivotal to the history of the club – the Scottish Cup final of April 24 was one; in a totally different way so was August 25. No-one knew it at the time, nor could possibly have predicted it, but it was the start of "nine in a row."

The teams were;

Dundee United:

Mackay, Millar and Briggs; Munro, Smith and Wing; Carroll, Gillespie, Dossing, Mitchell and Persson.

Celtic:

Fallon, Young and Gemmell; Murdoch, McNeill and Clark; Chalmers, Divers, McBride, Lennox and Gallagher.

Referee: *RH Davidson, Airdrie*

Celtic fans of this era were in the habit of seeing strange forward lines. This one was certainly strange, but the difference was that this one was successful and picked by a man who knew his football. Hughes was still unavailable, but Stein decided to drop Jimmy Johnstone, put Chalmers on the right wing, to keep John Divers and to put Charlie Gallagher on the left wing.

It was the night on which the young Dundee United supporters who had been far too uppity with their banners, rattles and bells before the start were taught a few things about the realities of footballing life. The crowd was about 20,000, and was about equally balanced, although proportionately there were an awful lot of Celtic fans with Dundee, Angus or Fife accents, with quite a few Glaswegians arriving straight from their work in their overalls with their piece bags – a phenomenon of midweek games in the 1960s!

Celtic started off playing towards the Shed or Dens Park end of the ground and attacked from the start. Within a couple of minutes, Charlie Gallagher rattled the bar and after a few corners, Celtic took the lead in the 13th minute when John Divers swept in a square pass from McBride. Murdoch, Divers and Gallagher were all superb as Celtic's play was relentless with inch-perfect passes and only a good display by Donald Mackay in the United goal and a great deal of bad luck prevented Celtic going further ahead before half-time. At the back, McNeill was in total control of Dossing in marked contrast to the League Cup game of 11 days ago, full-backs Young and Gemmell tackled determinedly and the United forward line never really got going.

If the first half was good, the second was immense. Joe McBride scored his first competitive goal for the club by taking a Chalmers pass and finding a home for it; then Bobby Lennox was sandwiched between Millar and Mackay and fouled by both simultaneously to gain a penalty kick, which Ian Young sank without much bother; and finally, Tommy Gemmell hammered home a fourth from well outside the box after the overwhelmed Dundee United defence could not clear the ball properly. Thus, both full backs had scored for Celtic in the same game, a rather unusual phenomenon.

It was nothing less than a rout. For a change, it was Dundee United supporters who disgraced themselves by throwing coins at John Fallon from the Shed, and their players were no better. Francis Munro (Celtic daft and a man who would eventually get a chance for the club years later) was booked for kicking the ball against the perimeter wall in a tantrum when he didn't get his own way, and then Orjan Persson (who would one day find his way to Ibrox) *"tried to put Tommy Gemmell into a wheelchair"* as a contemporary football magazine put it, and Bobby Davidson had no option but to *"invite him to depart"* as the coin throwing intensified from the failures of the Dundee educational system.

The Glasgow Herald says *"There was a champagne quality about the play of this latest Celtic blend. Victory was the product of teamwork and they were an impressive balance of speed, skill and spirit." The Dundee Courier* is a lot more down to earth with *"Celtic give United a Four Goal Dunt"* while Gair Henderson in *The Evening Times* wonders if there will even be a place in the team for John Hughes once he returns. Jock Stein described it as a *"resounding win."*

So the League was off to a good start, but now it was time to get back into the League Cup section. Stein, who had already in 1965 managed Hibs, Celtic, Scotland and Glasgow now added the Scottish League to this impressive list when he accepted an invitation to manage the League select at Ibrox on September 8 against the Irish League. He had now seen how Dundee United could be beaten and they were Celtic's next fixture at home on Saturday, 28 August as the League Cup resumed.

Following Wednesday night's game, it was hard to see Dundee United winning at Parkhead where they never really played well. Defeats in football, as we have seen, can be infectious in that one leads to another, and frankly, United were well beaten before they left Dundee, as the local DC Thomson Press (Tory to the core, but paradoxically pro-Celtic with Tommy Gallacher, son of Patsy, writing for them) was still chortling about Wednesday night.

Celtic had John Hughes back from his suspension, and he was given a great reception from the 36,000 crowd as Celtic came out in their all-green jerseys. The defence stayed the same as Wednesday night, but the forward line read *Chalmers, Divers, McBride, Lennox and Hughes*. The score was 3-0 this time, and the victory, although not so spectacular, was equally emphatic. Once again Ian Young scored with a penalty kick, awarded this time for handball, then John Hughes set up one for Steve Chalmers to tap in. There then followed a somewhat pedestrian second half before Joe McBride added a third near the end. Dundee United looked as if they had been a team who had been found out, and although they remained top of the section with five points, their number looked up. Celtic also got the result that they wanted at Dens Park when Motherwell came from behind to beat Dundee 2-1 in the last minute. All this meant that Motherwell and Celtic both had four points, and Dundee had three.

If anything, the favourites for the section were now Motherwell, who had two home games to play whereas Celtic had to visit Fir Park and Dens Park. Dundee United were still a point ahead but seemed now to have lost their way. On the other hand, if they won the Tayside Derby on Wednesday night at Dens Park, United would retain their advantage, no matter who won at Motherwell. It was still anyone's call.

The month of August ended on a strange note when 11,500 turned up at Parkhead to see Celtic v Motherwell Reserves, possibly the biggest-ever attendance for a reserve match, except perhaps a Celtic v Rangers game, and certainly larger than many Scottish First Division teams could expect for their home games. The attraction was the debut of the Brazilians Ayrton Inacio and Marco di Souza, probably the first time any Brazilian had ever participated in Scottish football. They both played well with Inacio scoring two goals in the 3-1 victory, but Jimmy Dunbar of *The Evening Times* was also impressed by Ronnie Simpson, Jim Craig, Jim Brogan and Jimmy Johnstone. These four might yet feature in Celtic's future plans, it was felt.

The word "Brazilian" had a mystique about it. The World Cups of 1958 and 1962 had shown supporters in this country some great football on their televisions, and an awful lot of it had been played by Brazilians. And, of course, there was Pele, and although no-one could pronounce his name - calling him *"Peely" "Pell" "Peels"* and even *"Pe-el,"* he was reckoned to be the best there had ever been (Those however who had seen Patsy Gallacher, begged to differ!). It was a short step from this towards believing that every single Brazilian had to be a great football player. These two players, and another two who came later - Jorge Fara and Fernando Consel, were probably good enough, but there were severe problems in adapting from the culture of Brazil to that of Scotland in the mid-1960s, and none of the four ever managed to get into the first team. It was a shame, but it kept Celtic on the back page of newspapers, always a very strong factor in Stein's thinking.

August 1965 had been a mixed month. The Vietnam war was intensifying with the Americans still possessed with the naïve belief that it was an easy conquest for them and beginning to try to persuade the British to join in. Fortunately for all concerned, Harold Wilson demurred, although the Americans had more success in trying to persuade the more gullible Australians.

For Celtic, League Cup qualification, so important for Celtic's credibility as a revanchist football cub, lay in the balance...

CHAPTER NINE

SEPTEMBER

The game at Fir Park on Wednesday, 1 September 1965 was a remarkable one. In the first place 25,000 were there, and although Fir Park had seen a few bigger crowds than that in its time, it was still a huge crowd for a Wednesday night. The accommodation was tight and far from comfortable, but they saw Celtic at their best. There was one controversial moment, but the score of 3-2 for Celtic was rather deceptive, for Motherwell's second goal was scored in the 88th minute, and was, by that stage of the game, not completely deserved.

Chalmers, Divers, Hughes, Lennox and Gallagher was the forward line tonight, showing Stein's belief in his policy of "horses for courses" with the team being changed to allow for different opposition, venue and team needs. It also had the side-effect of keeping all the players on their toes. Tonight, it was Hughes who was the star man in the forward line, although Lennox scored twice and was involved in a controversial incident. The omission of McBride was also a shrewd move by Stein who possibly felt that the Motherwell defenders knew their old teammate too well, and maybe it was better not to deploy him for this game.

The first goal was a funny one, and it arrived in only four minutes. A Charlie Gallagher corner was missed by John Hughes but came to Steve Chalmers who clipped it back to Lennox who scored. The equaliser came from Pat Delaney, who shot from well outside the penalty box, catching John Fallon and the rest of the Celtic defence unawares. One wonders what his father, the redoubtable Jimmy watching from the Fir Park stand, thought of that one?

But then Lennox, *"more eager than careful"* (as Gair Henderson put it in *The Evening Times*) barged into goalkeeper McCloy as he gathered a ball. A free-kick was awarded, and Lennox was lucky not to be booked for that, in the opinion of many supporters of both teams. But then again, a minute later, he tried the same thing – or at least he would have if Thomson had not intervened and barged him first. Quite correctly, referee Mr Watson of Glenrothes awarded a penalty kick. It did not go down well with the Motherwell crowd, but John Hughes took the penalty and Celtic went in at half time 2-1 to the good. Early in the second half, Celtic went 3-1 ahead after some good work from Tommy Gemmell, who ran to the by-line with the ball then chipped it back for Lennox. And that seemed to be that - until Murray scored that late counter, but it was so late that Celtic did not have too long to keep out any potential equaliser.

And of course, when things go well for you in football, they continue to go well. The news from Dundee was good, for at Tannadice, Dundee had beaten United 3-1, thereby, more or less, removing United from the top of the section, and allowing Celtic to go top. Once again, the other game in the section had gone the way that Celtic would have wanted it to, and it meant that Celtic had six points, both Dundee teams had five and Motherwell had four. Motherwell could not now win the section but both Celtic and Dundee could and so too could United, if they beat Motherwell by a huge margin and Dundee and Celtic drew. However, it looked as if a draw would be enough for Celtic at Dens Park, a ground where, for many years they had found it very difficult to win.

Things had changed, however, and changed utterly since the last time Celtic had been at Dens Park in March – the day that Jock Stein first gave Bobby Murdoch the right-half role. That day there had been empty spaces on the terracing and room for everyone. Not today. Long queues formed, and although the crowd was given as 28,000, there looked to be a lot more than that. It was one of those days in early September when it feels a shame that summer is now in retreat, for the weather is pleasant and warm but without being oppressive.

This time the forward line ran *Chalmers, Divers, McBride, Lennox and Hughes* with the defence remaining the same. It was a fine balance – the speed of Chalmers, the craft of Divers, the clinical finishing of McBride, the determination of Lennox and sheer unpredictability of Hughes. Many supporters believed that the left wing was in any case the best place for John Hughes, for he had more room and could find open spaces, whereas at centre-forward he could quite easily run into trouble.

With a huge contingent in green lending their support (easily outnumbering the home support), Celtic playing towards the Tannadice Park end of the ground roared into the attack and they had had several near things before Divers put them ahead in the 11th minute of the game. It followed some good movement from Hughes who made ground then sent the ball across the field to Chalmers, who deftly flicked the ball into Divers. Before the defence could get organised, Divers was able to hook the ball into the net from just inside the penalty box. Once again, the much-maligned John Divers had managed a goal for the club at a vital time.

Celtic remained on top after that, having the good sense not to fall back and allow Dundee back into the game. Dundee, having alienated so many of their support by their selling of Ure and Gilzean, had now regained a little credibility and enjoyed a reputation for quixotic unpredictability among their fans. They also possessed in Charlie Cooke a player of sublime footballing skill, so anything could happen. But then on the half-hour mark came one of the best goals that one is ever likely to see on any football field on any day, and it came from the mesmeric ability of Yogi Bear. Up till now, John Hughes had divided opinion on supporters' buses more than anyone else with words like *"liability," "useless,"* and *"poseur"* heard alongside *"matchwinner," "brilliant,"* and *"world-class."* And you could hear one man saying one thing before the game and another after. After this, the arguments ceased.

Celtic, on top and playing well, found Hughes halfway inside the Dundee half on the left wing on the same side of the field as the long, obtuse, angled stand which was such a characteristic of that famous old ground. He then evaded the tackle of International full-back Alex Hamilton (who had an innate capacity for annoying people by his sometimes-injudicious comments to the Press), and then to the amazement of the crowd charged across the field with the ball at his feet and pursued by a couple of Dundee players. He then suddenly turned and hammered home a shot from at least 25 yards past the bewildered Ally Donaldson in the Dundee goal. It all happened in a matter of seconds and caught everyone by surprise.

As often happens in such circumstances, there was a moment of stunned silence before Dens Park erupted into thunderous acclaim, with even the Dundee season ticket holders in the stand being seen to join reluctantly in the applause. Among the Celtic fans behind that goal, bedlam ensued for several minutes before things settled down and people started talking about *"Pele"* and even *"Patsy Gallacher"* in the context of what they had just seen! The applause rang out for a long, long time and this goal remained the main topic of conversation for many days in the area.

It was difficult to follow this, but Celtic were given a timely reminder that the job was not yet entirely done when, just before half-time, Andy Penman scored for Dundee after a good pass from Cooke. Nevertheless, Celtic going in for half-time at 2-1 ahead had reason to feel happy with themselves even though Dundee and their supporters were visibly animated by Penman's counter.

The second half was hard-fought with neither team able to break through for a long time and Celtic, with men like Ian Young and John Clark outstanding, containing the Dundee side. Celtic were 2-1 up but in reality they were, in effect, two goals up, for a draw would have suited them for qualification purposes. Now attacking the Provost Road end of that venerable old ground, Celtic found Dundee's defence difficult to crack, apart from the time when Chalmers scored but was pulled up for offside, a decision which did not meet with universal agreement, it has to be said. Then with five minutes to go, Joe McBride killed Dundee's fast-vanishing hopes with a header, and the game finished with the Celtic crowd in rare good humour.

Celtic had thus qualified from their difficult group from a position two weeks ago when Dundee had beaten a lacklustre side at Parkhead and qualification looked impossible. But this was a team with spirit and a Manager who knew his tactics, and that bright September day, the thought of another Hampden final and the League Cup was an attractive one. We now once again had the smell of silver in our nostrils.

The quarter-final of the Scottish League Cup would see Celtic paired with Raith Rovers, the first game at Stark's Park on September 15. But there was a League game before that against Clyde, and before Clyde, a game which involved four Celtic players plus their Manager – at Ibrox! This was the Scottish League v Irish League representative match. Even in 1965, quite a lot of fans and journalists were querying the value of such games against part-timers from a very poor League. At this point, Scottish domestic football was actually quite good and certainly too good for the honest journeymen of Ireland. The weather was wet, the crowd was low, the Scottish League won 6-2 in a game that did not prove very much, but Billy McNeill, John Hughes, Bobby Murdoch and Tommy Gemmell all took part in the very one-sided contest. The future of a fixture like this was now very much under the microscope.

Games between Celtic and Clyde did not enjoy a high reputation for being thrillers. *"You never get a good gemme atween those two"* was a frequent comment. But it was Celtic's first home League match of the season, and 35,000 turned up at Celtic Park to see the team who had qualified for the League Cup quarter final in such breathtaking style. Bertie Auld was still out injured and Charlie Gallagher was temporarily out of favour, so it was the same forward line that had played so well at Dundee.

But this time they did not function nearly so well. Neither winger really got going and Clyde, a well-organised, disciplined side who made it fairly obvious that they would be quite happy with a draw, played a tight game and the cries of frustration were audible and obvious long before half-time. One could not help believing, however, that the boos and the slow handclap were a bit hard on the players, given their other achievements so far this season, and it certainly did little to gee up their efforts. But then again Celtic supporters have never been known for their tolerance of a mediocre display.

Eventually, in the 72nd minute, Celtic got a breakthrough in a very unsatisfactory way through a penalty which most newspapers agreed was soft. It looked like nothing other than a clash of bodies between Clyde right-back Harry Glasgow and Joe McBride. Jock Stein in next week's *Celtic View* would concede that if it had been the other way round, he would have been very upset. But referee Mr Kelly of Motherwell thought that it was a penalty kick – and he is the only one who mattered - and after a prolonged Clyde protest, Ian Young put Celtic ahead. There was relief at this, and five minutes later Celtic scored again – once again the goal scored not by a forward but by the other full-back, Tommy Gemmell. Tommy was of course now established as an attacking full-back and encouraged to be so by Jock Stein – he hadn't always been in the past – and he came charging upfield as Hughes was taking a corner kick. He received the ball from a short corner and when the Clyde defence were expecting him to cross to someone else, he simply shot through a ruck of players and made the score 2-0.

That seemed to be that, but Clyde did not give in and with five minutes to go Ian Stewart took advantage of defensive uncertainty and brought them back into the game. The last five minutes took an age to pass, but eventually Mr Kelly brought proceedings to an end. If there was a lesson in all this, it was that League titles are not won by champagne football, but by the grinding out of victories. There was a long way to go, but Celtic were already top of the table, the only side which had won both its League games.

And so it was on to the compact little ground of Stark's Park, Kirkcaldy for the quarter-final and a really marvellous display of attacking football, which is still talked about yet in Kirkcaldy…and not only by Celtic supporters. Many Raith Rovers supporters agree that football of this kind should be preserved as an example of how the game should be played. Sadly, there does not seem to be any celluloid material of this occasion. It was a Wednesday night, and only the first leg of a quarter-final played at a ground some distance from Glasgow, so TV coverage did not happen.

Raith Rovers, managed by George Farm, were the only undefeated team in Scotland. They had been in the Second Division since 1963 but were clearly aiming to bounce back. Their centre-half was no less a person than Bobby Evans, who had played for Celtic between 1944 and 1960, and had now moved on from Third Lanark, making the unusual step of moving from being a Manager or Player-Manager back to being just a player! He was now, clearly, in the twilight of his career but still with a great deal of football left in him. It was largely due to him that Rovers had qualified for the quarter-final of the Scottish League Cup. And they had several other talented players in, for example, Pat Gardner who would go on and star for Dunfermline, scoring twice in their Scottish Cup triumph of 1968, and Ian Porterfield who would become a legend for Sunderland, scoring their goal in that epic English FA Cup final win of 1973.

About 18,000 packed into Stark's Park that night, with shoals of buses arriving from Glasgow and elsewhere and taking up their places on the Kirkcaldy Prom before disgorging their happy and enthused green-and-white clad supporters singing their songs about what a grand old team they had, and how they would no longer tolerate the despot or the slave, punctuated with the awe-inspiring chant of *"Cel-Tic"* followed by three hand claps, with the occasional friendly discussion with the locals about what Joe McBride or John Hughes were going to do to the Raith Rovers side.

The famous old compact ground featured an odd-shaped grandstand which went round a corner into an L shape (opened by Celtic in December 1922) and on the other side the old wooden coal shed of a standing enclosure in front of the Aberdeen to London railway line. It was as embarrassing to Raith Rovers supporters as the Jungle was to us, and it shook alarmingly when a train passed behind it. The ground had in recent years been supplemented by two more modern shelters behind each goal. It was a strange one but bristled with Scottish football history and it had provided entertainment now for many years for the Fife hewers of coal and the crafters of linoleum. And tonight "the queer like smell" of linoleum hit the nostrils immediately on disembarkation from the bus. Raith Rovers had never won anything of note, but they had often provided some tough opposition to Celtic, particularly in their heydays of the early 1920s and the mid 1950s.

The teams were:

Raith Rovers:

Reid, McKeown and Gray: Stein, Evans and Porterfield: Hutchison, Gardner, Richardson, Lyall and McLean.

Celtic:

Fallon, Young and Gemmell; Murdoch, McNeill and Clark; Johnstone, Gallagher, McBride, Lennox and Hughes.

Referee: *Mr W Elliott, Barrhead*

Much interest was displayed among the Celtic fans about how Jimmy Johnstone would play. He had missed a few games of late, and there was great speculation that this superbly talented redhead did not always get on well with Manager Jock Stein. Tottenham Hotspur were represented in the crowd that night by their Assistant Manager Eddie Bailey, and a bid for Johnstone was expected, although how the neurotic Uddingston man would have coped with the bright lights of swinging sixties London was a matter of some doubt. He and his Manager did indeed have more than a few run-ins with each other, but they had several things in common, one of them being a deep-rooted love of the west of Scotland, and a reluctance to leave!

Following a short delay to allow more of the crowd in through the turnstiles, which were, frankly, inadequate for the occasion, Celtic started off playing towards the Beveridge Park or the town end of the ground, and as early as the first minute Tommy Gemmell had hit the bar. It was Joe McBride, who had been in and out of the team since his arrival, who opened the scoring after some fine build-up play, and before Raith had a chance to come to terms with that one Bobby Lennox scored another. Soon after that came Raith's one moment of glory when Jockie Richardson pulled one back, but Celtic had made it 3-1 before half-time through Jimmy Johnstone and the wonder was that there had not been more as Celtic put on a devastating display of football.

The second half saw another five goals, a hat-trick from John Hughes who looked unstoppable as he rampaged down the left wing and another two from McBride to give him a hat-trick as well. It was pure football at its best, and to their credit, Raith Rovers never descended to dirty tactics and their supporters stayed and clapped the fine play of Celtic and the occasional good move from their own team.

One had to feel a little sorry for Bobby Evans. Now ageing, and with his bright red hair now greyer than Celtic fans had remembered when he last played for them five years ago, he had no answer to McBride and Lennox. He was still remembered with a certain amount of affection by the Celtic fans, even though it was no secret that the relationship between Evans and Jock Stein was nowadays a polite, formal one rather than a warm one. Some fans thought that Evans might have been a great asset as a backroom man for Stein, but no such invitation was ever issued. Still, the occasional good pass by Evans, now 38, was greeted with a ripple of applause from the green and white bedecked.

It was only, of course, the end of the first leg, with the return to be played at Celtic Park next week, but this result rendered that a formality. Those who saw the game at Stark's Park that autumn night, however, remain convinced that this was the way that football should be played, with the play of Bobby Murdoch especially recalled as he sent inch-perfect passes to Johnstone, Lennox, McBride and Hughes almost at will, while Charlie Gallagher showed tremendous trickery and skill. It was Celtic football at its best. History does not recall what Eddie Bailey of Tottenham Hotspur made of it all. No bid was made for any player, but he must have been mightily impressed.

It was not really a great night for the "wee teams" in the competition, for Rangers, Hibs and Kilmarnock all got the better of Airdrie, Alloa and Ayr United in the other quarter-finals, but Celtic were now aware that a stern test awaited them on Saturday in the shape of their first visit of the season to Ibrox to play a Rangers side who had so far been outshone by the events at Celtic Park, but who had watched it all with a grim determination to fight back.

There was still a certain mystique about Ibrox. Celtic seldom did well there in the past, like so many other teams "psyched out" by the size of the place and the feeling that, somehow or other, Rangers were meant to rule in Scotland. Stein had identified that as one of his main tasks – to persuade his men that they were entitled to win at Ibrox and that they could do it. It seemed that on the back of that great win at Raith Rovers, this might be the day.

Not, however, this time. The result was Rangers 2 Celtic 1, and although Peter Thomson on BBC TV (the legendary and notorious

"Blue Peter" whose face always told you Rangers' result before he announced it!) crowed about a *"convincing"* and *"decisive"* victory, it was in fact no such thing. The key point of the game was the injury to Billy McNeill early in the second half which really prevented a Celtic comeback. As it was, Celtic almost did snatch an equaliser through the services of the injured McNeill near the end, and a draw would have been a fair result.

Celtic were without Joe McBride, once again suffering from the injury problems that would be his bane for the rest of his short Parkhead career. This meant that John Hughes would have to be deployed in the middle, Divers replaced Gallagher, whom Jock believed to be too fragile for the hurly-burly and coarse tackling of the Rangers defenders, and Bertie Auld came back after an injury. The forward line thus read *Johnstone, Divers, Hughes, Lennox and Auld*.

For some strange reason, the game was not all-ticket, even though Glasgow and Scotland had talked about little else all week, and with 76,000 already inside Ibrox before kick-off time, the decision was made to close the gates with thousands still outside, particularly at the Broomloan Road or Celtic End of the ground. The result was chaos, and although a serious riot was narrowly avoided, we had the spectacle of literally hundreds of Celtic fans scaling the walls, even those walls with barbed wire on top. A considerable amount of them did indeed gain admission, but quite a few were arrested for their pains in a scene which was not dissimilar to a war film in which POWs escaped – except this was a break-in rather than a breakout.

The decision to close the turnstiles was not the best, for there probably was room on the terracing for everyone – just! As it was, such games were now more or less all-ticket after this, and a crowd of 76,000 is huge by any standards, even those of the 1960s.

The goals were all scored in the first half and two of them were penalties, correctly awarded by the bulky and stern Mr Wharton.

Jim Forrest had scored for Rangers after Tommy Gemmell miskicked his clearance, and then after John Hughes had equalised with a penalty, George McLean did likewise with his for Rangers. In the second half, Celtic tried hard but hampered by the injury to McNeill, simply could not get the equaliser, and 2-1 was the final score to the intense disappointment of the Celtic fans.

But there are times when one must lose a battle in order to win a war. There were three areas at least in which Celtic disappointed. One was goalkeeping and questions began to be asked about the likeable but fallible John Fallon; another was inside-right where John Divers simply found the game passing him by and there was one occasion near the end when he could have prodded home an equaliser, but opted to let the ball go thinking it was going in anyway… but it went past the post; and also for the first time, questions were asked about full-back Ian Young, hitherto a great success, but who definitely lost out today to Willie Johnston on several occasions. Gemmell too had made a mistake for the goal and one often wondered whether he might have been better as an out-and-out forward instead of trying to combine two roles. And was Jimmy Johnstone, brilliant player though he could be, mature enough as yet? And Bertie Auld seemed to be not quite as fit as he ought to be.

It was probably just a bad day. The result certainly meant more to Rangers and their supporters than it did to us. They had watched 1965 unravel with apprehension and horror, and this result did put on a brake, temporarily at least, to the Celtic juggernaut. It also lured Rangers and their fans into a false sense of security, and arrogance returned.

But Jock thought about these things. Europe now appeared, in the shape of the Dutch Cup-winners with the unlikely name of Go Ahead Deventer. First, however, there was the basically irrelevant second leg of the Scottish League Cup quarter-final against Raith Rovers at Celtic Park. Young Irish goalkeeper John Kennedy was given a game in the goal, and John Cushley replaced the injured

Billy McNeill. Surprisingly for a game in which a team was already 8-1 to the good, some 9,000 turned up at Parkhead. Bobby Evans was given a cheer, but the crowd were subdued in the first half, still suffering from Saturday and the lack of ability of the forwards to break down the Rovers defence. The tide eventually broke down the wall in the second half – first Murdoch, then Auld twice before Hughes, after 80 minutes of frustrating fecklessness, showed what he could do and broke through with a splendid run and a pass to Chalmers to finish it off.

And then Aberdeen came to town. Those with long memories recalled the day of January 30 when it all changed for Celtic and wondered whether a repeat was possible. To the delight of everyone in the 35,000 crowd, it was, and the Ibrox blues of last week were blown away with a splendid performance which ended in the famous score of 7-1.

There was a major surprise in the team selection, for Jock Stein fielded his third goalkeeper in eight days. It would be a fair bet that quite a few Celtic supporters had forgotten about Ronnie Simpson. He had played a few games last season but had disappeared from the first-team shortly after the arrival of Stein and many supporters might have just assumed that he had been given a free transfer. But here he was back again, at the age of nearly 35, in the Celtic goal with a very long career behind him including two English FA Cup medals for Newcastle United in 1952 and 1955 and an appearance for Great Britain in the 1948 Olympic Games. And little did we realise that the best was still to come! At the moment, he looked like a stop-gap, and the general view was that if Stein did not like John Fallon he would go into the transfer market sooner or later for another goalkeeper. The forward line read *Johnstone, Auld, McBride, Lennox and Hughes*, and a fit again Joe McBride made all the difference.

Frankly, in 1965, Aberdeen were a poor side. They had had their great days 10 years ago and would very soon come back but they had fallen into the trap of buying Scandinavians (a ploy that worked for Morton and Dundee United but not everyone) and were struggling, to the increasing disillusionment of their fans. Today they were swept aside by a Celtic side who were clearly angry at last week's disappointment, and the Dons were put to the sword. Every Celtic forward scored, with Lennox and Johnstone netting two, and the pick was another wonder goal from Hughes just before half time. For the Dons, suffering their second Parkhead hammering in 1965, there was not even the excuse of a frozen pitch this time!

It was a good game and a good day for Celtic. Rangers had drawn against Dundee at Dens Park that day, so it was reckoned that half of the damage last week had been repaired. In the meantime, an interesting scenario had unfolded in the Jock Stein, Celtic or Scotland saga. The rule in these days was that if more than two players from a club had been chosen for International duty, a game could be postponed. The agreement between Celtic and the SFA had been that Jock Stein could manage Scotland as long as Celtic were not in any way inconvenienced. This effectively meant that if three Celtic players were chosen for Scotland duty on October 2, when Northern Ireland played Scotland, then Motherwell v Celtic would be postponed, and Jock Stein would be the Manager of Scotland on that day. On the other hand, if only two Celts were on International duty, Jock would manage Celtic at Fir Park! It seemed a very amateurish and ad hoc method of running things, but there one was.

It was therefore a matter of some comment and amusement that Billy McNeill and John Hughes were picked for Scotland (deservedly and without any great argument or controversy in either case) and Bobby Murdoch was chosen as a reserve to travel. This was also a good choice because Murdoch could, of course, fill in, in emergency circumstances, either in the half-back line or the forward line. To what extent Stein himself had any say in the selection – in theory he didn't, for the Selectors chose the team! –

we do not know, but there is little doubt that the selection suited a lot of people! Celtic's trip to Motherwell was postponed and indeed would not be played for seven months when the circumstances would be totally different.

On September 29, Lennox scored a hat-trick, Johnstone two and Hughes one as Celtic beat Go Ahead Deventer 6-0 without any real bother. There had been an odd couple of days before the game (Celtic had arrived in the Netherlands on the Sunday night) when Mr Cor Van Es, the Go Ahead Deventer coach, went around telling everyone how good Celtic were and how his team had little chance against them. This may have been an attempt to unsettle Celtic but Stein, without ever being aggressive or anti-social to Mr Van Es, fed him a great deal of disinformation about what the team was going to be, ignored all the nonsensical grovelling and played his normal game, which made the second leg a formality.

No-one would wish ever to be disrespectful to Go Ahead Deventer, but their appearance in the European Cup Winners' Cup said something perhaps not about Dutch football necessarily but about how highly some countries rated their national Cup tournaments. In Scotland, and possibly even more so in England, the Cup is highly rated, being older than the respective Leagues. One would not say that the Scottish Cup was more important than the Scottish League, but it was certainly a very important part of the Scottish season. As far as the Netherlands were concerned, one wondered why Go Ahead were the representatives. The answer was that they had lost the Dutch Cup final to Feyenoord, who had also won the League and were therefore in the European Cup. Where were Ajax, Twente Enschede, Sparta Rotterdam, Eindhoven? To be tactful about it, Go Ahead had done well to earn the right to play against Celtic!

And thus Celtic finished the month of September. It had been a good month, the only black spot being the defeat at Ibrox. October would be a far more demanding month, and it would give Celtic an immediate chance to get back at Rangers. In some ways, October 1965 would be as vital and axiomatic a month in the future of Celtic as any.

CHAPTER TEN

OCTOBER

Scotland were disappointed in Belfast to lose 2-3 on Saturday, 2 October 1965. McNeill was not as dominant in the air as he usually was, and one or two chances were missed by the forwards. John Hughes did not star either and there was a palpable air of unhappiness about the squad.

But there were immediately other things on Stein's mind. Monday, 4 October was the date scheduled for the Scottish League Cup semi-final against Hibs at Ibrox, while Rangers were playing Kilmarnock at Hampden on the Wednesday night. There had already been a considerable amount of dispute about the venue, and the question was legitimately asked that unless both semi-finals were being played on the same night, why couldn't both of them be at Hampden? Or if Celtic had to play their match at Ibrox, why shouldn't Rangers be asked to play at Parkhead? There was also the question of the Ibrox floodlights, but that didn't come into the question until later.

It mattered not at the moment. The Scottish League, stubborn and unbending as always, decided that they were not going to give in to such emotional blackmail or even common sense, and the Celtic v Hibs game went ahead at Ibrox on 4 October. The weather was foul, and the ground was heavy, but that is exactly what Scottish football is all about!

Poor floodlights or not, inadequate cover or not, 46,074 spectators turned up to watch an absolutely thrilling game of football in which Celtic were perhaps lucky to get a replay. Yet no-one could grudge anyone anything on this night of splendid football. Hibs had been in great form recently, and Celtic saw why that night. Stein dropped Chalmers and Auld from the forward line which read *Johnstone, Gallagher, McBride, Lennox and Hughes*, and Ronnie Simpson was retained in the goal in place of John Fallon. Hibs had a mighty defence in Pat Stanton and John McNamee, and some wonderful forwards in Pat Quinn and Neil Martin – and of course, no-one knew that better than Jock Stein!

Celtic started off playing towards the Copland Road end of the ground and went ahead within the first ten minutes. John Hughes won a throw-in on the left and slipped it to Bobby Lennox, who sent over an inch-perfect cross for Joe McBride to get the better of McNamee and head home. In less than ten minutes, Hibs were back on level terms. Again, it was a cross and header. The cross came from Jim Scott and it found Neil Martin who beat ex-Hib Ronnie Simpson in the goal.

Half-time came with the scores still level and no-one able to separate the two teams, but it was Hibs who went ahead on the hour mark, when Eric Stevenson controlled a difficult ball and slipped it to Neil Martin who scored his second goal of the night. It was little wonder that Martin was in great demand by teams in England.

Things now looked black for Celtic as the minutes slipped away. The effort from the Celts could not be faulted, but McNamee was an absolute rock in the centre of the defence. He did of course have a point to prove against Celtic and may even have felt that he was better than McNeill, but certainly tonight there was little wrong with his performance as Celtic redoubled their efforts. Celtic felt that they should have had a penalty kick as Pat Stanton held Joe McBride in front of an empty goal, but Mr Davidson said no. As the game neared its end, the slighter-built Johnstone, Gallagher and Lennox seemed to tire ever so slightly, the raucous Celtic support, previously so animated and excited, went quiet and the weaker brethren began to head homewards to the Copland Road underground station and the waiting buses, while the smaller, but still substantial Hibs support began to sniff victory.

One wonders how life might have been changed if referee Bobby Davidson, much disliked by Celtic supporters for his perceived anti-Celtic feelings, had been a little more keen on his warm shower in his dressing-room. He was seen by supporters to look at his watch before Tommy Gemmell broke down the left and shot. Goalkeeper Willie Wilson had the shot covered but could not hold the wet ball, which rebounded off his chest to the eager feet of Bobby Lennox, who prodded the ball home for an equaliser which released delirium in the Broomloan Road end of the ground behind the goal.

"Kerrydale" in *The Celtic View* uses a rather brilliant historical parallel when he compares this to Alan Craig in the 1931 Scottish Cup final. The younger supporters had to ask more about this of their fathers (yet most Celtic families talked about this game endlessly!) but poor Craig was the Motherwell centre-half who had conceded an own goal in the last minute of the game to grant Celtic a replay in 1931 – which Celtic duly won 4-2. "Kerrydale" clearly knew his history and this had a great subliminal effect on the Celtic support, for it created the impression that Celtic were going to win the replay.

But before anyone could even think of a replay, there followed a period of 30 minutes extra-time, often an anti-climax between two exhausted teams, but not on this occasion. The 22 players found reserves of energy from somewhere and the pace never slackened. Both teams had chances, but no-one could score and indeed it had to be said that both teams were worth a replay when Bobby Davidson eventually signalled retreat. And so a replay it was.

But now football politics began to enter the equation. Using *The Celtic View*, and under the cover of "Kerrydale," Jock Stein had raised the issue of the Ibrox floodlights which he said were inadequate. Hibs joined in the fun as well. *"It is the unanimous opinion of both sets of players that the Ibrox lighting is not good enough. Neither Hibs nor Celtic want this game to be settled by some freakish error or accident caused by inability to follow the ball,"* said "Kerrydale," and that was plain enough.

Unlike Celtic Park and Hampden (and Easter Road for that matter), Ibrox did not have pylons and it was claimed that the lights along the roof of the stand and the enclosure did not illuminate certain areas of the pitch well enough, particularly on foggy nights. There may have been a certain justification for all this, but anyone who thought that this was NOT a deliberate plot to unsettle Rangers is guilty of extreme naivety. Teams like Tottenham Hotspur, Real Madrid and Inter Milan had played at Ibrox under these "inadequate" floodlights in recent years, and there had been no major protests or refusals to play.

Rangers had always been very proud of their stadium. As recently as 1962, *The Topical Times Football Annual* had featured the stadium as "Glasgow's Football Palace" and much had been made of marble staircases, plush lounges, huge dressing-rooms with pictures of the Queen and the like. Now here was a complaint about something as basic as floodlights! Using his contacts, Stein persuaded Hibs and their supporters (who didn't like Rangers either!) to join in the protest and to try to get the game moved to Hampden, with the Secretary of the Hibs Supporters Federation even making the dubious claim that, for a midweek game, Hampden was easier to reach from Edinburgh than Ibrox was.

There had to be a replay, but where and when? It couldn't be next midweek because there was a Scotland v Poland World Cup match, and the game had to be scheduled for Monday, 18 October, only five days before the final. The venue was the bone of contention, and both teams, Hibs in particular, made a dignified appeal for the game to be played at Hampden, *The Celtic View* giving prominence to a letter from Mr Forbes of the Hibs Supporters Association about how Hampden would be preferable. A couple of readers' letters also appeared deploring the inadequacy of the Ibrox floodlights. But the

Scottish League, stubborn to the last and clearly impervious to the suspicions that they were in the pay of Rangers, decreed that it would have to be Ibrox again.

The other semi-final, at Hampden on Wednesday, 6 October, was an astonishing game. Rangers, playing brilliantly, were 6-1 ahead midway through the second half, but then they suddenly lost control. Kilmarnock's Tommy McLean scored three goals, and Rangers were mighty glad to hear Mr Paterson's final whistle with the score at 6-4. It showed that Rangers could be quite majestic, but that they could be vulnerable if someone put pressure on them. Killie's three goals caused the Ibrox supporters more than a little anxiety.

There then followed (on Thursday night, and no-one seemed to see any problem in Celtic playing on Monday, Thursday and Saturday of that week!) one of the more pointless games in this season when Go Ahead Deventer, already 0-6 down, came to Celtic Park to play the second leg of the European Cup Winners' Cup tie. The game is only notable for it being the debut of Jim Craig (Stein having decided to give Ian Young a deserved rest) and a headed goal by Joe McBride as Celtic won 1-0 in front of a disappointed crowd of about 18,000. There was a certain amusement and admiration in the attitude of the Dutchmen to the Celtic team, of whom they were clearly in awe. Jimmy Johnstone was badly fouled and before Jimmy could retaliate (he was often guilty of this) several Go Ahead men apologised to him and told the perpetrator that he was out of order! When Steve Chalmers was injured, following an accidental collision with the goalkeeper, three Dutchmen rushed to his aid! It was actually the way that the game should be played, but as a football match, this was a disappointment.

It was a totally different matter on Saturday when Hearts came to town. The events of April 24 of this year had effectively caused Celtic and Hearts to reverse roles. Celtic had won the Scottish Cup, but Hearts had lost the League on the same day and their supporters were now sentenced to a generation and several decades of mediocrity. They would now turn nasty as well, beginning to ape the songs of Rangers supporters and failing to see the sheer incongruity of Derry and sashes in Dalry and Gorgie, and this abominable trait was beginning to develop when the Edinburgh men came to Celtic Park on Saturday, 9 October.

It was a fine autumn day, and the crowd was well over 35,000. Stein brought back Charlie Gallagher, that fine passer of a ball, and it turned out to be a wise move. In fact, although Charlie had played several games for Celtic this season in the first eleven and the reserves, this was actually his first game at Celtic Park, and today the Parkhead crowd saw just exactly what they had been missing.

The forward line read *Johnstone, Gallagher, McBride, Lennox and Hughes*. It had been rumoured for some time that Stein was interested in Willie Wallace of Hearts, but he did little to boost his chances of a transfer or indeed a Scottish cap when he got the ball just outside the penalty box but shot hurriedly high and wide past Ronnie Simpson's goal.

Joe McBride at the other end was far more clinical when Bobby Lennox put him through to tuck a neat ball past Jim Cruickshank in the 12th minute, then 20 minutes later repeated the process to make it 2-0. This time Joe lashed the ball home from about 20 yards, and it was one of these moments when there was a split-second of total bewildered silence before the crowd erupted in acclaim. Just before half-time came another goal, this time from Bobby Lennox after Jimmy Johnstone remembered the golden rule that the fleet-footed Lennox needed the ball in front of him so that he could score without breaking stride, and Bobby had the simplest of tap-ins.

Seconds later, referee Mr Henderson of Dundee blew for half-time with Parkhead in an uproar and reflecting, not without cause, that this was the best Celtic team they had seen for years. They had put seven goals past Aberdeen a fortnight ago, and now they were

3-0 up against Hearts. And it continued in the second half, when a long ball out of defence found Lennox who ran on and hooked the ball over the head of Cruickshank. That was on the hour mark, and then ten minutes later, Charlie Gallagher scored a great goal when he sent a swerving shot past the goalkeeper to put Celtic 5-0 up.

There was a slight sting in the tail however, when Celtic visibly relaxed, possibly lulled into a sense of false security by the songs of triumph resounding all over the stadium, and Hearts managed to pull a couple of goals back through Alan Gordon. It was too late to make any significant difference to the scoreline, but it did not save the Celtic defenders from the wrath of Jock Stein at the end. They were forgiven, however, by the fans who left Parkhead that night in rare good humour. They were now confident that form like this would be sufficient to deal with what was to come in the near future.

And it was a difficult programme with Falkirk at Brockville, then the League Cup semi-final replay (which could of course lead to a Cup final against Rangers) before a trip to Dens Park to take on Dundee, all before the end of October. But the immediate midweek would see Celtic take a back seat, because Scotland had a crucial World Cup game when Poland came to Hampden. McNeill, Hughes, and of course Stein would be very much involved in that one.

So Jock went off to Largs with the Scotland squad, while *The Celtic View* kept beating the drum about the Ibrox floodlights, this time adding the point that the game between Rangers and Celtic on September 18 had seen problems of crowd congestion. This was an irrelevant factor, it has to be said, because the Celtic v Hibs game was never likely to attract anything like as large a crowd as an Old Firm game, but it still remained a stick to beat Rangers with.

But the Scottish League remained obdurate. Celtic and Hibs both reluctantly accepted the decision, but the point had been made. Rangers were duly rattled and from now on, European opposition and even Scottish teams who played at Ibrox in midweek games would look upwards at the floodlights and ask questions. It was one of the many propaganda battles that Celtic won against Rangers. The immediate story had now run its length, however, and the replay would go ahead at Ibrox.

Meanwhile the attention of the nation turned to Scotland v Poland. In theory, although Jock Stein was in charge of the team, the eleven players were actually still chosen by the Selectors. To what extent Jock "talked" to the Selectors and expressed his preferences we do not know, but when the team was announced on the Tuesday afternoon, there was only one Celtic player in Billy McNeill, and no place for John Hughes.

It was at this point that the nation really began to take seriously the possibility of Scotland playing in the World Cup finals in England. The idea of travelling to a place like Sunderland or Liverpool to support Scotland had its attractions, and a huge crowd of 107,580 turned up at Hampden to see this game. The idea that Scotland could even win the World Cup was not entirely fanciful. It would be more or less a home tournament for Scotland, and we knew (did we not?), that we are at least as good as the real hosts, England.

The game itself was of an exceptionally painful nature, and even those who trotted out the old clichés of *"the Scottish penchant for self-destruction"* were aware that even that was not enough to verbalise the pain that was felt in the crowd and the millions listening to the game throughout the world on radio. It was not on television until later that night and it was in highlights form, but by that time, the result was known, and the TV viewers duly turned their backs on Scotland.

Billy McNeill had opened the scoring for Scotland. He had come up for a corner kick, hoping to repeat what had happened at Hampden in April in the Scottish Cup final, but this time the ball came to his foot. 1-0 for Scotland, and things looked good. A strong penalty claim was then turned down, as was another more half-hearted one, and several other chances were missed, one in particular by the man who divided the Scottish support more than anyone else, Denis Law.

Half-time came and went and Scotland were still 1-0 up. This was an accident looking for a place to happen, as the Scottish saying goes, and Scotland still failed to increase their lead. What we all suspected would happen duly did, and Scotland conceded two late and infinitely preventable goals in the 80th and 85th minutes. Poland's World Cup hopes were immediately resurrected, and Scotland's plunged into extreme doubt, while the supporters despaired. Two qualifying games remained against Italy, home and away, but Scotland would now have to win them both, and that was unlikely. The crowd expressed their feelings strongly at the end before departing into one of the worst traffic jams that Glasgow had ever seen.

Two men were particularly blamed for this catastrophe – Denis Law and Alex Hamilton. Law had missed chances and had not seemed too bothered about the defeat. It had been recalled that when Scotland lost 10 days ago in Ireland, Law seemed to find it funny. He was blamed all the more for this game because everyone knew that he had the ability to change things – and didn't! Hamilton was simply caught out of position too often and, in truth, had never really recovered from the goal John Hughes had scored against him at Dens Park on September 4!

Jock Stein was not blamed for it all, except of course by the lunatic fringe of the Rangers support, but he must have been deeply hurt by all this, and possibly even begun to doubt his abilities at that level, but he had no time to dwell on things or to indulge in self-pity. He returned to Celtic Park on Thursday and turned his attentions to Falkirk.

Before that game, melancholic news reached Celtic Park and the older generation of supporters of the passing of Joe Dodds at the age of 77. This removed the last remaining link of *Shaw, McNair and Dodds*, the iron defence of 1913/14. Dodds could also play at centre-half and left-half and he was a much-loved old Celt. McMenemy had died in the summer, and now the only Celt of the great pre-World War I days left was Davie McLean, a somewhat peripheral figure at Celtic Park admittedly, but one who was by no means finished yet and who, as we shall see, still came to Celtic Park and Hampden to see big games.

But now for Brockville! If there was any club which symbolised in a way the fortunes of the under-performing Celtic teams of the late 1950s and early 1960s it was the Bairns of Falkirk. Celtic had played some good games against them, but far too often Celtic let themselves down at Brockville, as often as not to the accompaniment of hooliganism with memories of men like Pat Crerand and Dunky Mackay standing with a bottle in their hands appealing to the supporters to behave themselves. Slowly, Jock was winning the hooligan battle in tandem with the playing battle. Today, October 16 saw all that was good about Celtic and Scottish football, and give or take the odd hiccup, the behaviour of both sets of fans was exemplary.

Many of the problems at Brockville in the past had centred on overcrowding. Today the crowd was about 18,000 but they were well-marshalled and controlled. Ronnie Simpson failed a fitness test on his shoulder (something that was to cause him more problems in future years and would eventually lead to his retirement in 1969) and John Fallon was brought back. Apart from that, the team was the same as had defeated Hearts at Parkhead last week.

Falkirk scored first and it was through the agency of a man who would become a real character in Scottish football, particularly when Manager of Partick Thistle, John Lambie, the man who kept pigeons, swore like a trooper on Saturday and went to Church on Sunday! Every one of the seven goals scored that day would be a cracker and the first one set the trend as right-back Lambie was in the right place to hammer home a cutback from a corner kick. A couple of minutes later, Bobby Lennox equalised from a

Joe McBride feed, but after chances and good goalkeeping at both ends, Falkirk scored before half-time when Sammy Wilson (not the Sammy Wilson of Celtic's 7-1 League Cup win) swivelled and scored a cracker of a goal for Falkirk.

Bobby Murdoch equalised for Celtic in 60 minutes with a shot from outside the penalty box, but then Johnny Graham put the Bairns back in front by dribbling past Fallon. A minute later, a shot from Jimmy Johnstone hit the post and bounced in, and one felt that that might have been enough for everyone. A 3-3 draw would not have been unfair to either side, but it was Bobby Lennox within the last ten minutes with a fierce drive which beat Willie Whigham.

The game finished to great cheers from both sets of supporters, and Jock Stein and the Celtic party were full of admiration for the Falkirk team. At Easter Road that day, Rangers beat Hibs 2-1. Naturally, this was a disappointment for Celtic supporters, but it did have the benefit of perhaps unsettling Hibs in view of the replay showdown now appearing on the horizon for Monday night.

Celtic now decided to have an extra training session on Sunday, so that potential injures could be checked, but it was a gentle workout followed by baths and massage to keep the muscles in trim. It was ascertained that Ronnie Simpson was in fact fit, but that did not necessarily mean that he was playing, for Jock said that nothing would be divulged until kick-off time. Hibs said likewise, so both sets of fans set out for Ibrox without any clear insight as to what or whom they were going to see.

In the event, before a crowd of 51,423 in a thin film of fog which did not impair anyone's vision in spite of the alleged inadequacy of the Ibrox floodlights, the teams were on predictable lines. Simpson was in the goal and the forward line read *Johnstone, Gallagher, McBride, Lennox and Hughes*. Hibs were also as expected, but what was not expected was the scale of the Celtic victory. The first game had been a classic between two equally matched teams; this one saw Celtic at their best and Hibs more or less totally outclassed in a way that baffled their supporters and journalists alike, although a clue was perhaps given when Neil Martin left for Sunderland soon afterwards.

McBride scored first with the Hibs defence appealing in vain for offside, then Hughes added a second before 20 minutes were up. Celtic were well on top and when Lennox scored in the second half the game was over. We then saw John McNamee bringing on himself one of the silliest dismissals you could imagine. He fouled John Hughes (and one suspects there may have been something personal in this) by scything him down. Rightly he was booked by referee Bobby Davidson for this, but then he persisted in arguing – never the wisest course of actions with Davidson – and he was sent off. Even then, he still would not go, and was eventually escorted from the field by a couple of his teammates. Bobby Murdoch then scored a fourth to put the tin lid on a fine night's performance. No more was said about the floodlights, although apparently at half-time there had been a loudspeaker appeal, presumably a wind up, for an electrician to make himself known!

Many years later, a story emerged about Jock Stein that night. The players were in the dressing-room celebrating and singing. Jock disapproved, because although it had been a good victory, the big job remained to be done on Saturday. Apparently, he slapped his own face so that it was red and angry-looking, burst open the door and tore into everyone for premature celebration and lack of respect to defeated opponents Hibs. No-one knows if this story is true, but it would certainly be echoed in Wednesday's Celtic View when Stein said that he wanted Saturday's team to be *"the most determined ever to have worn the green and white striped shirts."*

The days between the Hibs game and the final saw the propaganda battle in full spate. Celtic had no injury worries and mentioned this every time a journalist looked in their direction, whereas Rangers were compelled to admit that George McLean would be unfit and unable to play. Sean Fallon wrote a series of articles in the normally

Rangers-orientated Scottish Daily Express in which he predicted a Celtic victory, and he wrote it in such a way that he was almost assuming that Celtic would win anyway. Much was made about how nice it would be if Ronnie Simpson who had assumed that his career was over several years ago could win a Scottish League Cup medal to add to the two FA Cup medals he had won with Newcastle United in 1952 and 1955. By Friday night, Gair Henderson in *The Evening Times* was predicting a Celtic victory as long as they managed to keep the *"touchline terrors"* of Henderson and Johnston quiet.

There was little wonder that a huge crowd turned up. Last year had seen a 2-1 win for Rangers in the same League Cup final, but now the tables had turned and Celtic, full of confidence, were managed by Jock Stein, from whom positivity radiated. The main question seemed to be *"Could Celtic win another trophy in 1965 to maintain their improvement or could Rangers fight back and prove that Celtic's April triumph was simply a one-off?"* The stakes could hardly be higher.

This was possibly the most significant Celtic v Rangers game of them all. This was the game which swung the balance of power, more or less irreversibly, from Rangers to Celtic for the next 10 years and more, and this was the game which guaranteed Celtic a permanent place at the top of Scottish football, when for a few years in the early 1960s, they had slipped dangerously close to insignificance.

The reasons for all this were complex, and yet they were simple too. The game must be seen in the context of the last few years of the early 60's, when Celtic teams came out to play Rangers with an almost visible and tangible look about them, as if they knew that they were expecting to lose. No matter how well they had played up till then, there was almost an immutable law of Heaven that Celtic had to lose to Rangers. Since the glorious 7-1 game of 1957, children had grown up knowing little else and were almost schooled and programmed into accepting it. Season 1963/64 in particular had seen a fine Celtic team, but one who had lost five times to

Rangers with an eerie pattern in every case of holding them well for the first half-hour, missing a few chances, then encountering some bad luck in the shape of a refereeing decision or a defensive error... then a complete, dismal, collapse in the second half...and loads of complaints and moaning, but nothing tangible.

The difference was now Jock Stein. The Scottish Cup had been annexed in April 1965, but, other than in a Glasgow Cup tie at the end of the 1964/65 season, Stein's Celtic had still not yet beaten Rangers. When the clubs met at Ibrox a month previously, Celtic had lost 1-2 – a narrow defeat, at least partly to be explained by an injury to Billy McNeill, but a defeat nevertheless, and in the context of the Old Firm, that meant everything. It followed then that a defeat here today might mean that Paradise had NOT in fact arrived in April, and that the long dismal tunnel of defeats to Rangers was to continue.

The precedents were hardly encouraging. Last year at this time, the Scottish League Cup final had seen Celtic well on top, but the "death wish" took over in the missing of vital chances and the lapses of concentration in defence, and there were the vivid memories, still fresh in the mind, of the Scottish Cup replayed final of 1963, when 60,000 supporters turned their backs on Celtic in protest at a spineless and spiritless surrender to the arrogant Rangers. Others recalled the semi-final of the Scottish Cup in 1960, when there had been a competent 1-1 draw followed by a dismal collapse in the replay.

Today attracted a massive crowd of 107,609 (still a record for the Scottish League Cup final) to see this game, which had clearly caught the imagination of both sets of supporters and quite a few of the neutrals as well. The game was by no means the best there has ever been between the two of them – for example, there wasn't a single good goal in the 90 minutes, and very few defence-splitting passes – but what the crowd saw was a different Celtic, a Celtic who were prepared to lower their much-vaunted standards of behaviour and good conduct (so cherished by Chairman Bob Kelly) in pursuit of victory. In short, Celtic descended to the same level as Rangers, and the game, though devoid of the finer touches of football, nevertheless gave some great entertainment, and lacked nothing in passion.

The teams were;

Celtic:

Simpson, Young and Gemmell; Murdoch, McNeill and Clark; Johnstone, Gallagher, McBride, Lennox and Hughes.

Rangers:

Ritchie, Johansen and Provan; Wood, McKinnon and Greig; Henderson, Willoughby, Forrest, Wilson and Johnston.

Referee: *Mr H Phillips, Wishaw*

The first sight of the new Celtic was the foul by Ian Young on Willie Johnston. Johnston - from Cardenden in Fife, the home of John Thomson, had impressed recently for both Rangers and Scotland and he had to be stopped. Young mercilessly scythed him down. This was a clear indication that there was to be "no more Mr Nice Guy" from Celtic. Both players were booked by referee Hugh Phillips, generally regarded as one of the best around, Young for the foul and Johnston for retaliation. Young, apparently, regretted that tackle for the rest of his life; Johnston, on the other hand, went on to collect what is claimed to be a world record for the number of times that he got himself sent off! And of course, the Scotland in Argentina story of 1978 features Johnston as one of its stars!

There would be three more bookings in the game – Bobby Murdoch and Jimmy Johnstone of Celtic and Ron McKinnon of Rangers. Five bookings in a game in 1965 was considered a lot, but possibly by the standards of the 1960s, the game was not quite as dirty as the banner headlines *"Orgy of crudeness"* and the *"X*

Certificate Cup final" of *The Sunday Post* implied. But certainly, few prisoners were taken.

Celtic's two goals came from the penalty spot at the Celtic End of the ground. One was when Ron McKinnon of Rangers - in a moment that he himself could never understand, handled a harmless ball in the box, and the other was when Davie Provan (no relation to the Celtic Davie Provan of the 1980s) brought down Jimmy Johnstone. He claimed there was no contact, but Mr Phillips said there was, and that was that, even though Rangers Chairman John Lawrence allowed himself to be quoted as saying that *"what we wanted to say about that decision could not be printed!"* An odd quote that, come to think of it.

It was interesting to recall an occasion twelve months earlier, in last year's League Cup final, involving the same three characters - Johnstone, Provan and Phillips. A stonewall penalty was turned down at the same end at the same stage of the game. Now, Celtic got the benefit of a debatable decision, and it was hard to resist the conclusion that the difference was the massive figure in the Celtic dugout. *"He cowed referees into fairness,"* was the way that it was put by John Divers.

Anyhow, all this meant that twice the lumbering figure of John Hughes had to come up to the mark. John, that quixotic, moody, temperamental, idiosyncratic, individualistic sort of player, the subject of many a discussion and argument on the terracings and the supporters' buses, must have felt that destiny was calling him on those two occasions. He had already in this campaign scored a marvellous goal at Dens Park, Dundee on the day that we qualified, and today he did not let us down. Billy Ritchie got a hand to one of them, but both went in, and Celtic now reached half-time 2-0 up. The Celtic End cheered, but there was anxiety as well, for 45 long minutes remained.

It was not an easy 45 minutes to watch. There was little in the way of good attacking play by either side, but Celtic had the edge in midfield. Such times as Rangers came close, the Celtic defence dealt with it competently and well, and we began to breathe just a little more easily as the minutes ticked away. Bobby Murdoch was immense and men like Charlie Gallagher and Joe McBride proved their versatility by acting as emergency midfielders and even defenders when required. Behind them all stood Ronnie Simpson, who had twice won an English FA Cup winners' medal with Newcastle United. By no means a tall man, Ronnie nevertheless radiated confidence and re-assurance. It was also apparent that Rangers forwards, Alex Willoughby and Jim Forrest, had their limitations when up against a good defence which stood up to them.

It was neither pretty nor relaxing to watch, and there were even some Celtic supporters who saw it as some sort of affront to the traditions of the club which demanded all-out attack, even when the situation in the game did not lend itself to cavalier, champagne, attacking football. This was a new, more pragmatic, practical Celtic doing what was needed of them. If you want to win honours, you have to do that sometimes.

But then within the last ten minutes, disaster struck when Ronnie Simpson, Ian Young and John Greig all went up for the same ball, and the ball went in off the face of Young! It was a bizarre own goal. Now the heat was turned up as Rangers redoubled their efforts, and we became very introverted and worried on the terracing. McNeill had had a great game but was now showing signs of tiring and beginning to lose the plot. But how comforting it was to see Ronnie Simpson talk quietly to him, banging one fist into the palm of his other hand, and generally taking control of the situation! A father figure indeed, and much loved by the 50,000 anxious hearts behind that goal.

The full-time whistle came, the Cup was presented amidst great scenes of joy, and Celtic set off on their half-lap of honour to show the beautiful three-handled trophy to their own fans. It did not go down well among the "thickos" at the Mount Florida end and some managed to get on to the pitch. No real damage was done, although both trainer Neil Mochan and Ian Young were manhandled, and the real heroes of it all were the Celtic supporters who did not retaliate. It was possibly just as well that superbly fit athletes like John Hughes and Tommy Gemmell did not turn on the undernourished youths of Govan and Larkhall. What a mess they would have made of them!

Breathtakingly, some newspapers managed to say that it was Celtic to blame for it all because of their *"provocative"* lap of honour (cheerfully ignoring all the times that Rangers had held a lap of honour!) and the upshot was that such laps of honour were banned for several years, something that punished Celtic almost exclusively! *The Celtic View* wrote eloquently in Celtic's favour and managed to remind readers of the night of the 7-1 victory in 1957 and how the BBC had managed to lose its pictures of the game! It had nothing to do with 1965, of course, but it kept the pot stirring! To be honest, the BBC had been one of those who had indeed played down, even eschewed, the disorder at the end, and had stressed what a poor, disappointing game it had been. The bottom line, however, had been that Celtic had now won the Scottish League Cup for the third time.

Indeed, *The Celtic View* enjoys itself this week. Reluctant to let a good story go, it gives a couple of precedents about League Cup semi-final venues being changed when it came to a replay. It features Billy McPhail, the hat trick hero of the 7-1 game, has a picture of some Rangers players playing in Celtic shirts in a benefit game, and has a story about Davie McLean who played for Celtic in the 1900s (indeed Davie had attended the game on Saturday with his brother George) but fails to mention that Davie also played for Rangers!

That was, of course, by way of a sideshow. The important thing was that Celtic had won the Scottish League Cup and had shown to the world that they were no longer going to lie down to Rangers as they had done so often, so abjectly and so abysmally in the past. The anonymous writer of *The Times*, in an excellently restrained and thoughtful piece of writing, puts things very well when he sums it all up perspicaciously by saying, *"They (Celtic) are moving into a new era of success."* No-one knew just how successful we were going to be, but everyone agrees that things might have been different, if we had not beaten Rangers in this final which was low on skill, but high on significance for the future.

And Rangers and their fans knew it! It was my misfortune that evening to be "caught behind enemy lines" as it were, "cut off from my unit" and to be travelling back into Glasgow Central from Mount Florida Station rather than King's Park. My fellow travellers were downcast and even a little angry with the turn of events. I had my Celtic scarf crunched into my pocket and lived in fear of it being exposed as the others in the crammed carriage moaned, swore and blamed it all on a man who lived in the Vatican in Italy, whereas I knew perfectly well that it was a man who came from the Lanarkshire coal mines and started playing for Albion Rovers who was the cause of it all. I didn't feel like telling them that, though! Oh, what an uncomfortable journey it was, and how glad I was to see Central Station with all the women laden with their shopping, bearded students, and above all else, policemen!

I was aware that two men on that train kept looking at me. One of them insisted on talking to me and asking me what I felt about the game while I confined myself, contrary and alien to my nature, to saying things like *"Aye"* and *"That's richt,"* nodding sagely and continuing to employ my theatrical skills in trying to look unhappy. It was the other man who accosted me once I had left the train and was walking through the huge (and safe) concourse of Glasgow Central Station. *"You're a Celtic supporter,"* he said, pointing a finger at me. As bravely as possible, I said, *"Whit maks ye think that?"* *"Because Ah'm one tae!"* was the reply as he took his green and white scarf from his pocket. *"Ye can always tell!"* We laughed with relief and joy, and after that, I more or less flew home on a cloud of happiness!

And so once again, we had a trophy! Two in 1965 or three if you counted the Glasgow Cup! Happy days were indeed here again! And everyone now knew that Stein's Celtic were going places, and we simply could not wait for Wednesday night and Dens Park to play the game that should have been played on League Cup final day.

And once again, we had a Monday morning on which we could look forward to going to work and to school. And slowly, slowly, we now began to see the waverers and the neutrals (if there are such things in Scottish football) beginning to side with Celtic in arguments. No-one could now dismiss the Scottish Cup final triumph in April as a temporary blip. Celtic's return was permanent and real.

The supporters were in a buoyant joyful mood that night as they travelled the road and the miles to Dundee to meet a team whom we had both beaten and lost to in the League Cup (which we now of course possessed!). In spite of their crazy, self-seeking Directors who would sell anything for money, they still had a good side and on their own pitch they were always a difficult side to beat with Charlie Cooke, who had been indifferent for Aberdeen, beginning more and more to impress everyone who watched him play for Dundee. Indeed, he was now being freely compared with Billy Steel, which was the Dundee equivalent of someone saying that Bertie Auld was as good as Patsy Gallacher!

The crowd was about 18,000 and they saw a really good game which Celtic deserved to win, although it was a close-run thing. Those who thought that Jock might change the team which won the Scottish League Cup were disappointed when the same team ran out, each and every one of them with the new-found spring in the step that the recent capture of a trophy always brings.

Celtic started off playing towards the goal into which John Hughes had scored that marvellous counter some seven weeks ago, and it was John who was prominent early in the game, beating defenders and sending over crosses which were just out of the reach of Joe McBride or Bobby Lennox. But Dundee gave as good as they got with

The CELTIC VIEW

PURPOSE OF THE NEW PAPER

SCOTLAND TEAM BOSS AND CELTIC

Best Wishes for the New Season

Celtic Public Relations Officer Jimmy McGrory wishes his successor as manager Jock Stein a successful season.

A new season begins for the Scottish Cup-winners Celtic with the launch of the club newspaper. This iconic Celtic line-up includes new signing Joe McBride, fifth from right.

A piper leads the Celtic and Motherwell teams onto the field in Douglas, Isle of Man on 28 July 1965 for a pre-season friendly. This was Joe McBride's Celtic debut and he played against his former club.

Roker Park, Sunderland. 7 August 1965. Jim Baxter facing familiar opposition on his debut in English football, following his transfer from Rangers. Celts in the photo are Bobby Lennox, Bobby Murdoch and John Clark on an afternoon when they won 5-0.

Our first reserve team of the new season.
Back row: Craig, McCarron, Simpson, Brogan, Cushley, O'Neill;
Front row: Connelly, Divers, Quinn, Sweeney, Taylor.

Celtic's first competitive goal of the new season is scored by Bertie Auld, who hurt himself in the process. Whilst he was off the pitch receiving treatment, Dundee United striker Dennis Gillespie scored the winner in the League Cup section match played at Tannadice on 14 August 1965.

Celtic's reserves had better luck that afternoon, beating United's second-string 3-1 at Parkhead.

Action from Celtic's League Cup section matches.

Top: Billy McNeill attacks the Motherwell defence.

Bottom: Bertie Auld nips the ball away from Dundee goalkeeper Ally Donaldson as Bobby Lennox and Joe McBride look on.

Top: Joe McBride rounds off Celtic's 3-0 victory over Dundee United on 28 August 1965.

Centre and Bottom: John Hughes scores THAT goal against Dundee at Dens Park on 4 September 1965, much to the delight of the travelling support.

For the second time in 1965 Celts go goal-crazy against Aberdeen at Celtic Park. These goals are from the 7-1 demolition of the Dons on 25 September 1965.

Top: Bobby Lennox opens the scoring. Centre left: Jimmy Johnstone makes it 2-0.

Centre right: Lennox is in the net but Bertie Auld was the scorer of Celtic's sixth goal.

Bottom: It's Jinky again on target as Celts go 5-0 up.

Images from Jock Stein's first European match in charge of Celtic, played in the Netherlands on 29 September 1965. Celts beat Go Ahead Deventer 6-0 on the night.

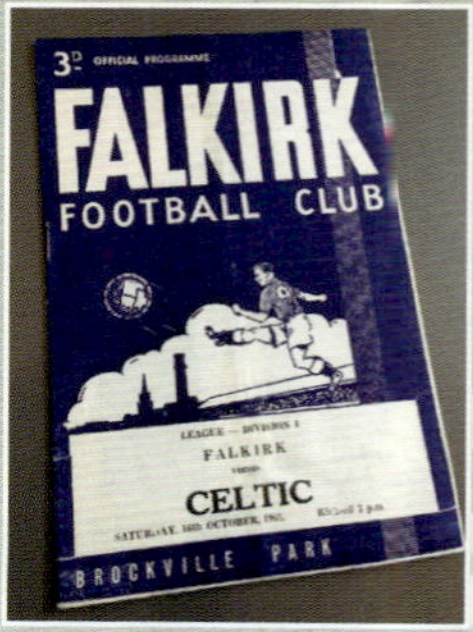

Joe McBride heads Celts into the lead against Hibernian in the League Cup semi-final at Ibrox, beats Hearts keeper Jim Cruickshank in the 5-2 win at Celtic Park on 9 October 1965 then tussles with former Celt Jimmy Rowan in the 4-3 victory over Falkirk at Brockville seven days later.

Action from the League Cup final played at Hampden on 23 October 1965.

Top: Tommy Gemmell clears the danger as John Clark and Billy McNeill provide cover.

Centre: Billy Ritchie and Ron McKinnon combine to thwart Bobby Lennox in the air.

Bottom: Ian Young makes a vital clearance in the first half at Hampden.

Breakthrough at Hampden.

John Hughes sends Billy Ritchie the wrong way from the spot to give Celts the lead, then leaps high in the air to take the congratulations of his teammates.

Top: Joe McBride goes to the aid of Jimmy Johnstone after the winger is felled for Celtic's second penalty at Hampden.

Bottom: Ritchie guesses correctly this time but the shot from John Hughes has too much power and Celtic have one hand on the League Cup at 2-0.

Top: It's all over and Celtic have won the League Cup for the first time since 1957. Jock Stein greets his team as they leave the Hampden pitch.

Bottom: All smiles…for now. Captain Billy McNeill and matchwinner John Hughes lead the jubilant Celtic team on that ill-fated lap of honour.

Winners and losers. Celebrations turn ugly as Rangers supporters invade the field to confront the victorious Celtic players and staff.

THE CELTIC VIEW

ISSUE No. 12 OCTOBER 27, 1965 PRICE 4d.

THE LEAGUE CUP VICTORY

The Winners' Case

CELTIC Football Club wish this week to offer sincere congratulations to their League Cup winning team. The club directors and officials are strongly of the opinion that no amount of talk or writing about the scenes that followed the final whistle at Hampden last Saturday should be allowed to distract attention from the fact that CELTIC WON THE LEAGUE CUP.

Celtic are also convinced that it was the winning of the trophy by Celtic which was the primary cause of the serious misconduct of followers of the beaten finalists.

The Celtic officials also wish to compliment

WINNING PICTURES

Left: John Clark, John Hughes, and Billy McNeill leave Hampden pavilion with the League Cup.

Below: Clearly apparent is the concern of McNeill, Hughes, and Bobby Murdoch as they see Rangers' followers invade the field.

Top: Jock Stein, Neil Mochan and the League Cup-winning Celtic team.

Centre: Happy ballboys parade Celtic's latest trophy around the pitch at half-time during the match against Stirling Albion on 30 October 1965.

Bottom: The Celtic View reflects on the victory and the aftermath.

Top: Aarhus goalkeeper Bent Martin saves from Bobby Lennox in Denmark. He would later sign for Celtic.

Centre: Celts celebrate a goal in the return leg against Aarhus.

Bottom: St Johnstone keeper Mike McVittie clearing the danger at Muirton Park on 13 November 1965.

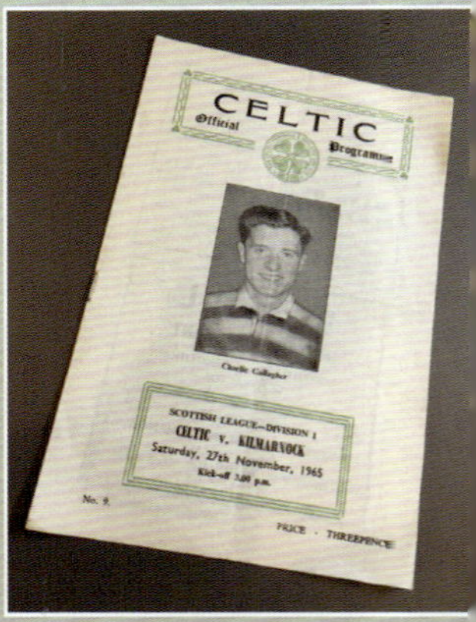

Top: Kilmarnock goalkeeper Bobby Ferguson taking no chances at Celtic Park on 27 November 1965.

Bottom: Three out of three! The Glasgow Cup, Scottish Cup and League Cup - all won in 1965 - are proudly displayed at Celtic Park. The other trophies on show are the St Mungo Cup of 1951 (second left), the Coronation Cup of 1953 (second from right) and the British League Cup of 1902 (extreme right).

Andy Penman and Charlie Cooke looking sharp and centre-forward Kenny Cameron getting the better of Billy McNeill now and again.

On Saturday, McNeill had similarly been hesitant against Forrest and Willoughby, but had rallied and taken charge immediately after Celtic went ahead. The same thing happened here when first McBride scored from a Johnstone pass, then Lennox from a McBride pass within about ten minutes of each other. Dundee came close as well, but now that Celtic were ahead, McNeill was back in charge and in control of the dangerous Cameron.

Half-time came with Celtic two goals up, but Dundee pulled one back in ten minutes from a free-kick needlessly conceded on the edge of the box. It was well-taken by Andy Penman and deceived Ronnie Simpson who had not expected a lob into the corner of the net. From now on, it was a tremendous game of football, with Celtic's defence just asserting sufficient control and Bobby Murdoch just getting the better of Charlie Cooke. Bobby Davidson's final whistle was greeted with a great deal of relief, and no-one could have seriously complained if Dundee had managed to scrape a draw.

It was like another game - in reverse. In August 1962, at the same old ground in the Scottish League Cup, Celtic had played well enough to get at least a draw, but it was the League Champions who won 1-0 with a goal from Gordon Smith, once of Hibs and Hearts and now Dundee. Now, here was another example of the roles having been reversed. Jock Stein was getting Celtic to win games. Previously, the standard of football had been good enough, but Celtic just couldn't win games. They could now. It was a good result and the only fly in the ointment was that Rangers had also won tonight, beating Dundee's neighbours United 2-0 at Ibrox.

There was one other game to be played in that triumphant month of October 1965, and that was when Stirling Albion came to Celtic Park on October 30. No-one really expected a shock against THIS Celtic side (they might have a few seasons earlier) and they didn't get one as Celtic in their all-green strip beat the all-white Stirling

Albion 6-1 with a hat-trick from John Hughes (who could do no wrong these days), two goals from Joe McBride and one from Bobby Murdoch. It was the same team that had won the last three games and the 26,000 crowd who had seen the League Cup paraded at half-time with green and white ribbons, left for home in rare good humour. The team were two points behind Rangers (it was two points for a win in 1965) but with a game in hand – that game at Fir Park which had to be postponed because of the International in Ireland on October 2.

There was of course no let up now (nor would anyone have wanted there to be one). Europe now returned to the agenda. A trip to Denmark awaited in the first midweek of November to play Aarhus in the European Cup Winners' Cup.

CHAPTER ELEVEN

NOVEMBER

"When chill November's surly blast laid field and forest bare..." is the way that Robbie Burns describes the onset of winter. There is a lot less warmth, a lot less daylight and yet, metaphorically, it is when the heat intensifies in the Scottish football season. The gloves are now off, and the good football teams are expected to deliver. For the first time in many years, Celtic were this winter to be involved in a League race. Previously, it had come almost to be expected that Celtic would be struggling. Not this year.

One man who was very impressed by Celtic's performance against Stirling Albion on Saturday, 30 October 1965 was Henri From, the Manager of Aarhus, where Celtic were bound on Wednesday night. The players came in for light training on the Monday morning under the supervision of Sean Fallon (Jock Stein was in Rome watching Italy play Poland and spying on a few players for the visit of the Italians to Scotland next week) and then intended to fly to Aarhus that night. The squad was the eleven who played on Saturday plus John Fallon, Jim Kennedy, Steve Chalmers, Bertie Auld and John Cushley.

A gale kept their chartered Aer Lingus flight in Dublin, and instead of trying their luck on some other aeroplane on Monday night, Fallon made the decision to stay overnight in a hotel in Troon and to fly on the Tuesday. This would not have been good news for the many "fear of flying" sufferers in the Celtic party, including of course Jimmy Johnstone, who made a meal of it! But they arrived safely enough in Aarhus, where they met Jock Stein who had just seen Italy inflict a dreadful hammering on Poland, something that was hardly good news for Scotland.

There had been a suggestion that Bertie Auld, now fit again after a thigh injury, might play in place of Charlie Gallagher but Stein decided to play safe and keep faith with Gallagher. The rest of the team more or less picked itself in those days, but this team was instructed tonight to keep things quiet and not to do anything silly against the enthusiastic Danish amateurs who were still clearly in awe of their mighty Scottish opponents. It was therefore a really rather dull game which Celtic won 1-0, thanks to a Joe McBride header from a John Hughes corner kick. Both goalkeepers played well, the Danish one a fellow called Bent Martin whom Stein would keep an eye on for future reference, and the only other matter of interest was Jimmy Johnstone, the winger making what *The Glasgow Herald* coyly describes as *"an indiscreet gesture with his hand"* while being booked for prolonged dissent and being therefore rather lucky that Billy McNeill sprinted up and told him to calm down before the Belgian referee took any further action.

There was a certain criticism of Celtic for not putting the game to bed, but there are times when things do not go the way one wants, and it was a pleasant, albeit cold, experience for everyone, not least the Chairman of Aarhus who at the after-match dinner, nevertheless raised a cheer from the Celtic party for his ability to quote Robbie Burns! Possibly even the referee Mr Henri Burgucht was in awe of Celtic, for after very clearly writing (this was before yellow cards) the name of Jimmy Johnstone in his notebook, he then decided not to report him and told the Celtic party so before he left Denmark. Jimmy was then reputed to have made another "gesture with his hand" but this was a cheery thumbs-up.

Celtic now returned to Glasgow to play the in-form Partick Thistle, who had delighted their supporters and *"set Maryhill alight"* (as it was somewhat exuberantly described) by beating Hibs. A larger

Thistle support than had been seen for a long time appeared at Celtic Park to support the Jags, their yellow and red colours mingling agreeably with the green and white to lighten what was a rather dull, typically November day in Glasgow.

This game was a disappointing 1-1 draw. It was the first bad game for a while, and possibly a timely reminder that you don't always get all the breaks that you perhaps feel you deserve. The team was still the same (possibly a change or two might have been, to advantage, made) but today they came up against tough opposition. It is tempting to assume that this was one of the "parking the team bus" sort of games that one sees so often at Celtic Park, but this was not the case. Thistle took the game to Celtic, might have scored twice but for Ronnie Simpson, and for long periods in the second half were clearly the better team. Once again, Joe McBride was the Celtic scorer, this time sweeping home a Bobby Lennox cross. That was just before half-time, but ex-Celt Jim Conway scored for Thistle early in the second half.

It was generally agreed by the Press as being a good game, and of course, Partick Thistle supporters were over the moon at the result, but Celtic fans were not at all happy. News that Rangers were beating Falkirk 3-0 did not help the mood, but it hardly excused the boos that were heard at the end with even men like McNeill and Johnstone not exempt from such criticism. It did mean that Celtic were now three points behind Rangers, but with only nine games played out of 34, it was hardly a terminal decline. It was indeed one of these setbacks from which lessons can be learned and did not really justify the overwhelming mood of depression which hung over the fans.

One man exempt from criticism in the eyes of the supporters was Ronnie Simpson, whose career showed absolutely no sign of coming to an end. He had been a hero in the Scottish League Cup final a fortnight ago, and now he stayed a hero. A letter to *The Celtic View* suggested that it might be a good idea for John Fallon and John

Kennedy, the other two goalkeepers, to stand behind Ronnie's goal and learn from him! Yet he was from an unlikely background for a Celtic hero. His father was of course Jimmy Simpson, who had played for Rangers in the 1930s but who was now as committed a Celtic fan as anyone and very proud of his son who now had a Scottish medal to add to his English ones.

Ronnie's love for the game was infectious and it was for good reason that he was called *"Faither,"* for he was never reluctant to share his lifetime's experiences in the game with the younger and sometimes wilder elements. He was the confidant of Billy McNeill, and a great source of strength to the other defenders in the side.

He also had a surprising relationship with John Fallon, whom he had ousted from the side. Often in such circumstances, the dispossessed, aggrieved party takes umbrage and even plots against his replacement, trying to unsettle him. Not so in this case. John Fallon, a man whose love of the club took precedence over everything else, went out of his way to become friends with Ronnie. They sat together on the bus for away trips, exchanging tips and talking about today's opposition and aspects of the art of goalkeeping, like the way to save penalty kicks, where to stand at corner kicks, how to throw a ball out etc.

There was a lovely picture of them embracing each other at the end of the Scottish League Cup final and the bond was clearly strong. They both shared the view (possibly mistakenly) that Jock Stein didn't like them. Certainly, Stein as Manager of Hibs had been quite keen to unload Ronnie to Celtic, and John always felt that Stein didn't trust him. It may be that Jock did not trust goalkeepers generally – he had been captain of Celtic that awful day of the Scottish Cup final of 1955 when John Bonnar misjudged a corner kick and gave Clyde a late equaliser – and his subsequent dealings with goalkeepers in the transfer market were far from satisfactory (in contrast with his dealings with strikers, for example, where he made three excellent buys in Wallace, Hood and Deans), but here in 1965, Stein now decided that the goalkeepers were a breed apart and that they should be allowed to get on with it.

All this had been going on with significant international events taking place in the background. Rhodesia (the country that we now know as Zimbabwe) had been wanting independence from Britain. It was something that the Labour Government of Harold Wilson was reluctant to grant unless there were "unimpeded progress towards majority rule," which was not really on the agenda of Ian Smith, the Rhodesian Prime Minister. The two men held a series of meetings, one of them on board a ship, but failed to reach agreement. Rhodesia eventually declared UDI (Unilateral Declaration of Independence) and things were at an impasse. The tragedy of Robert Mugabe's Zimbabwe in the 21st century might not have happened if the obdurate Ian Smith had come to an agreement with the benign and enlightened Harold Wilson.

Meanwhile, Celtic and their disappointing show against Partick Thistle on November 6 were put to one side while Scotland faced Italy in the World Cup. To reach the finals, after their dreadful game against Poland, Scotland probably had to beat Italy twice, home and away. Frankly, this did not seem likely, but optimism has always been a characteristic of the Scottish football fan, and a crowd of 100,393 turned up at Hampden to see Scotland take on Italy.

It turned out to be one of the very few Scotland triumphs in the World Cup, as John Greig of Rangers scored a late winner with time running out, after 88 minutes of not really looking as if they could achieve anything against a brick wall Italian defence. But they did, and all Scotland enjoyed the triumph. It meant now that a win in Naples in December would qualify Scotland, and a draw would earn a play-off.

It was of course very easy and very tempting to be carried away with the euphoria of it all. Scotland, as a country, is bad for that, as the prelude to Argentina in 1978 would prove. But at least there was a chance of making it to England. The crunch game was a month away, however, and a very tall order. Other things had to be seen to before then. Celtic were due at Muirton Park, Perth on Saturday to play St Johnstone, and that was never an easy fixture.

Ah! But what a difference a year makes! Twelve months earlier, on 7 November 1964, they went down 0-3 to St Johnstone a couple of weeks after the defeat in the League Cup final to Rangers in one of the most dismal performances that Celtic had ever given. Now the roles had been reversed and Celtic, with the League Cup gracing the Parkhead sideboard, won 4-1 in a very competent display of football with virtually the same team as had played in the League Cup final. The only difference was Jim Craig coming in for Ian Young, who was out with an ankle injury.

It was a game which had a curious incident in the first half. St Johnstone were awarded a free-kick outside their own box at the ice rink end of Muirton Park. The defender took it and passed it back to the goalkeeper, but unfortunately omitted to tell his goalkeeper and the ball rolled into the net! "Goal!" we all shouted and so did our players, whose ignorance of the Laws of Football was abysmal, for you cannot score a goal that way. Mr Fleming of Banknock correctly awarded a corner kick for Celtic, but no amount of calm reassurance from those of the support who knew what they were talking about could persuade the others that Mr Fleming didn't necessarily wear an apron and play a flute every July!

Not that it mattered, for before half-time Joe McBride scored with a simple tap-in after Charlie Gallagher's drive was parried by goalkeeper Mike McVittie, who was at least paying more attention this time than he had been a few moments previously.

Half-time saw a massive movement of troops to be behind the goal into which Celtic were shooting in the second half, and we were rewarded with a fine display of attacking football with both wingers in particular on song, Hughes scoring twice and Johnstone once, as the game finished 4-1. The walk back to the railway station that evening was not so much a walk back as a parade with songs, chants and cries of a risen people. Last year's walk back had been like a funeral procession, but what a difference now! In every sense, Celtic were now a team of winners!

Two other pieces of news emerged that day. The death was reported of Hugh Delaney of the Celtic Supporters' Association – a good man and much missed – and the other was the transfer of Jim Kennedy to Morton. Jim had been one of the unlucky Celts who had missed out on the trophies and the medals of the Stein era, but he had made a great contribution to Celtic for several years and had deservedly won a handful of Scottish caps. He was a solid rather than a brilliant player and a Celt through and through. In his Morton incarnation, he would meet Celtic again.

There then followed the rather unremarkable 2-0 win over Aarhus in the second leg of the European Cup Winners' Cup. The weather was miserable, but there were 27,000 there to see Celtic put the tie to bed, the goals scored by the somewhat unlikely combination of Billy McNeill and Jimmy Johnstone. The aggregate score was 3-0, but it should have been a great deal more. So far, so good for Celtic in Europe, but their next challenge would be much more demanding than part-timers from Denmark and the Netherlands.

Hamilton Accies now came to Parkhead. Frankly, the gallant men from Douglas Park, who had done so well to earn promotion from the Second Division last season, were misfits in the First Division this year, and they were not expected to do very much against the strong going Celtic. John Hughes had hurt his leg against Aarhus on Wednesday night and was rested in favour of Bertie Auld, who was given a great welcome back from his fans in the crowd. What was a great deal more unsettling was the sight of Billy McNeill being carried off near the end by Neil Mochan and Bob Rooney with a leg injury, following a collision with Hamilton's goalkeeper Billy Lamont.

Lamont in fact had a great game for Hamilton, restricting the Celtic forwards to 5-0. It was not really much of a contest with

Celtic so much on top and either unable or even unwilling to put Hamilton to the sword more than was necessary. The goals were scored by five different men – Auld, Johnstone, Gemmell, Murdoch and McBride. The 15,000 crowd were somewhat unsatisfied with this performance, more so when they discovered that Rangers had also won 5-0, but their victory was against far more demanding opposition in Kilmarnock, who were due at Parkhead next Saturday.

But before that, we had another International, this time against Wales at Hampden. 49,888 supporters were there to see a much-improved Scottish performance and a 4-1 win. Stein had to leave out McNeill and Hughes for injury reasons, so the only Celtic player on view that night was Bobby Murdoch. Bobby had one of his best-ever games that night, scoring twice and removing any possible lingering doubts that he was not a world-class wing-half. The performance did a great deal to restore Scottish credibility. It proved that the result against Italy at Hampden was not a fluke, and optimism, that most dangerous of emotions, began to spread about that game in Naples on December 7.

Four Celtic players – McNeill, Hughes, Murdoch and Lennox - were chosen in the 21-man squad for the game in Italy, and this meant that the game against St Mirren at Love Street on December 4 would be postponed as the Scottish authorities decided to give Stein every possible chance for qualification to the World Cup finals. Games in England, however, were not postponed on December 4 – why should they be? – and this was going to have its effect on relationships between the two countries, as we shall see.

One fixture remained for Celtic in November, and this was against League Champions Kilmarnock at Celtic Park. Now managed by ex-Celt Malky MacDonald, Kilmarnock were involved in a struggle in the European Cup at that moment against, of all teams, Real Madrid, so it was expected that, although they would fight hard – they always did against Celtic – their eye might be slightly off the ball, as far as Celtic were concerned.

This game was tough. The pitch was hard and had had to be protected by straw and then sprinkled with sand - a process that was still going on as many of the 24,000 spectators arrived. Hughes was back for Celtic but McNeill wasn't, and John Cushley took over as centre-half while Bobby Murdoch was the acting captain. Craig was still in for Ian Young, but there was a surprise in the forward line as Charlie Gallagher was dropped and Joe McBride moved to inside to allow Steve Chalmers to play in the centre. The weather was cold, and there was a hint of freezing fog in the air. It was Scottish football in winter and a long way away from Madrid and Naples where some of the players would soon be playing!

The first half was even – indeed a credit to both teams for trying so hard in difficult circumstances, and the game turned on two decisions in the second half by referee Alistair McKenzie from Coatbridge, a man with a reputation for the occasional eccentricity. It was Kilmarnock who went ahead with a goal from Brian McIlroy, who looked offside when he picked up a pass from Tommy McLean. Clearly the referee himself had some doubts and consulted his linesman, but the goal stood to the loud sound of booing from all round the ground. That was in the 60th minute.

But 10 minutes later, Celtic were on level terms from a penalty kick which did not look like a penalty kick and was not claimed for with any particular enthusiasm by the home support. Goalkeeper Bobby Ferguson and Steve Chalmers went for the same ball, and Ferguson got there first. There was some bodily contact, but it did not really look like any kind of a foul, until the referee pointed to the spot. It was controversial, to put it mildly, and frankly looked very much like a "compensation" award for a dodgy offside goal.

Kilmarnock protested long and loud, but Hughes did not hesitate as he hammered the ball home to put Celtic level. From then on, Celtic pressed and pressed with McBride now back in the centre, Chalmers on the right wing and Johnstone in a sort of a midfield role – the "roving commission" role that Jock loved to give him, and this move reaped its reward when Jimmy passed a through ball to McBride who beat Ferguson for the winner.

Kilmarnock felt robbed, and no-one was ever really convinced about the penalty, but it was a win. No-one was convinced about the Kilmarnock goal either, so, in a sense, things had cancelled each other out, and Celtic had the two points. Yet it was a very unsatisfactory sort of a win as well, for Rangers - who beat Motherwell 3-0 today, had defeated the same opponents 5-0 last week. But, as wise Celtic supporters pointed out, League Championships are seldom won by champagne, flamboyant football. Often one has to grind out a victory, as was certainly the case here. Nor are they ever won in November. That dull month closed with Celtic three points behind Rangers but with a game in hand, and Dunfermline Athletic in the mix as well. The League race would now take a backseat for a fortnight.

Celtic supporters may have been a little underwhelmed by some recent performances in the Scottish League, but they were still enjoying what was really a novel experience for so many of them. By the onset of winter, Celtic were usually well out of the title race and attendances were dropping, but now for the first time in over a decade, one could honestly say that Celtic were in the race. There was still a spring in the step of so many supporters, and there was always the very comforting thought that even if everything went pear-shaped in the League, there was still the Scottish League Cup sitting on the sideboard, draped in green and white ribbons! And the cold weather did not even seem all that cold!

CHAPTER TWELVE

DECEMBER

The first few days of December 1965 were dominated by two topics of conversation. One was the extreme cold and frost, and the other was Scotland's team for Italy.

Celtic would have been playing against St Mirren at Love Street on the first Saturday of the month, but the game was off to allow for preparation for the World Cup qualifier, and it would have been postponed anyway because of the frost. In the event, only two senior games were played in Scotland that Saturday and the venues (Montrose and Stranraer) give a clue as to the extent of the frost in central Scotland. There had been a half-hearted attempt to arrange a game between a Celtic-Rangers Select and Moscow Dynamo, who had played a few games in England on tour, but in spite of confident assertions that the game would go ahead at Hampden on Friday, 3 December, it did not (even though the turnstiles had been opened and some intrepid fans had braved the cold and paid their money) and then a brave, desperate last-ditch attempt to arrange it for the following day at Parkhead failed as well. It was probably just as well. The crowd would have been a pitiful one. Spectators hate uncertainty about fixtures and they also know when they are being taken to the cleaners.

All this meant that attention fixed even more on projected events in Italy on Tuesday afternoon. It is important to nail a myth that went around for years afterwards, namely that Scotland would have won but for wicked English clubs who refused to cancel games on the previous Saturday and to release their players. There is an element of truth in this, but only an element. Sadly for those of the Scottish paranoia, the facts simply do not back this up in its entirety. The reasons for Scotland's defeat were quite simply injuries, which forced Stein into a rather unwise team selection, and the fact that they were playing Italy in Italy. Scotland did not lose the World Cup in Naples on December 7; they lost it against Poland at Hampden on October 13, a game that was thrown away by complacency. We were never really likely to beat Italy in Italy. But it is handy to be able to blame everything on the English!

There were several memorable things about December 7, however. One was the sheer obsession about the game all over Scotland. The lunchtime kick-off on TV saw huge absenteeism among schools and works who were not enlightened enough to allow the bending of rules a little. Rootes at Linwood had to close down for the afternoon! Men were sacked, schoolboys were belted but the country made it its business to see the game. The disappointment was all the keener, but there was no country on earth that took its football any more seriously than Scotland did.

Ex-Prime Minister Gordon Brown tells the story of his own experience that day. He was in sixth year at Kirkcaldy High School and was thinking of making a dignified approach, along with some others, to his Headmaster Mr Adam to ask for time off. Mr Adam got wind of this, and duly belted Brown and some of his friends for even thinking of it!

Another curious business was a remarkable interview given on the Saturday before the match to BBC TV from two Scottish-born managers of English clubs – Tommy Docherty of Chelsea and Bill Shankly of Liverpool – in which they managed to upset everyone in both Scotland and England. They upset Scotland by saying that although they would like to release men like Eddie McCreadie and Ron Yeats for Tuesday, clubs had to come first, and no games would be postponed on the Saturday. They then upset the English by saying that if England had had to qualify for the World Cup, again they wouldn't have been able to do so!

And the third was the sheer volume of injuries to Scotland – Billy McNeill, Jim Baxter, Billy Stevenson, Denis Law, Willie Henderson among others – which led to Ron Yeats playing as a double centre-half! It is of course not unusual – in fact it is common practice - for injuries to be faked to avoid playing in an International friendly, but this was the World Cup, and the injuries were all genuine. Scotland tried hard but were beaten by a better side – yet one which managed in the World Cup itself the next summer to lose one famous day in Middlesbrough to North Korea!

Anyway, it was over, and Jock was now released from Scotland duties. He was now solely in charge of Celtic, and it was probably true to say that Celtic supporters were happy about that. Three games remained in December 1965 – Hibs at Celtic Park, Dunfermline at East End Park and on Christmas Day, Morton at Celtic Park. They were all good ones, and the remarkable year of 1965 finished on a high note.

Celtic's players who were not with Scotland (everyone except Bobby Murdoch and John Hughes) had gone to Largs with Sean Fallon, hoping to find the conditions more congenial for training. They were in fact a lot better on the coast but, in any case, a thaw had arrived and there was no great danger for the game against Hibs. The bad news was that Billy McNeill was still out, but there was a ray of sunshine in the return of Ian Young, the right-back now fit again.

Stein was given a round of applause as he came out with the team before the start. It was a way of saying *"thank you"* for being exclusively with Celtic now! It was also possibly an expression of sympathy and solidarity with Jock for his "near miss" with Scotland. For Celtic, Young was in for Craig and Cushley for McNeill and the forward line was *Johnstone, Gallagher, McBride, Lennox and Hughes*. But Hibs sprung a surprise by dropping Pat Quinn, generally reckoned to be one of the best players at Easter Road at that time. Alan Cousin, once of Dundee and much admired by Bob Shankly who had brought him to Easter Road, was in for Hibs.

It was a good game between two good teams. The game started in minuscule daylight and without the floodlights. Was this Celtic trying to save on their electric bill? After about 10 minutes, referee Mr Rodger of Stonehouse called a halt and signalled to the electrician that a shilling in the meter might be no bad idea, and on came the floodlights, *"turning dark December into something like the sunshine of June,"* according to *The Evening Times*.

The 22,000 crowd enjoyed this game. It was fast and even with loads of goalmouth action and missed chances, but Celtic won 2-0 because of some excellent goalkeeping by Ronnie Simpson against his old club and a couple of great goals. They were scored towards the end of each half, both fashioned by Jimmy Johnstone, who now seemed to be adding consistency to his craft and wizardry. The first was a corner kick, which found John Hughes. Very calmly, John took his time to tee the ball up and crash it home past Billy Wilson.

Then towards the end of the game, with Hibs looking more and more as if they were going to equalise, Jimmy ran 40 yards with the ball, beating a few men, and then crossed for Joe McBride to score a second and settle the Parkhead crowd who were beginning to get a little agitated and apprehensive. The game finished 2-0 and it was generally agreed to be one of the best games of the season. Celtic v Hibs games are often reckoned to be the best combination, and so it turned out on this occasion. Both Rangers and Dunfermline also won today, so there was no change at the top with Rangers on 26 points, Celtic on 23 and the Pars on 22, but Celtic had a game in hand. All three teams were to play each other soon. Next Saturday would see Celtic at East End Park, then Dunfermline came to Ibrox on Christmas Day before Celtic played Rangers at Parkhead on January 3.

The week before the trip to Dunfermline was a quiet one. Celtic learned that they had been drawn against Dinamo Kiev in the Cup Winners' Cup after the New Year. The scheduling of these games would cause some problems for Celtic, but the problem was that there was no opportunity to watch Dinamo at this point because the Soviet season had closed down for the winter. But Jock could always phone his old friend Bertie Peacock, now manager of Coleraine, who had been knocked out by Kiev in the previous round.

On the injury front, the luckless Ian Young had hurt himself again, so he was out, and although Billy McNeill was recovering, Stein decided not to risk him against Dunfermline. There had been some talk of playing McNeill or John Cushley at right-back and using a double centre-half formation, but Jim Craig was chosen at right-back again. Then, on the day of the game, there was a surprise with Stevie Chalmers in the forward line in place of Bobby Lennox in a Celtic team that read, *Simpson, Craig and Gemmell; Murdoch, Cushley and Clark; Johnstone, Gallagher, McBride, Chalmers and Hughes.*

The choice of Chalmers was another of Stein's "horses for courses" policy decisions, and on this occasion, (as indeed on most occasions) he was absolutely spot on, for it was Stevie who got the two goals which earned Celtic their 2-0 win. That, together with a surprise result at Shawfield where Clyde drew 2-2 with Rangers, meant that it was a good day for Celtic. Rangers were still on top, but the lead was now only two points and Celtic had a game in hand.

It was a cold day with an east wind blowing at East End Park. Snow threatened but did not appear, and the result was a very good game of football (as was the tradition of these two teams when they met) in which Celtic were certainly the better team, although possibly there were not two goals of a difference. Not that it mattered in the slightest to those who travelled back to their buses and trains chanting (more than a little prematurely) *"Champions"* and singing the praises of Jock Stein.

The goals came after an even first half. Celtic, playing against the wind, started off well and were unlucky not to score in the first minute, but then the Pars fought back. In the second half, Celtic, now with the wind behind them, gradually took command. The first goal came when Chalmers raced on to a hopeful upfield punt by Cushley, then seemed to have lost the opportunity by not shooting first time as he took the ball to the right, but then crashed the ball home off the post. It was a great goal. His second was more of an opportunist's goal, when Jim McLean was short with a header back to goalkeeper Eric Martin, and Chalmers nipped in to lob the ball over Martin's head.

That made it 2-0, and Cushley then took control of the centre of the field and no fightback materialised. Cushley was, like John McNamee, unfortunate in that he arrived at Celtic Park at the same time as Billy McNeill. He was good enough, as he would prove for Dunfermline and West Ham United, but not quite as good as Billy who, on his game, was a superb player. It was a very competent and professional performance from Celtic, and they really looked like League Champions that day. They had shown that they knew how to win at a difficult venue in a game that was pretty even. But it was not yet Christmas and there was a very long way to go.

Indeed, it was an unusual position to be in – buying Christmas shopping, going to parties and dances and to have a team which had a realistic chance of winning the Scottish League. No-one could remember a Christmastime like it, and not only that, but we were in Europe as well, and already had the Scottish League Cup in the bag! The big hit at the moment was The Beatles "We Can Work It Out" and that seemed to be so appropriate to Celtic and the future, while we could not help feeling that for Rangers it was "The Carnival Is Over" from The Seekers. The week before Christmas had stories about Aarhus keeper Bent Martin coming to Celtic on trial in the New Year, and the first shots being fired in the saga about where and when to play the ties between Celtic and Dinamo Kiev. It was an interesting and informative example of what the Soviet Union was really all about.

Football was played on Christmas Day in those days, if it fell on a Saturday. Some people queried the value of this, for by 1965 Christmas was rapidly taking over from the New Year in Scotland as the main midwinter festival – it had been a Public Holiday now for a few years since 1958 - and there were certainly problems with transport for getting to games. But for the meantime, Christmas Day in 1965 continued to have football, and welcome it was too.

Merry Christmas did not quite come into it. At Parkhead, the same Celtic team as had beaten Dunfermline at East End Park last week (Billy McNeill was still out) faced Morton, who had the luckless Jim Kennedy playing for them at left-half and thumped them 8-1. A hat-trick from Joe McBride, two from John Hughes, two from Stevie Chalmers and one from acting captain Bobby Murdoch did the trick for Celtic. The standard of play was magnificent, and each one of the goals was a great goal to watch – the two from Hughes were particularly good – and had Celtic played with the same intensity in the second half after they had been 7-0 up at half-time, the score could well have been over 20! Fortunately, for the sake of respectability, Morton rallied a little in the second half or Celtic eased up, but whatever it was, 8-1 was the final scoreline.

And it did not stop there. As if realising that Celtic were doing well, over at Ibrox Rangers decided to lose their first League game of the season. There were more mundane reasons for their defeat as well. One was that it was against Dunfermline at Ibrox, and Willie Cunningham's men had a point to make after last week's defeat to Celtic, and also John Greig was out for Rangers with tonsillitis. Whether they liked to admit it or not, Rangers depended to a very large, even unhealthily large, extent on Greig, and today proved it. In spite of scoring in the very first minute, Rangers then lost three goals as their fans turned nasty. They did pull one back near the end, but the final result was Rangers 2 Dunfermline 3.

Evening papers that night (they still appeared on Christmas Day in 1965) showed both Glasgow teams on 27 points with Dunfermline now on 24. Goal average was minimally in favour of Rangers, but Celtic, crucially, had played one game fewer. The trek home that night was a pleasant one, the spring in the step was visible, audible and even tangible. 1965 was now finished as far as the playing of games went. It had been a good year, but the contrast between now and Christmas 1964 was astonishing.

What a difference a year makes! Last Boxing Day had seen frosty wintry weather (no change there) but a minuscule crowd of about 5,000 watching a Celtic team going nowhere. Granted they had played not all that badly that day against Motherwell, with two good goals from John Hughes, but there was no real prospect of any sustained improvement with the "death wish" palpable, and the paralysing presence of Rangers everywhere. New Year's Day 1965 would contain a few new motifs, like a player being sent off and someone else missing a penalty (ironically, possibly the players who would become the acknowledged stars of the Lisbon Lions), but the outcome was so predictable.

But that was now "the name of another town," as the phrase went. Things had not so much changed or improved as revolutionised. *"Things had changed, changed utterly,"* as WB Yeats said of Dublin in 1916. There seemed to be no limit to what could now be achieved, with even a few utopians and optimists saying things like, *"You know, I even think this team could do well in Europe."* Really, these chaps had no sense of reality at all, did they? Some who had been ecstatic and rapturous in April after the Scottish Cup final qualified their own joy by saying *"Mind you, they are no world beaters."* Now, they were beginning to wonder. Maybe they were world beaters?

The New Year fixtures saw Celtic at Shawfield on New Year's Day, then Rangers at Celtic Park on January 3 with a 2.00pm kick-off. These games dominated everyone's thoughts as the Bells approached. One must never remain in the past, for the future is always more important – but it was difficult not to think of the

Scottish Cup, the Glasgow Cup and the Scottish League Cup all sitting in the Parkhead Boardroom with green and white ribbons on them and permit oneself a smile!

If someone had made any comment about three trophies and being top of the League a year earlier at a Hogmanay party, he would have been considered to have had too much to drink. It would have been considered bizarre in the context of what was happening at Celtic Park in the meantime. And yet, the odd thing was that there had not been any great change in personnel, apart from Bertie Auld and Joe McBride. There had been one major positional change in the moving of Bobby Murdoch from inside-right to right-half, but the other factor was that so many players had simply raised their game. And what had made them raise their game was nothing other than the new management set-up of Jock Stein. The future seemed optimistic *"…and westward look, the land is bright."*

EPILOGUE

THE PROMISED LAND

1965 having been a massive year in the history of the club, what did 1966 bring? It was a curious time, with everything in the balance in the nerve-wracking month of April before early May brought what was seen as the main target of the season, namely the Scottish League Championship. But it was not an easy ride!

Astonishingly, the League title had only been won once since the Second World War and only another five times since the Great War. It was quite simply a tournament that Celtic did not do well in! An even more astonishing statistic was that they were usually not even close. Since Celtic won the League in 1954, they had come second in 1955 but in no other season (with the possible exception of 1962, when brilliant play alternated with appalling inconsistency) could one honestly say that they had been in with any kind of chance of lifting the flag. It was therefore considered the priority to win the Scottish League.

As the 1966 League fixtures got underway, Celtic duly beat Rangers 5-1 on January 3, but then by the end of the month they had lost twice, admittedly on difficult away grounds at Pittodrie and Tynecastle and each time with some excuse – a frosty pitch in Aberdeen and an odyssey of a return from Georgia before the Tynecastle game, but then suffered an appalling defeat at the end of February at Stirling Albion for no real rational reason and which reminded one of the bad old days.

The 5-1 victory at the New Year was a highly significant occasion, but before the game even started, there was a vivid and telling indication of just who was running Scottish football now. The day was frosty and foggy, and the game was in some doubt even after the turnstiles had been opened. The early arrivals had been allowed in, and they saw two bulky men walking round the pitch. They were not dissimilar in appearance and both were wearing similar coats – what was called in the mid 1960s a "top" coat and very necessary to fend off the cold on that freezing day. Closer inspection revealed that the two men were Jock Stein and Tom "Tiny" Wharton, the referee.

It was rumoured that these two did not like each other and they were certainly a clash of personalities. Today, there was no indication of acrimony or dispute, but the conversation was clearly animated and to an untrained eye seemed to centre on whether or not today's game should go ahead, with Jock repeatedly digging his boot into the ground, and Tom doing likewise. It looked as if Jock was keener on the game going ahead than Tom was, and the Celtic Manager was exercising his debating skills to that effect to the less convinced referee.

Eventually the two men shook hands and went off together. No announcement came to the effect that we were to get our money back or to keep our tickets for when the game might go ahead in the future. So the game went ahead and Celtic, 0-1 down at half-time, turned on a dazzling exhibition in the second half and won 5-1.

The interesting thing about the Stein-Wharton confab was that no representative of Rangers was in sight. This was odd. They seemed to be happy to be told that the game was to be played without having been consulted. They stayed in the background. To their credit, they never complained about the pitch being unplayable even after their heavy defeat, but it did show the growing influence of big Jock. It was another indication that Rangers were being worsted on the political as well as the football front.

Things looked grim at the end of February, but although there were further draws at Partick Thistle and Hibs, the team won every other game, particularly the last three vital ones at the end of April and the beginning of May, at Morton and Motherwell and at home to Dunfermline. It was Fir Park, Motherwell in an undistinguished 1-0 victory that saw Celtic's 21st League Championship secured.

It was not as simple as all that, though, and the League fortunes were intertwined with our fortunes in the Scottish Cup and European Cup Winners' Cup, particularly in that tense month of April, where it seemed possible that we could throw them all away!

Europe saw a great performance against Dinamo Kiev at Celtic Park and a competent one in Georgia (Ukraine being out of action for the winter), the beginning of a nightmare trip home brought about by a combination of bad weather and the sheer awkwardness of the tyranny of the Soviet Union. However, Celtic recovered and faced Liverpool in the semi-final. All the clichés about a battle of Britain and Bannockburn were trotted out, ludicrously so, as Liverpool's Manager and several players were Scottish. Celtic played well in the first leg at Parkhead, but a 1-0 victory was scant reward for their efforts.

The second leg was a travesty and one of the very few times in Celtic history when everyone (including those who were not Celtic minded) admitted that Celtic had had a raw deal in a refereeing decision. This was when Lennox scored a goal which was definitely onside but chalked off because the linesman could not believe how fast Bobby actually was! The nightmare continued when the supporters misbehaved. Bottle-throwing can never be condoned, but the frustration of the fans was totally understandable. When Liverpool eventually lost the Hampden final to German opposition in Borussia Dortmund, very few Celtic fans wept for them. What goes around, comes around, as they say.

That game at Anfield was played on Tuesday, 19 April 1966. Saturday, 23 April was the Scottish Cup final – Celtic v Rangers! Celtic's path to the final had been interesting. Stranraer provided few problems at Parkhead, but then there was a tough game at Dens

Park, Dundee on a Wednesday night after it had been postponed on the Saturday, followed by a trip to Tynecastle, where there was serious overcrowding in a 3-3 draw. Celtic won the Parkhead replay before an astonishing 72,000 crowd and then in the semi-final beat Dunfermline Athletic, who provided surprisingly little resistance on a wet and windy day at Ibrox.

The final against Rangers was 0-0 the first time around, and a similar result looked likely in the replay, but it was Kai Johansen who scored the winning goal for Rangers. It was looked upon as an unlucky result, but so too was the Liverpool one. You get nothing for hard luck! In Rangers circles, their Scottish Cup triumph was praised not without cause but without end.

The serious side now was that the League had to be won. Celtic's confidence had taken a jolt, whereas Rangers were now buoyant. Both Glasgow teams (Dunfermline had long since fallen by the wayside) were equal on points but Celtic had a game in hand and a slightly less favourable goal average, although that could change. Celtic had three games to play and Rangers two. Saturday, 30 April, the last scheduled day of the League season, saw both teams with tricky away fixtures – Celtic at Greenock and Rangers at Dunfermline. Celtic won 2-0 (after a struggle and surviving a penalty kick) and Rangers 2-1, but the goal scored by Dunfermline made a difference to the goal average and tilted it ever so slightly in favour of Celtic. The Morton result, incidentally, had the side effect of relegating the Greenock side, including that doughty old Celtic warrior Jim Kennedy.

And so it was on to Wednesday night. It was long and hard but eventually Celtic got the better of Dunfermline 2-1. Rangers beat Clyde 4-0, so the League wasn't yet settled, but on the Saturday Celtic travelled to Motherwell knowing that unless they lost 1-4 they would win the League. We travelled in a relaxed frame of mind, having also enjoyed a little nemesis being visited on the arrogant Liverpool, who on the Thursday night in the final of the Cup

Winners' Cup lost 1-3 to Borussia Dortmund at Hampden. Celtic did not play well that day at Motherwell but won 1-0 thanks to a late Lennox goal, and a long 12-year nightmare was finally over.

It is remarkable how many Celtic historians use the word "free" to describe their emotions on this night. It is of course a word that appears frequently in Celtic mythology with lyrics like *"A hymn for the dawn of the free"* and *"nothing matters, Mary, when you're free,"* along with no more despots or slaves. Our slavery was now over. It had been a self-inflicted slavery, but it was real none the less. It was indeed a liberating experience to find that Celtic could be champions again. We were indeed now free. The team could now go to the USA on a close-season tour as Scottish Champions and face the 1966/67 season knowing that they would be competing in the European Cup. But that is another story!

As for the rest of Jock Stein's managerial career at Celtic, it is easier perhaps to concentrate on the failures rather than the successes. From summer 1965 until summer 1975, when Jock was involved in a very serious motor accident and laid off for a year, there were 30 available Scottish tournaments to be played for. Celtic won nine Scottish League titles, six Scottish League Cups and six Scottish Cups – a total of 21 out of 30, something like 70%. During that time where Celtic won 21 honours, Rangers won four and Dunfermline, Aberdeen, Dundee, Partick Thistle and Hibs one each. Such statistics simply cannot be argued against.

There was the European Cup triumph of 1967, one defeat in the final of 1970 and two in semi-finals, when a penalty shoot-out in 1972 and sheer thuggery and intimidation in 1974 prevented Celtic from reaching the final in those years.

But perhaps the biggest testimony to the success of the Stein Revolution in 1965 was what Celtic now expected. In 1967, when they lost (in contentious circumstances – but that is another totally different story!) to Racing Club in the World Championship, and in 1970 when they lost to Feyenoord through sheer complacency in the European Cup final, they were still second in the World in 1967 and in Europe in 1970. They were Champions of Europe in 1967 in spite of the defeat to Racing, and the best team in Britain in 1970 through their glorious defeat of Leeds United.

One would have thought that this level of success might have been enough, but no, on both of these occasions in 1967 and 1970 there began the most intense spell of navel-gazing and self-examination that one could have imagined. And all because they were not quite the best! There had been times in the 1950s and 1960s when you would not necessarily have put Celtic in the top five in Scotland! Regular defeats to the likes of Falkirk, St Mirren, Dundee, Dunfermline and Airdrie were the order of the day to the immense dismay of the huge but disorientated support. But things changed and changed utterly in 1965. It was indeed the year of the Celtic revolution.

"Before Stein we never had a victory; after Stein we never had a defeat."

This statement is not literally true ... but it is close enough to be going on with.

THE CLASS OF 1965

GOALKEEPERS:

FALLON, John *(Born 16 August 1940)*
Appearances - 184: Shut Outs - 61

An immensely likeable character who still follows Celtic to this day. John played for the club between 1959 and 1972 and enjoyed some tremendous performances, particularly in 1969 when he was part of the side which won the three domestic Scottish honours in the month of April. He was technically a Lisbon Lion because he was the substitute goalkeeper (only a substitute goalkeeper was allowed in 1967) but had to give up his medal to Chairman Bob Kelly. The club later struck a medal for him to compensate. Arguably his best-ever game for Celtic was in Argentina when he was called upon to play at the last minute, after Ronnie Simpson had been felled with a missile, and he played superbly. His low point was against Rangers at the New Year of 1968, when they were gifted an undeserved 2-2 draw. Some supporters never forgave him for that, but he came back magnificently the following year. When John lost his place to Ronnie Simpson, there were no tantrums or transfer requests, instead he and Ronnie became friends, learning a great deal from each other.

KENNEDY, John (Jack) *(Born 4 September 1939)*
Appearances - 1: Shut Outs - 1

Jack played only one game for Celtic, against Raith Rovers in the League Cup quarter-final, but he earned seven caps for Northern Ireland and won the Irish League with Distillery. After leaving Celtic in 1967, he played for Detroit Cougars in the USA and English side Lincoln City.

SIMPSON, Ronnie *(11 October 1930-19 April 2004)*
Appearances - 188: Shut Outs - 91

A remarkable and scarcely believable career! Ronnie's father was Jimmy Simpson of Rangers, and he played for Queen's Park, (as an amateur he represented Great Britain in the 1948 Olympic Games) Third Lanark and Newcastle United (for whom he won two English FA Cup medals) before he returned to Scotland in 1960 to join Hibs. Ronnie was then sold by Jock Stein to Celtic only as a cover for injuries four years later, and he cannot have believed that he would start, in his mid-30s, winning medals for Celtic. He certainly played a great part in the winning of the League Cup in 1965, and from then on his career never looked back with 1967 seeing a European Cup-winners medal and the first of his five Scottish caps in the famous 3-2 win over World Champions England at Wembley. Only a shoulder injury in 1969 brought to an end this remarkable career. Apart from all this, Ronnie was a City Councillor (for the Conservatives!) in Edinburgh, ran a sports shop, was a member of the Pools Panel, managed Hamilton Accies and was a goalkeeper coach for Dunfermline Athletic.

FULL-BACKS:

CRAIG, Jim *(Born 30 April 1943)*
Appearances - 209: Goals - 6

By no means, your normal run-of-the-mill Celtic player. Jim was the son-in-law of a Celtic Director, he is still the only Celtic player to have been a dentist, and he is still the only dentist to have won a European Cup-winner's medal. His nickname was "Cairney" because of a BBC series called "This Man Craig" based on a Glasgow comprehensive school, in which the main character was Mr Craig played by John Cairney (In real life, John Cairney, who did many programmes of Robert Burns as well, is a Celtic supporter who wrote a biography of Jimmy McGrory). He was a fine right-back, and although he gave away that penalty in Lisbon, most people including Jock Stein himself absolved him from blame, and in any case he more than made up for it in the rest of the game. He played for Celtic until 1972, his double-century of appearances including a rare goal scored in the League Cup final of 1969. Following the Scottish Cup final win of May 1972, he departed with his wife temporarily to South Africa, but soon returned and has appeared frequently hosting programmes on Celtic TV. He is interested in other sports, and his son, also called James Craig, played four times for Scotland at rugby.

GEMMELL, Tommy *(16 October 1943-2 March 2017)*
Appearances - 434: Goals - 69

A larger-than-life character forever immortalised by his goal in Lisbon (He also scored in Celtic's other European Cup final in Milan in 1970). Many fans had qualms about Tommy in 1965 because of his unreliability, but his career took off under Jock Stein and he was undeniably one of the best players of that era. A good penalty kick taker, and never afraid to attack, Tommy had an infectious swagger about him that inspired confidence. He did not always see eye-to-eye with Jock Stein, and on one particular occasion, he was dropped for a League Cup final after being sent off when playing for Scotland! On another occasion, he was sent home in disgrace from the USA. Tommy was transferred to Nottingham Forest in 1971 but was not a success there. He came back to Scotland to play for then manage Dundee, winning a League Cup-winners medal for them in that awful final of December 1973 against Celtic on an unplayable pitch. He was particularly hated by Rangers supporters because he made no attempt to hide his non-Catholic background.

KENNEDY, Jim *(31 January 1934-2 December 2003)*
Appearances - 241: Goals - 2

It is a shame that Jim never won a major medal for Celtic because no-one deserved one more for his effort and love of the club. By the time that Jock Stein arrived, Jim was possibly just a little on the old side and he was transferred to Morton, having played only a handful of games under Jock. He had been a very reliable left-back for Celtic, having had some particularly good games in the 1961/62 season, and when Tommy Gemmell arrived on the scene, he found a new niche for himself at left-half in season 1963/64, another season when Celtic almost made it, and indeed would have done so but for their Rangers complex. Jim was a creative left-half, and yet he was still playing at left-back for Scotland, including the famous 1-0 win over England at Hampden in April 1964, which made it three victories in a row over the English. He played six times for Scotland but lost both his Cup Finals against Rangers (in the Scottish Cup final of 1963 and the League Cup final of 1964/65), while he had the misfortune to go down with appendicitis on the eve of the replay against Dunfermline in the 1961 Scottish Cup final.

O'NEILL, Willie *(30 December 1940-28 April 2011)*
Appearances - 79: Goals - 0

Willie never really let Celtic down and was a fine reserve for many years before he moved to Carlisle United in 1969. He played the first half of the 1966/67 season, when the two full-backs were Gemmell and O'Neill, before Jim Craig was brought back in January and Gemmell was moved to left-back. Willie is chiefly remembered for two things. One was when he made his debut in that horrendous Scottish Cup final replay defeat of 1961 – albeit Willie played well enough – when Jim Kennedy went down with appendicitis, and the other was in the Scottish League Cup final of October 1966, when he appeared from nowhere to clear his lines at a time when Rangers were pressing hard. He was a great team man and a great friend of Jimmy Johnstone. Stein tried to ensure that the two of them would sit together on aeroplanes, so that Willie could tell Jimmy jokes and keep him from panicking!

YOUNG, Ian *(21 May 1943-11 December 2019)*
Appearances - 164: Goals - 3

A hard-working full back, who perhaps deserved more out of the game than what he got. It is a shame that Ian tends to be recalled for his famous crunching tackle on Willie Johnston in the 1965 Scottish League Cup final, which earned him a booking but effectively put Johnston out of that game. But there was so much more to him than that. He had a curiously hunched run, and could indeed tackle hard, but he was also capable of playing out of defence, although he was never really an attacking full-back. A Rangers supporter as a boy, he attracted their attention, but he always felt ill done by them and would say that as a Celtic player he would play so much harder against Rangers. He came to the fore in 1963, when changes had to be made after an appalling 0-4 defeat to Rangers at Ibrox at the New Year, and he held his place, frequently earning good reviews until 1966. He lost his place to Jim Craig, but there was not really very much between the two of them. He played one game in the 1966/67 season, and then moved on to St Mirren. In later years, he was a social worker and a committed Christian, apparently regretting very much his infamous tackle on Willie Johnston, but Celtic fans did not share his feelings of remorse! A fine player who served the club in bad times and good.

HALF-BACKS:

BROGAN, Jim *(5 June 1944-24 September 2018)*
Appearances - 341: Goals - 9

A tremendous servant for Celtic who played in midfield and at full-back for many years before opening a string of pubs. He was the younger brother of Frank, whom Celtic released prematurely, but Jock Stein saw talent in Jim. He did not quite make it to Lisbon, but he was the first man to fight his way into that team, replacing John Clark as a defensive sweeper. Jim won seven Scottish League titles, four Scottish Cups, three Scottish League Cups and played in the 1970 European Cup final in Milan, as well as being chosen four times for Scotland. He was a very hard tackler, earning nicknames like "Crazy Horse" from the appreciative Celtic fans. Jim was not an attack-minded player, but he once scored a famous goal on 3 January 1972, when he appeared out of nowhere to score a last-gasp winner against Rangers at Parkhead. He played for Celtic until 1975, and then appeared for Coventry City and Ayr United. Very sadly, he spent the last 10 years of his life suffering from dementia, caused, his family believed, at least partly by his footballing career.

CLARK, John *(Born 13 March 1941)*
Appearances - 318: Goals - 3

Commonly known as "the quiet man," "Luggy" or "John the brush" (because he was the "sweeper up"), John was born in Chapelhall in 1941 and joined Celtic in 1958. He scored a famous goal in the quarter-final replay of the Scottish Cup against Hibs at Easter Road in 1961, when fellow Lisbon Lion Ronnie Simpson was the beaten goalkeeper. For a while he was a right-half, but Jock Stein spotted that his best position was behind Billy McNeill as almost a double centre-half or a "sweeper up." John was a very unspectacular sort of player, and his lifestyle was like that as well. But he was very reliable and never caused any trouble, often being seen as a calming influence on McNeill. He was the first of the Lions to lose his position on a regular basis, but John was right to feel that he still had some football left in him when he departed to Morton in 1971. When his playing career was over, he became Assistant Manager to Billy McNeill at both Aberdeen and Celtic. John finished his working life officially as the Kit Man at Celtic Park, but one suspects that he was often consulted by various Managers for a few words of wisdom.

CUSHLEY, John *(21 January 1943-24 March 2008)*
Appearances - 41: Goals - 0

A fine centre-half who filled in more than adequately for Billy McNeill when Billy was injured, John moved to West Ham United and later Dunfermline Athletic in order to get first-team football. He was simply unfortunate to be around when McNeill was in his prime. John was a teacher of French and Spanish and was taken to Spain as an interpreter with the Celtic party which tried unsuccessfully to sign Alfredo di Stefano in 1964. When his football career was finished, he continued as a teacher. John died in 2008 of Motor Neurone Disease.

McNEILL, Billy *(2 March 1940-22 April 2019)*
Appearances - 789: Goals - 37

It would be difficult to overestimate the contribution of Billy McNeill to Celtic. As a player, he won nine Scottish League titles, seven Scottish Cups, six Scottish League Cups and of course one European Cup. Then, as a Manager, he had five seasons in which he won one trophy every year, before, as if it were all meant, Billy was brought back to win the League and Cup double in Celtic's Centenary year. And there is still more to it than that! Billy was an inspiring leader and centre-half, and he was with the club through bad times. He made his debut in 1958, and although a regular in the Scotland team was sometimes prone to errors, having a particularly bad time in 1964/65 when he was thinking of going south. But Jock Stein and Bertie Auld came back and his life took off, with Billy symbolically heading Celtic to glory in the 1965 Scottish Cup final, and from then on it was glory all the way. Billy has a strong claim to being considered the most influential Celt of all time.

MURDOCH, Bobby *(17 August 1944-15 May 2001)*
Appearances - 484: Goals - 105

Arguably the best player of the Lisbon Lions - and that is some claim! - Bobby was also the first of that wonderful team to die. He succumbed to a stroke in 2001 at the age of just 56. He made his Celtic debut in 1962 as an inside-forward, at which he was only a moderate success, but wise supporters wondered whether he might be a better wing-half. It was Jock Stein's decision to move him to that position which made Celtic one of the best teams in the world and Bobby Murdoch one of the best players in the world. He suffered a few weight problems in later years, causing him to go twice to health farms in England. Bobby moved to Middlesbrough in 1973 and starred for them under Jack Charlton before becoming their Manager, and he is considered to be one of the all-time Boro greats. Bobby played 12 times for Scotland but never with any great success, although he did score a fine goal against West Germany at Hampden in 1969.

FORWARDS:

AULD, Bertie *(23 March 1938-14 November 2021)*
Appearances - 279: Goals - 85

Bertie was the game-changer in 1965. He should never have been allowed to go in the first place in 1961, but his return from Birmingham City in January 1965 was the first step to the Celtic revival and resurrection of this year. He had clearly upset Mr Kelly by his slightly unconventional approach to authority in 1961 and his transfer occurred round about the same time as the Scottish Cup final defeat to Dunfermline Athletic. Bertie was much missed and managed to win an English League Cup-winners medal with Birmingham in 1963, when we were on our knees and unable to win anything. His return was greeted with great enthusiasm by the support, and after an anonymous second debut against Hearts, he moved inside to allow Bobby Lennox to go outside, and the team suddenly picked up, feeding on Bertie's infectious enthusiasm. He was the mainstay of the team in Lisbon and hung around until 1971 before moving to Hibs. Bertie was the Manager of Hamilton Accies, Partick Thistle and Hibs, but his heart was always with Celtic, attending games regularly and being always willing to turn up at supporters' functions, where he was a popular entertainer.

CHALMERS, Stevie *(26 December 1935-29 April 2019)*
Appearances - 406: Goals - 228

A remarkable character from the old Garngad, who was once given only weeks to live when suffering from meningitis, Stevie nevertheless came back to score the most famous goal in Celtic's history, the winner in Lisbon in the 1967 European Cup final. Stevie was in the RAF before he joined Celtic via junior outfit Ashfield in 1959. A total gentleman, whose calm and dignified demeanour sometimes belied his grim determination to do well, he also excelled at golf. Stevie was equally at home on the right wing as he was in the centre. He suffered terrible abuse from the ignorant during the bad old days of the early 1960s, but he stuck to his game and, although out for several spells with injuries, Stevie was a vital player in Jock Stein's team. His five appearances for Scotland included a goal scored against Brazil in June 1966 at Hampden. Stevie's Celtic career effectively ended when he broke his leg in the 1969 Scottish League Cup final against St Johnstone, but he later played for both Morton and Partick Thistle. For a while after he retired, Stevie worked for the Celtic Development Pools.

DIVERS, John *(8 March 1940-23 September 2014)*
Appearances - 232: Goals - 102

Son of the John Divers who played in the Empire Exhibition Trophy-winning side of 1938 and the great-nephew of Patsy Gallacher, John's career was ultimately a disappointment, and yet it did have its moments. A great ball player, but fatally too slow and sometimes appearing to lack the urgency required, John broke through in the 1950s and for a while looked the part. On one occasion, for the first match of season 1962/63, he was dropped for being late, having forgotten his boots, having to go back for them and getting delayed in traffic jams! John suffered like everyone else from the erratic team selections of the day, and when Jock Stein arrived it looked as if there were no place for him. But he was given a surprise recall in the second game of the 1965/66 season, and in the first League game at Tannadice Park on 25 August 1965, he scored the first goal of the original "nine in a row." Sadly, John's Indian summer did not last long, and he was dropped after a disappointing performance against Rangers in September 1965. John finished his football career playing for Partick Thistle, before becoming a Teacher of Commercial subjects.

GALLAGHER, Charlie *(3 November 1940-11 July 2021)*
Appearances - 171: Goals - 32

One of the best Celtic players of this era, even though he struggled to secure a regular first-team place and indeed a regular position. In modern terms, Charlie would have been a midfielder with superb passing ability and also with a devastating shot. He was famous for his ability to take corner kicks, setting up at least two iconic goals (against Dunfermline in the 1965 Scottish Cup final and Vodjvodina in the European Cup two years later) for Billy McNeill and also on one occasion - in a Scottish Cup tie at Morton - scoring from one directly. A silky player, with a clear ability to read a game, the wonder was that Charlie did not play oftener, but the 1968 Scottish League title win is often referred to, quite rightly, as "Gallagher's Championship." Celtic were behind in the race and did not have the opportunity to play Rangers again after a damaging draw at New Year. All that they could do was win their games and hope that Rangers would crack. Bertie Auld was injured, and Charlie stepped in, instrumental as Celtic won, for example, difficult away games at St Johnstone, Dundee United, Hearts and Aberdeen with such panache that Rangers did indeed "crack" under the psychological pressure of it all. Having done that job, Gallagher then retired from the scene, although he did later have some successful seasons with Dumbarton.

HUGHES, John *(3 April 1943-1 August 2022)*
Appearances - 416: Goals - 189

No player ever caused so many arguments amongst Celtic supporters as John Hughes did. On a good day, he could be the best in the world, and he has many fine goals to his credit – one at Dens Park springs to mind and another two against Morton, one at Cappielow and another in a League Cup semi-final at Hampden – but the problem was that he could not always be relied upon to produce the goods, and this was possibly why he did not get a game in Lisbon. Yet there were few better sights than "Yogi Bear" in all his glory, and he was deservedly considered by the support to be a cult hero. John was particularly good on heavy pitches and also on the hard ground, when he ditched his football boots for sandshoes. The personality clash between him and Jock Stein, however, was not subtle and came to a head one day in March 1971 when John walked out of Parkhead after being dropped. It seemed to stem from a game at Muirton Park, when he was taken off injured, insisted on going back on, and then had to come off again. Yogi was transferred to Crystal Palace in October 1971, then went briefly to Sunderland in 1973 before injury curtailed his career. Things might have been different for John in the latter part of his career at Celtic, if he had taken his opportunity to score at the start of extra-time in the Milan European Cup final.

JOHNSTONE, Jimmy *(30 September 1944-13 March 2006)*
Appearances - 515: Goals - 130

Words sometimes fail the historian as he tries to assess the contribution of Jimmy Johnstone. We must analyse his relationship with his Manager. Both Jock Stein and Johnstone owed an awful lot to each other, but their fallings-out were frequent and legendary. On at least two occasions, Stein had Johnstone suspended and there were several other occasions when Jimmy was dropped and ignored. Yet without Stein, the likelihood would have been that Johnstone would have drifted away from the game, and that would have been a terrible loss, because Jimmy on his game was a sight to behold. Like most ball players of that era, he was subjected to some terrible abuse from defenders, and one of Stein's great successes was in persuading him not to retaliate, but to get up and come back for more. On one famous occasion, Stein indulged Jimmy's fear of flying by allowing him to miss a game in Belgrade if he helped Celtic build up a four-goal first-leg lead, which he duly did; when Jimmy tried the same another time, it was *"Get oan that f---in' plane like a'body else"* but Jock instructed Willie O'Neill or Bobby Lennox to sit beside him and tell him jokes! Jimmy is rightly considered to have been one of the best football players of all time, but he wasn't always the best team man. In spite of all that, Jimmy along with Lennox and Billy McNeill stayed with Stein for every one of the nine-in-a-row League titles won by Celtic from 1965/66 until 1973/74.

LENNOX, Bobby *(born 30 August 1943)*
Appearances - 608: Goals - 304

One of the real success stories. For a while, when he was playing all over the forward line, Bobby's Celtic career seemed to be going nowhere. The arrival of Bertie Auld, however, saw the pair of them link up on the left side of the field, and the goals began to come. He had a great deal of infectious enthusiasm and teamed up with Jimmy Johnstone on and off the field. Known as "the Buzz Bomb," Lennox's speed was phenomenal, and he was likened to a greyhound or a whippet, sometimes running so fast that he was wrongly flagged for offside by a linesman who simply could not believe how fast he was. A case in point was the game against Liverpool in the European Cup Winners' Cup semi-final of 1966, but a typical Lennox goal came in the Scottish League Cup final of the same year when he ran on to a Joe McBride knock down and scored at speed without breaking stride. Bobby played for the club for 20 years, although there was a brief break when he spent the summer of 1978 in the USA with the Houston Hurricanes, and he was never known to complain. With

304 goals, Bobby is second only to Jimmy McGrory in terms of scoring goals for Celtic, *"the only team he ever wanted to play for."* Others said that, but Bobby Lennox meant it.

MAXWELL, Hugh *(14 May 1938-January 2010)*
Appearances - 8: Goals - 2

By no means one of Celtic's best-ever players, Hugh joined Celtic from Falkirk in November 1964 in a move that smacked of desperation. He was then given his debut the following day in a game against Dundee which should have been abandoned because of torrential rain. Hugh scored within 10 seconds in his next game, against his old team Falkirk, but sadly he did little else in his time at Parkhead. Under Jock Stein, he played just two games, and Celtic lost both! Hugh was transferred to St Johnstone in summer 1965 and later enjoyed spells with Dunfermline and South African outfit Hellenic. Back in 1962, Hugh had famously scored all seven of Falkirk's goals in a 7-3 League win at Brockville over a Clyde side which featured a very young Harry Hood.

McBRIDE, Joe *(10 June 1938-11 July 2012)*
Appearances - 94: Goals - 86

Born in Govan near Ibrox Park on the very day that Celtic were winning the Empire Exhibition Trophy, Joe took a long time before eventually joining Celtic in June 1965 as Jock Stein's first major signing. He had already played with Kilmarnock, Wolves, Luton Town, Partick Thistle and Motherwell (giving Billy McNeill a bad time in the 1965 Scottish Cup semi-final). Joe was not an instant success, but once he settled down goals came with regularity, and he was particularly impressive in the first half of the 1966/67 season until sustaining a bad injury at Pittodrie on Christmas Eve. He required surgery and was out for the rest of the season, missing out on Lisbon, but still finished up the top goalscorer in the country! His comeback from this injury was limited with Celtic, but he did tmove on to Hibs and then Dunfermline before finishing his career with Clyde. Joe was a prolific striker, and it is a great pity that Celtic didn't get him earlier and hold on to him a little longer.

BACKROOM & MANAGEMENT STAFF

FALLON, Sean *(31 July 1922-18 January 2013)*

Celtic's "Iron Man" (a reference to his toughness as a player) was Assistant Manager to Jimmy McGrory in 1965, and it is believed that Chairman Bob Kelly intended to make Fallon the Manager and Jock Stein his Assistant, but Stein refused. Sean had played for Celtic in the 1950s, mainly as a left-back although he did as a centre-forward score the winning goal in the 1954 Scottish Cup final against Aberdeen. He remained very loyal to Jock and deserves a fair amount of praise for his part in the team's incredible success. Sean was particularly adept at spotting and developing young talent.

KELLY, Bob *(17 October 1902-21 September 1971)*

Often portrayed as the villain of the piece, Bob Kelly does indeed have a lot to answer for, particularly with regard to the disastrous years of the early 1960s. But this is perhaps to ignore his other great qualities. He was the son of James Kelly, who played in and was captain of Celtic's first-ever team in 1888, but a boyhood accident prevented Bob from having a career in football himself. On the death of his father in 1932, he became a Director of Celtic and he proved to be an able administrator, taking over as Chairman of the club in 1947. Kelly would also become President of the Scottish League and, later, of the SFA. He earned credit for his stand in 1952 against the removal of the Irish flag from Celtic Park, and no-one could doubt his love for the club. But as Chairman he kept interfering in team selection, did not invest nearly enough in the playing side of the club and some of his ideas were crazy. As a result, the club was going through a very bad spell due to his ill-thought-out youth policy, sometimes called "The Kelly Kids," until he realised, belatedly, in late 1964 or early 1965 that he was in the wrong and appointed Jock Stein to the Manager's job – a job that Stein should have had years earlier. To his credit, Kelly backed Stein unreservedly, and deserves some praise, at least, for the club reaching such dizzy heights in European and World football. Bob was knighted at New Year 1969 for his services to Scottish football.

McGRORY, Jimmy *(26 April 1904-20 October 1982)*

Undeniably one of Celtic's greatest-ever players and certainly their most prolific-ever goalscorer, having broken all top-flight records in the 1920s and 1930s. Jimmy endured a less productive spell as manager from 1945 until 1965, during which Celtic, in spite of a few exceptional successes which hinted at a return to the glory days, failed to make any real impact on Scottish football. One League title in 20 years is really not good enough for a club like Celtic. Yet Jimmy remained a much loved and respected figure, and as such was a handy "shield" for the Kelly regime.

MOCHAN, Neil *(6 April 1927-28 August 1994)*

Neil was the trainer of the Lisbon Lions, and deserves all the credit he can get for producing such fit young men. Not only did he understand football, but he also understood human psychology, knowing how to deal with the fragile creatures that professional footballers can sometimes be. Neil had played with distinction for Celtic in the 1950s, not least in the 7-1 League Cup final win over Rangers in 1957, and in May 1953 he managed the unusual feat of winning two Cup medals (the Glasgow Charity Cup and the Coronation Cup) before he played a game at Parkhead! He was appointed as Celtic trainer in 1964 and together with Bob Rooney and Jim Steele provided a formidable and very supportive backroom team. Having played in the same team as Jock Stein, he enjoyed the Manager's confidence in everything, and Stein frequently stated how much he owed to Mochan. The man known as "Smiler" died of leukaemia in Falkirk in 1994.

STEIN, Jock *(5 October 1922-10 September 1985)*

A colossus of a man in more senses than one, Jock first came to public attention when he captained Celtic to the Coronation Cup in 1953 then the League and Cup double the following year. Following a spell in the Celtic backroom, he became Manager of Dunfermline in 1960, then moved to Hibs before returning to Celtic in early 1965. What he achieved at Celtic is truly breathtaking – nine consecutive League titles and then another one, eight Scottish Cups, six Scottish League Cups and, of course, a European Cup. Jock even survived a serious road accident in the summer of 1975 to come back and win a sparkling League and Cup double in 1977. But he never really survived the transfer of Kenny Dalglish to Liverpool in August 1977 and departed a year later after a dismal final season. Briefly Manager of Leeds United, Jock then took over the Scotland job and restored some degree of pride after the Argentina fiasco. He took Scotland to World Cup qualification in 1982 and had more or less done that job again in September 1985 at Ninian Park, Cardiff against Wales when he tragically collapsed and died just minutes after the end of the game.

Appendix - 1965 Statistics

List of competitive games played by Celtic in 1965

Friday, 1 January 1965
Scottish League
Rangers 1 Celtic 0

Rangers: *Ritchie, Provan and Caldow; Greig, McKinnon and Wood; Wilson, Millar, Forrest, Beck and Johnston.*

Celtic: *Simpson, Young and Gemmell; Clark, McNeill and Kennedy; Johnstone, Murdoch, Hughes, Divers and Gallagher.*

Referee: *Mr T Wharton, Clarkston*

Scorer: *Forrest.*

Saturday, 2 January 1965
Scottish League
Celtic 1 Clyde 1

Celtic: *Simpson, Young and Gemmell; Clark, McNeill and Kennedy; Lennox, Maxwell, Hughes, Divers and Gallagher.*

Clyde: *McCulloch, Glasgow and Mulheron; McHugh, Fraser and White; Bryce, Gilroy, Knox, McLean and Hastings.*

Referee: *Mr J McConville, Wishaw*

Scorers: *Celtic – Hughes; Clyde – Gilroy.*

Saturday, 9 January 1965
Scottish League
Dundee United 3 Celtic 1

Dundee United: *Mackay, Millar and Briggs; Munro, Smith and Gillespie; Dick, Berg, Dossing, Mitchell and Persson.*

Celtic: *Simpson, Young and Gemmell; Clark, McNeill and Brogan; Johnstone, Murdoch, Hughes, Divers and Gallagher.*

Referee: *Mr W Mullen, Dalkeith*

Scorers: *Dundee United – Dossing 2, Millar; Celtic – Hughes.*

Saturday, 16 January 1965
Scottish League
Celtic 1 Hearts 2

Celtic: *Fallon, Young and Gemmell; Brogan, McNeill and Kennedy; Johnstone, Murdoch, Hughes, Gallagher and Auld.*

Hearts: *Cruickshank, Shevlane and Holt; Ferguson, Anderson and Higgins; Hamilton, Jensen, Wallace, Gordon and Traynor.*

Referee: *Mr J Kelly, Motherwell*

Scorers: *Celtic – Gemmell; Hearts – Hamilton 2.*

Saturday, 23 January 1965
Scottish League
Morton 3 Celtic 3

Morton: *E Sorensen, Boyd and Johansen; Smith, Kiernan and Strachan; Bertelsen, J Sorensen, Caven, McGraw and Stevenson.*

Celtic: *Fallon, Young and Gemmell; Clark, McNeill and Brogan; Johnstone, Murdoch, Hughes, Lennox and Auld.*

Referee: *Mr J Stewart, Paisley*

Scorers: *Morton – Bertelsen 2, Strachan; Celtic – Lennox, Hughes, Gemmell.*

Saturday, 30 January 1965
Scottish League
Celtic 8 Aberdeen 0

Celtic: *Fallon, Young and Gemmell; Clark, McNeill and Brogan; Chalmers, Murdoch, Hughes, Lennox and Auld.*

Aberdeen: *Ogston, Bennett and Shewan; Petersen, McCormick and Smith; Fraser, Winchester, Ravn, Kerrigan and Mortensen.*

Referee: *Mr JP Barclay, Kirkcaldy*

Scorers: *Hughes 5, Lennox, Murdoch, Auld (pen).*

Saturday, 6 February 1965
Scottish Cup (R1)
St Mirren 0 Celtic 3

St Mirren: *Liney, Murray and Riddell; Gray, Clunie and Wilson; McIntyre, Queen, Carroll, Ross and Gemmell.*

Celtic: *Fallon, Young and Gemmell; Clark, McNeill and Brogan; Chalmers, Murdoch, Hughes, Lennox and Auld.*

Referee: *Mr T Wharton, Clarkston*

Scorers: *Lennox 2, Chalmers.*

Saturday, 13 February 1965
Scottish League
St Mirren 1 Celtic 5

St Mirren: *Liney, Murray and Riddell; Gray, Clunie and Wilson; Robertson, Carroll, Hughes, Queen and Gemmell.*

Celtic: *Fallon, Young and Gemmell; Clark, McNeill and Brogan; Chalmers, Murdoch, Hughes, Lennox and Auld.*

Referee: *Mr A Crawley, Glasgow*

Scorers: *St Mirren – Carroll; Celtic – Chalmers, Lennox, Brogan, Hughes, Murdoch.*

Saturday, 20 February 1965
Scottish Cup (R2)
Queen's Park 0 Celtic 1

Queen's Park: *Clark, Gilmour and Pollatschek; Robertson, Neil and McLaughlin; Hopper, Millar, Buchanan, Mackay and Waddell.*

Celtic: *Fallon, Young and Gemmell; Clark, McNeill and Brogan; Chalmers, Murdoch, Hughes, Lennox and Auld.*

Referee: *Mr JW Paterson, Bothwell*

Scorer: *Lennox.*

Saturday, 27 February 1965
Scottish League
Celtic 2 Kilmarnock 0

Celtic: *Fallon, Young and Gemmell; Clark, McNeill and Brogan; Chalmers, Murdoch, Hughes, Lennox and Auld.*

Kilmarnock: *Forsyth, King and Watson; Murray, McGrory and Beattie; McIlroy, McInally, Hamilton, McFadzean and Sneddon.*

Referee: *Mr JRP Gordon, Newport-on-Tay*

Scorers: *Hughes, Chalmers.*

Saturday, 6 March 1965
Scottish Cup (Q/Final)
Celtic 3 Kilmarnock 2

Celtic: *Fallon, Young and Gemmell; Clark, McNeill and Brogan; Chalmers, Murdoch, Hughes, Lennox and Auld.*

Kilmarnock: *Forsyth, King and Watson; Murray, McGrory and Beattie; Brown, McInally, Hamilton, McFadzean and McIlroy.*

Referee: *Mr H Phillips, Wishaw*

Scorers: *Celtic – Lennox, Auld, Hughes; Kilmarnock – McInally 2.*

Wednesday, 10 March 1965
Scottish League
Airdrie 0 Celtic 6

Airdrie: *Samson, Jonquin and Caldwell; Rowan, Hannah and Reid; Ferguson, McMillan, Mooney, Murray and Newlands.*

Celtic: *Fallon, Young and Gemmell; Clark, McNeill and Brogan; Chalmers, Murdoch, Hughes, Lennox and Auld.*

Referee: *Mr N Watson, Glenrothes*

Scorers: *Auld 5, Hughes.*

Saturday, 13 March 1965
Scottish League
Celtic 0 St Johnstone 1

Celtic: *Fallon, Young and Gemmell; Clark, McNeill and Brogan; Chalmers, Murdoch, Hughes, Lennox and Auld.*

St Johnstone: *McVittie, McFadyen and Coburn; Richmond, McKinven and Renton; Kerray, Whitelaw, McCarry, Duffy and McGrogan.*

Referee: *Mr RH Davidson, Airdrie*

Scorer: *Duffy.*

Saturday, 20 March 1965
Scottish League
Dundee 3 Celtic 3

Dundee: *Donaldson, Hamilton and Cox; Cousin, Easton and Stuart; Murray, Penman, Cameron, Cooke and Robertson.*

Celtic: *Fallon, Young and Kennedy; Murdoch, McNeill and Clark; Johnstone, Chalmers, Hughes, Lennox and Auld.*

Referee: *Mr WJ Mullen, Dalkeith*

Scorers: *Dundee – Cameron 2, Murdoch own goal; Celtic – Lennox 2, Johnstone.*

Monday, 22 March 1965
Scottish League
Celtic 2 Hibs 4

Celtic: *Fallon, Young and Gemmell; Brogan, McNeill and Clark; Chalmers, Murdoch, Hughes, Maxwell and Lennox.*

Hibs: *Wilson, Fraser and Davies; Stanton, McNamee and Baxter; Martin, Quinn, Cormack, Hamilton and Stevenson.*

Referee: *Mr RH Davidson, Airdrie*

Scorers: *Celtic – Lennox 2; Hibs - Martin 3, Young own goal.*

Saturday, 27 March 1965 (Hampden)
Scottish Cup (S/Final)
Celtic 2 Motherwell 2

Celtic: *Fallon, Young and Gemmell; Murdoch, McNeill and Clark; Johnstone, Gallagher, Hughes, Lennox and Auld.*

Motherwell: *Wylie, Thomson and R McCallum; Murray, Delaney and W McCallum; Lindsay, McCann, McBride, Weir and Hunter.*

Referee: *Mr AJF Webster, Falkirk*

Scorers: *Celtic – Lennox, Auld (pen); Motherwell – McBride 2.*

Wednesday, 31 March 1965 (Hampden)
Scottish Cup (S/Final replay)
Celtic 3 Motherwell 0

Celtic: *Fallon, Young and Gemmell; Murdoch, McNeill and Clark; Chalmers, Gallagher, Hughes, Lennox and Auld.*

Motherwell: *Wylie, Thomson and R McCallum; Murray, Delaney and W McCallum; Carlyle, McCann, McBride, Weir and Lindsay.*

Referee: *Mr AJF Webster, Falkirk*

Scorers: *Chalmers, Hughes, Lennox.*

Saturday, 3 April 1965
Scottish League
Celtic 1 Third Lanark 0

Celtic: *Fallon, Young and Gemmell; Murdoch, McNeill and Clark; Chalmers, Gallagher, Hughes, Lennox and Auld.*

Third Lanark: *Williams, D MacKay and May; Connell, Little and A Mackay; McGuire, Jackson, Murray, Fyfe and Kirk.*

Referee: *Mr W Syme, Glasgow*

Scorer: *D MacKay own goal.*

Wednesday, 7 April 1965
Scottish League
Hibs 0 Celtic 4

Hibs: *Wilson, Simpson and Davies; Stanton, McNamee and Baxter; Cormack, Hamilton, Scott, Quinn and Martin.*

Celtic: *Fallon, Young and Gemmell; Murdoch, McNeill and Clark; Chalmers, Gallagher, Hughes, Lennox and Auld.*

Referee: *Mr JP Barclay, Kirkcaldy*

Scorers: *Auld 2, Chalmers, Murdoch.*

Wednesday, 14 April 1965
Scottish League
Falkirk 6 Celtic 2

Falkirk: *Whigham; Lambie, Hunter; Houston, Baillie, Fulton; Graham, Gourlay, Wilson, Moran, Halliday.*

Celtic: *Fallon, Young and Gemmell; Murdoch, Cushley and O'Neill; Johnstone, Gallagher, Hughes, Lennox and Auld.*

Referee: *Mr J McConville, Wishaw*

Scorers: *Falkirk – Moran 2, Halliday, Graham, Fulton, Wilson; Celtic - Auld 2 (1 pen).*

Saturday, 17 April 1965
Scottish League
Celtic 1 Partick Thistle 2

Celtic: *Fallon, Young and Kennedy; Murdoch, McNeill and Clark; Johnstone, Lennox, Chalmers, Auld and Hughes.*

Partick Thistle: *Gray, Campbell and Muir; Gibb, Harvey and Cunningham; Cowan, Hainey, Hogan, Ewing and McParland.*

Referee: *Mr J Callaghan, Glasgow*

Scorers*: Celtic – Chalmers; Partick Thistle – Gibb, Hogan.*

Saturday, 24 April 1965 (Hampden)
Scottish Cup Final
Celtic 3 Dunfermline Athletic 2

Celtic: *Fallon, Young and Gemmell; Murdoch, McNeill and Clark; Chalmers, Gallagher, Hughes, Lennox and Auld.*

Dunfermline Athletic: *Herriot, W Callaghan and Lunn; Thomson, McLean and T Callaghan; Edwards, Smith, McLaughlin, Melrose and Sinclair.*

Referee: *Mr H Phillips, Wishaw*

Scorers: *Celtic – Auld 2, McNeill; Dunfermline Athletic – Melrose, McLaughlin.*

Wednesday, 28 April 1965
Scottish League
Dunfermline Athletic 5 Celtic 1

Dunfermline Athletic: *Herriot, Thomson and W Callaghan;*

Smith. Fraser and T Callaghan; Edwards, Ferguson, McLaughlin, Sinclair and Melrose.

Celtic: *Fallon, Gemmell and O'Neill; Clark, McNeill and Brogan; Johnstone, Murdoch, Hughes, Maxwell and Lennox.*

Referee: *Mr W Elliott, Barrhead*

Scorers: *Dunfermline Athletic – McLaughlin 2, Melrose, Ferguson, Clark own goal; Celtic – Hughes.*

Friday, 30 April 1965
Glasgow Cup (R1)
Celtic 2 Rangers 1

Celtic: *Fallon, Young and Gemmell; Murdoch, McNeill and Clark; Chalmers, Gallagher, Hughes, Lennox and Auld.*

Rangers: *Martin, Provan and Caldow: Hynd, McKinnon and Greig; Henderson, Wood, McLean, Brand and Wilson.*

Referee: *Mr D Weir, Glasgow*

Scorers: *Celtic – Auld, Chalmers; Rangers – Henderson.*

Monday, 3 May 1965 (Celtic Park)
Glasgow Cup (S/Final)
Celtic 3 Clyde 0

Celtic: *Fallon, Young and Gemmell; Murdoch, McNeill and Clark; Johnstone, Gallagher, Chalmers, Lennox and Auld.*

Clyde: *McCulloch, Glasgow and Soutar; Mulheron, Fraser and White; Bryce, Kilroy, Knox, McLean and Hastings.*

Referee: *Mr T Wharton, Clarkston*

Scorers: *Auld, McNeill, Lennox.*

Tuesday, 11 May 1965 (Hampden)
Glasgow Cup Final
Queen's Park 0 Celtic 5

Queen's Park: *Donaldson; Gilmour and Pollatschek; Stewart, Neil and Hunter; Buchanan, Carter, Ingram, Mackay and Hay.*

Celtic: *Fallon, Young and Gemmell; Murdoch, McNeill and Clark; Chalmers, Gallagher, Hughes, Lennox and Auld.*

Referee: *Mr W Brittle, Glasgow*

Scorers: *Lennox 2, Auld, Chalmers, Murdoch.*

Saturday, 14 August 1965
Scottish League Cup
Dundee United 2 Celtic 1

Dundee United: *Mackay, Millar and Briggs; Munro, Smith and Wing; Carroll, Gillespie, Dossing, Mitchell, Persson.*

Celtic: *Fallon, Young and Gemmell; Murdoch, McNeill and Clark; Johnstone, Gallagher, Chalmers, Lennox and Auld.*

Referee: *Mr AJF Webster, Falkirk*

Scorers: *Dundee United – Carroll, Gillespie; Celtic – Auld.*

Wednesday, 18 August 1965
Scottish League Cup
Celtic 1 Motherwell 0

Celtic: *Fallon, Young and Gemmell; Murdoch, McNeill and Clark; Johnstone, Divers, Chalmers, Lennox and Auld.*

Motherwell: *McCloy, M Thomson and McCallum; Aitken, Martis and Murray; Lindsay, Hunter, Delaney*, I Thomson and Weir.

Referee: *Mr W Elliot, Barrhead*

Scorer: *Divers.*

Saturday, 21 August 1965
Scottish League Cup
Celtic 0 Dundee 2

Celtic: *Fallon, Young and Gemmell; Murdoch, McNeill and Clark; Johnstone, Divers, McBride, Lennox and Auld.*

Dundee: *Donaldson, Hamilton and Stuart; Cousin, Easton and Houston; Murray, Penman, Bertelsen, Cooke and Cameron.*

Referee: *Mr J Hamilton, Renfrew*

Scorer: *Cameron 2.*

Wednesday, 25 August 1965
Scottish League
Dundee United 0 Celtic 4

Dundee United: *Mackay, Millar and Briggs; Munro, Smith and Wing; Carroll, Gillespie, Dossing, Mitchell, Persson.*

Celtic: *Fallon, Young and Gemmell; Murdoch, McNeill and Clark; Chalmers, Divers, McBride, Lennox and Gallagher.*

Referee: *Mr RH Davidson, Airdrie*

Scorers - *Divers, McBride, Young (pen), Gemmell.*

Saturday, 28 August 1965
Scottish League Cup
Celtic 3 Dundee United 0

Celtic: *Fallon, Young and Gemmell; Murdoch, McNeill and Clark; Chalmers, Divers, McBride, Lennox and Hughes.*

Dundee United: *Mackay, Millar and Briggs; Munro, Smith and Nelson; Soutar, Gillespie, Rooney, Mitchell, Persson.*

Referee: *Mr D Smail, Selkirk*

Scorers: *Young (pen), Chalmers, McBride.*

Wednesday, 1 September 1965
Scottish League Cup
Motherwell 2 Celtic 3

Motherwell: *McCloy, M Thomson and McCallum; Aitken, Martis and Murray; I Thomson, Howieson, Delaney, McLaughlan and Hunter.*

Celtic: *Fallon, Young and Gemmell; Murdoch, McNeill and Clark; Chalmers, Divers, Hughes, Lennox and Gallagher.*

Referee: *Mr N Watson, Glenrothes*

Scorers: *Motherwell – Delaney, Murray; Celtic – Lennox 2, Hughes (pen).*

Saturday, 4 September 1965
Scottish League Cup
Dundee 1 Celtic 3

Dundee: *Donaldson, Hamilton and Stuart; Cousin, Easton and Houston; Murray, Penman, Cameron, Cooke and Bertelsen.*

Celtic: *Fallon, Young and Gemmell; Murdoch, McNeill and Clark; Chalmers, Divers, McBride, Lennox and Hughes.*

Referee: *Mr H Phillips, Wishaw*

Scorers: *Dundee – Penman; Celtic – Divers, Hughes, McBride.*

Saturday, 11 September 1965
Scottish League
Celtic 2 Clyde 1

Celtic: *Fallon, Young and Gemmell; Murdoch, McNeill and Clark; Chalmers, Divers, McBride, Lennox and Hughes.*

Clyde: *Wright, Glasgow and Mulheron; McHugh, Fraser and White; Bryce, Gilroy, Staite, Stewart a*nd Hastings.

Referee: *Mr JM Kelly, Motherwell*

Scorers: *Celtic – Young (pen), Gemmell; Clyde – Stewart.*

Wednesday, 15 September 1965
Scottish League Cup (Q/Final)
Raith Rovers 1 Celtic 8

Raith Rovers: *Reid, McKeon and Gray; Stein, Evans and Porterfield; Hutchison, Gardner, Richardson, Lyall and McLean.*

Celtic: *Fallon, Young and Gemmell; Murdoch, McNeill and Clark; Johnstone, Divers, McBride, Lennox and Hughes.*

Referee: *Mr W Elliott, Barrhead*

Scorers: *Raith Rovers – Richardson; Celtic – McBride 3, Hughes 3, Lennox, Johnstone.*

Saturday, 18 September 1965
Scottish League
Rangers 2 Celtic 1

Rangers: *Ritchie, Johansen and Provan; Watson, McKinnon and Greig; Henderson, Sorensen, Forrest, McLean and Johnston.*

Celtic: *Fallon, Young and Gemmell; Murdoch, McNeill and Clark; Johnstone, Divers, Hughes, Lennox and Auld.*

Referee: *Mr T Wharton, Clarkston*

Scorers: *Rangers – Forrest, McLean (pen); Celtic – Hughes (pen).*

Wednesday, 22 September 1965
Scottish League Cup (Q/Final)
Celtic 4 Raith Rovers 0

Celtic: *Kennedy, Young and Gemmell; Murdoch, Cushley and Clark; Johnstone, Lennox, Chalmers, Auld and Hughes.*

Raith Rovers: *Reid, Selfridge and Gray; Stein, Evans and Porterfield; Christie, Gardner, Richardson, Lyall and McLean.*

Referee: *Mr W Elliot, Barrhead*

Scorers: *Auld 2, Chalmers, Murdoch.*

Saturday, 25 September 1965
Scottish League
Celtic 7 Aberdeen 1

Celtic: *Simpson, Young and Gemmell; Murdoch, McNeill and Clark; Johnstone, Auld, McBride, Lennox and Hughes.*

Aberdeen: *Clark, Bennett and Shewan; Burns, McCormick and Smith; Wilson, Little, Ravn, Winchester and Mortensen.*

Referee: *Mr JRP Gordon, Newport on Tay*

Scorers: *Celtic – Lennox 2, Johnstone 2, Auld, McBride, Hughes; Aberdeen – Winchester.*

Wednesday, 29 September 1965
Cup Winners' Cup (R1)
Go Ahead Deventer 0 Celtic 6

Go Ahead Deventer: *Van Zoghel, Butter and Thiemann; Kanselaar, Warner and Somer; Grebing, Niehaus, Buekestein, Veenstra and Adelaar.*

Celtic: *Simpson, Young and Gemmell; Murdoch, McNeill and Clark; Johnstone, Gallagher, Chalmers, Lennox and Hughes.*

Referee: *MM Zuimers, Luxemburg*

Scorers: *Lennox 3, Johnstone 2, Hughes.*

Monday, 4 October 1965 (At Ibrox)
Scottish League Cup (S/Final)
Hibs 2 Celtic 2

Hibs: *Wilson, Simpson and Davis; Stanton, McNamee and Baxter; Cormack, Quinn, Scott, Martin and Stevenson.*

Celtic: *Simpson, Young and Gemmell; Murdoch, McNeill and Clark; Johnstone, Gallagher, McBride, Lennox and Hughes.*

Referee: *Mr RH Davidson, Airdrie*

Scorers: *Hibs – Martin 2; Celtic – Lennox 2.*

Thursday, 7 October 1965
Cup Winners' Cup (R1)
Celtic 1 Go Ahead Deventer 0

Celtic: *Simpson, Craig and Gemmell; Murdoch, McNeill and Clark; Johnstone, Chalmers, McBride, Lennox and Hughes.*

Go Ahead Deventer: *Van Zoghel, Butter and Thiemann; Kanselaar, Warner and Somer; Wustefeldt, Niehaus, Groving, Veenstra and Adelaar.*

Referee: *Mr H Sigurdsson, Iceland*

Scorer: *McBride.*

Saturday, 9 October 1965
Scottish League
Celtic 5 Hearts 2

Celtic: *Simpson, Young and Gemmell; Murdoch, McNeill and Clark; Johnstone, Gallagher, McBride, Lennox and Hughes.*

Hearts: *Cruickshank, Ferguson and Shevlane; Polland, Anderson and Cummings; Jensen, Barry, Wallace, Gordon and Traynor.*

Referee: *Mr RD Henderson, Dundee*

Scorers: *Celtic - McBride 2, Lennox 2, Gallagher; Hearts – Gordon 2.*

Saturday, 16 October 1965
Scottish League
Falkirk 3 Celtic 4

Falkirk: *Whigham, Lambie and Hunter; Rowan, Baillie and Scott; Lowrie, McManus, Wilson, Graham and Gourlay.*

Celtic: *Fallon, Young and Gemmell; Murdoch, McNeill and Clark; Johnstone, Gallagher, McBride, Lennox and Hughes.*

Referee: *Mr R Rodger, Stonehouse*

Scorers: *Falkirk – Lambie, Wilson, Graham; Celtic – Lennox 2, Murdoch, Johnstone.*

Monday, 18 October 1965 (At Ibrox)
Scottish League Cup (S/Final Replay)
Celtic 4 Hibs 0

Celtic: *Simpson, Young and Gemmell; Murdoch, McNeill and Clark; Johnstone, Gallagher, McBride, Lennox and Hughes.*

Hibs: *Wilson, Simpson and Davis; Stanton, McNamee and Baxter; Cormack, Quinn, Scott, Martin and Stevenson.*

Referee: *Mr RH Davidson, Airdrie*

Scorers: *McBride, Hughes, Lennox, Murdoch.*

Saturday, 23 October 1965 (At Hampden)
Scottish League Cup Final
Celtic 2 Rangers 1

Celtic: *Simpson, Young and Gemmell; Murdoch, McNeill and Clark; Johnstone, Gallagher, McBride, Lennox and Hughes.*

Rangers: *Ritchie, Johansen and Provan; Wood, McKinnon and Greig; Henderson, Willoughby, Forrest, Wilson and Johnston.*

Referee: *Mr H Phillips, Wishaw*

Scorers: *Celtic – Hughes (2 pens); Rangers – Young own goal.*

Wednesday, 27 October 1965
Scottish League
Dundee 1 Celtic 2

Dundee: *Donaldson, Ryden and Cox; Cousin, Easton and Houston; Murray, Penman, Cameron. McLean and Cooke.*

Celtic: *Simpson, Young and Gemmell; Murdoch, McNeill and Clark; Johnstone, Gallagher, McBride, Lennox and Hughes.*

Referee: *Mr RH Davidson, Airdrie*

Scorers: *Dundee – Penman; Celtic – McBride, Lennox.*

Saturday, 30 October 1965
Scottish League
Celtic 6 Stirling Albion 1

Celtic: *Simpson, Young and Gemmell; Murdoch, McNeill and Clark; Johnstone, Gallagher, McBride, Lennox and Hughes.*

Stirling Albion: *Taylor, Cunningham and Murray; Reid, Rogerson and Robb; Fyfe, Anderson, Fleming, Thom and Hall.*

Referee: *Mr W Anderson, East Kilbride*

Scorers: *Celtic – Hughes 3, McBride 2, Murdoch; Stirling Albion – Fyfe.*

Wednesday, 3 November 1965
Cup Winners' Cup (R2)
AGF Aarhus 0 Celtic 1

AGF Aarhus: *Martin, A Sorensen and Nilson; Amidsen, Olmar and Petersen; Jensen, Bjerregard, Enoksen, O Sorensen and Hermansen.*

Celtic: *Simpson, Young and Gemmell; Murdoch, McNeill and Clark; Johnstone, Gallagher, McBride, Lennox and Hughes.*

Referee: *Mr H Bergacht, Belgium*

Scorer: *McBride.*

Saturday, 6 November 1965
Scottish League
Celtic 1 Partick Thistle 1

Celtic: *Simpson, Young and Gemmell; Murdoch, McNeill and Clark; Johnstone, Gallagher, McBride, Lennox and Hughes.*

Partick Thistle: *Gray, Campbell and Muir; Cunningham, Harvey and Gibb; Conway, Hainey, Roxburgh, McParland and Gallagher.*

Referee: *Mr JW Paterson, Bothwell*

Scorers: *Celtic – McBride; Partick Thistle – Conway.*

Saturday, 13 November 1965
Scottish League
St Johnstone 1 Celtic 4

St Johnstone: *McVittie, Richmond and Coburn; Collumbine, McKinven and Renton; Cowan, Kerray, Anderson, Duffy and Kemp.*

Celtic: *Simpson, Craig and Gemmell; Murdoch, McNeill and Clark; Johnstone, Gallagher, McBride, Lennox and Hughes.*

Referee: *Mr AD Fleming, Banknock*

Scorers: *St Johnstone – Duffy; Celtic - Hughes 2, Johnstone, McBride.*

Wednesday, 17 November 1965
Cup Winners' Cup (R2)
Celtic 2 AGF Aarhus 0

Celtic: *Simpson, Craig and Gemmell; Murdoch, McNeill and Clark; Johnstone, Gallagher, McBride, Lennox and Hughes.*

AGF Aarhus: *Martin, Laursen and A Sorensen; Amidsen, Olmar and Petersen; Bjerregard, Jensen, Enoksen, O Sorensen and Hermansen.*

Referee: *J Riseth, Norway*

Scorers: *McNeill, Johnstone.*

Saturday, 20 November 1965
Scottish League
Celtic 5 Hamilton Accies 0

Celtic: *Simpson, Craig and Gemmell; Murdoch, McNeill and Clark; Johnstone, Gallagher, McBride, Lennox and Auld.*

Hamilton Accies: *Lamont, Gauchan and Holton; Hinshelwood, Small and Anderson; McClure, McCann, Forsyth, Gilmour and Frye.*

Referee: *Mr J Hamilton, Renfrew*

Scorers: *Auld, Johnstone, Gemmell, Murdoch, McBride.*

Saturday, 27 November 1965
Scottish League
Celtic 2 Kilmarnock 1

Celtic: *Simpson, Craig and Gemmell; Murdoch, Cushley and Clark; Johnstone, McBride, Chalmers, Lennox and Hughes.*

Kilmarnock: *Ferguson, King and Watson; Murray, McGrory and McFadzean; McLean, McInally, Hamilton, O'Connor and McIlroy.*

Referee: *Mr A McKenzie, Coatbridge*

Scorers: *Celtic – Hughes (pen), McBride; Kilmarnock – McIlroy.*

Saturday, 11 December 1965
Scottish League
Celtic 2 Hibs 0

Celtic: *Simpson, Young and Gemmell; Murdoch, Cushley and Clark; Johnstone, Gallagher McBride, Lennox and Hughes.*

Hibs: *Wilson, Simpson and Davies; Stanton, McNamee and Baxter; O'Rourke, Cousin, Scott, Cormack and Stevenson.*

Referee: *Mr R Rodger, Stonehouse*

Scorers: *Hughes, McBride.*

Saturday, 18 December 1965
Scottish League
Dunfermline Athletic 0 Celtic 2

Dunfermline Athletic: *Martin, Callaghan and Lunn; Smith, MacLean and Thomson; Edwards, Paton, Fleming, Ferguson and Robertson.*

Celtic: *Simpson, Craig and Gemmell; Murdoch, Cushley and Clark; Johnstone, Gallagher, McBride, Chalmers and Hughes.*

Referee: *Mr RD Henderson, Dundee*

Scorer: *Chalmers 2.*

Saturday, 25 December 1965
Scottish League
Celtic 8 Morton 1

Celtic: *Simpson, Craig and Gemmell; Murdoch, Cushley and Clark; Johnstone, Gallagher, McBride, Chalmers and Hughes.*

Morton: *Sorensen, Boyd and Loughlan; Gray, Strachan and Kennedy; McIntyre, McGraw, Harper, Stevenson and Watson.*

Referee: *Mr D Smail, Selkirk*

Scorers: *Celtic - McBride 3, Chalmers 2, Hughes 2, Murdoch; Morton – Watson.*

Year-end Summary

Games played	*56*
Won	*39*
Drawn	*6*
Lost	*11*

List of competitive appearances in 1965 (Possible 56)

Bobby Murdoch	55
John Clark	54
Tommy Gemmell	53
Bobby Lennox	51
Billy McNeill	50
John Hughes	50
Ian Young	48
Jimmy Johnstone	35
John Fallon	34
Charlie Gallagher	32
Stevie Chalmers	31
Bertie Auld	28
Joe McBride	24
Ronnie Simpson	21
Jim Brogan	13
John Divers	12
Jim Craig	7
John Cushley	6
Jim Kennedy	6
Hugh Maxwell	3
Willie O'Neill	2
John Kennedy	1

List of competitive goals scored in 1965

John Hughes	34
Bobby Lennox	31
Joe McBride	24
Bertie Auld	22
Stevie Chalmers	14
Jimmy Johnstone	10
Bobby Murdoch	10
Tommy Gemmell	5
John Divers	3
Billy McNeill	3
Ian Young	3
Charlie Gallagher	1
Jim Brogan	1
Own goals	1